Export Challenges and Strategies in Indian Industry

Export Challenges and Strategies in Indian Industry

Editors

S. Shanmugasundaram
Assistant Professor
Department of Business Administration
Annamalai University
Annamalai Nagar, India

N. Panchanatham
Professor & Head
Department of Business Administration
Annamalai University
Annamalai Nagar, India

I.K. International Publishing House Pvt. Ltd.

NEW DELHI • BANGALORE

DISCLAIMER

The authors are solely responsible for the contents of the papers compiled in this volume. The publishers or editors do not take any responsibility for the same in any manner. Errors, if any, are purely unintentional and readers are requested to communicate such errors to the editors or publishers to avoid discrepancies in future.

Published by

I.K. International Publishing House Pvt. Ltd.
S-25, Green Park Extension
Uphaar Cinema Market
New Delhi – 110 016 (India)
E-mail: info@ikinternational.com
Website: www.ikbooks.com

ISBN 978-93-81141-93-9

10 9 8 7 6 5 4 3 2 1

Published by Krishan Makhijani for I.K. International Publishing House Pvt. Ltd., S-25, Green Park Extension, Uphaar Cinema Market, New Delhi – 110 016 and Printed by Rekha Printers Pvt. Ltd., Okhla Industrial Area, Phase-II, New Delhi – 110 020.

Foreword

Engaging in export trade is a never-ending challenge for a host of reasons: political turmoil, market uncertainties, compliance requirements, payment problems, shipping delays and lot of changing procedures and documentation to contend with in every country, including our own. While there is a favourable trend towards global harmonization, we are not there yet.

And on top of all these issues, there is the global recession that started in late 2008, with plummeting consumer demand and shrinking trade finance. Only time will tell how long these conditions will prevail. But global trade with new and different opportunities will endure, as it always has. Most experienced exporters confirm their belief that the overall rewards are still worth the risk and difficulties.

While the economic competition in world markets is greater than ever, so are the potential benefits. Practical knowledge, training, and persistence by Indian business community are vital to our future success in the international arena. We need to maintain our efforts to produce high-quality products and services and to market them aggressively and competitively abroad.

At the same time, Indian companies more than ever recognize that to be globally competitive in their exports, they must also look to other countries for raw materials, components, and final products and compare them with those that are produced in this country. That is what the global economy is all about breaking down international barriers and encouraging the free flow of goods, services, technology and capital.

While this book covers all the basic export/import challenges in Indian industry especially, procedures and documentation challenges, experienced foreign traders also are likely to find many new nuggets of practical, cost saving information and advice. The learning process never stops. The authors meet many exporters and importers every year and motivate them to attend seminars and workshops to update themselves of the problems that surface in trading operations due to currency fluctuations, cultural differences, or a penalty imposed because of incorrect documentation or security infractions.

This volume is an excellent compilation of various facets of export processes in Indian industry, and is a wonderful effort to showcase the different strategies used by people in different industries.

As in most endeavours, the basic ingredients of enthusiasm, interest and hard work are important for achieving success in exporting and importing, but that alone is not sufficient.

The additional critical factors needed are technical knowledge and training, which will lead to success for those who carefully apply what they learn.

I congratulate the editors S. Shanmugasundaram and N. Panchanatham, for their dedicated effort in bringing out this book, which will definitely be a guide to all future export professionals.

G. Loganathan
Managing Director, The Imperial, Tirupur
Tamil Nadu, India

Prof. Dr. M. Ramanathan
M.S. (G.S.), F.R.C.S.(Glasg), F.A.B.M.S.
Vice-Chancellor

Phone: Office : 04144-238283
Res. : 04144-238214
Fax : 04144-238925
04144-238080
E-mail : auvc_mr@hotmail.com
ANNAMALAI UNIVERSITY
ANNAMALAINAGAR P.O. 608 002
INDIA

Foreword

14-5-2012

I am very pleased to write the Foreword for this innovative book "**Export Challenges and Strategies in Indian Industry**". This edited volume includes chapters by leading researchers and experts in their respective fields, each providing a comprehensive review of current issues that are important in Indian export.

Engaging in export trade is a never-ending challenge for a host of reasons: political turmoil, market uncertainties, compliance requirements, payment problems, shipping delays and lot of changing procedures and documentation to contend with in every country, including our own.

While there is a favourable trend towards global harmonization, we are not there yet. And on top of all these issues, there is the global recession that started in late 2008, with plummeting consumer demand and shrinking trade finance.

While the economic competition in world markets is greater than ever, so are the potential benefits. Practical knowledge, training, and persistence by Indian business community are vital to our future success in the international arena. We need to maintain our efforts to produce high-quality products and services and to market them aggressively and competitively abroad.

At the same time, Indian companies more than ever recognize that to be globally competitive in their exports, they must also look to other countries for raw materials, components, and final products and compare them with those that are produced in this country. That is what the global economy is all about breaking down international barriers and encouraging the free flow of goods, services, technology and capital.

While this book covers all the basic export/import challenges in Indian industry especially, procedures and documentation challenges, experienced foreign traders also are likely to find many new nuggets of practical, cost saving information and advice.

This volume is an excellent compilation of various facets of export processes in Indian industry, and is a wonderful effort to showcase the different strategies used by people in different industries.

As in most endeavours, the basic ingredients of enthusiasm, interest and hard work are important for achieving success in exporting and importing, but that alone is not sufficient. The additional critical factors needed are technical knowledge and training, which will lead to success for those who carefully apply what they learn.

I congratulate the editors S. Shanmugasundaram and N. Panchanatham, for their dedicated efforts in bringing out this book, which will definitely be a guide to all future export professionals.

(Dr. M. Ramanathan)

Preface

In the present-day scenario, the high priority goal of our nation is to increase exports as much as possible, using export as the driving force for growth and job generation. While, the advantages of exporting by far outweigh the disadvantages, small and medium size enterprises especially face some challenges when venturing in the international marketplace. Entering an export business requires careful planning, management commitment, knowledge on capital and market know-how, competitive pricing strategy and access to quality products. It is almost impossible to succeed in export business without realizing the challenges and opportunities. While there are no hard-and-fast rules that can help companies make decision to export and to become successful, understanding the opportunities and challenges of exporting can help smooth entry into new markets, keep pace with competition and eventually realize profit.

Export Challenges and Strategies in Indian Industry covers a wide range of topics relating to export business in India viz., production challenges, procurement challenges, technological challenges, cost challenges, supply chain challenges, HR challenges, financial challenges, quality challenges, research & development challenges, international poricing challenges, infrastructure challenges, government policy challenges, international packing and marketing challenges, export shipping challenges, export marketing, WTO related issues, trade and non-trade barriers, market survey, India's export potential, export competitiveness, market–related issues, policy issues, issues from Indian standard, issues relating to foreign direct investment, labour issues, and so on.

This volume is an attempt to augment the existing resources on export business. The editors foresee more collaborative efforts in creating such rich pool of knowledge for export business.

Editors

Preface

Acknowledgements

We first thank the God Almighty for His boundless grace and blessings. We place on record our sincere thanks to the authorities of Annamalai University for all their support in bringing out this volume successfully.

We sincerely thank and acknowledge the valuable contributions made by the authors in this emerging and important field of study. Without their contribution this book would not have seen the light of the day. We extend our deep sense of gratitude to them.

We acknowledge, with sincere gratitude, the cooperation and encouragement given by our colleagues and friends in preparing this book.

Our families have always supported us in every academic activity. We are privileged to extend our deepest gratitude for their continuous support in accommodating our ambitions and making their social life to suit this rigor.

Editors

Contents

1

Indian Agricultural Exports: Constraints for External Trade

Rajesh C. Jampala, P. Adi Lakshmi and Srinivasa Rao Dokku

Professor & Head, Department of Commerce and Business Administration, P.B. Siddhartha College of Arts & Science, Siddhartha Nagar, Vijayawada, Andhra Pradesh
E-mail: rajeshjampala@yahoo.com

Professor & Head, Department of Business Administration, P.V.P. Siddhartha Institute of Technology, Kanuru, Vijayawada, Andhra Pradesh
E-mail: lakshmi_jampala@yahoo.com

Assistant Professor, P.V.P. Siddhartha Institute of Technology
E-mail: srinu_dokku@yaoo.co.in

ABSTRACT

Agriculture, a core sector of the Indian economy, accounts for 30 per cent of the country's Gross Domestic Product (GDP), 20 per cent of total export earnings, two-thirds of country's workforce and livelihood for 70 per cent of the total population. India's share in world production is nearly 10 per cent in fruits and 14 per cent in vegetables. India produces 50 per cent of world's mangoes, 19 per cent of banana, 36 per cent of cashew nut, more than 10 per cent of onion, 38 per cent of cauliflower, 28 per cent of green peas, etc. Despite all this, our share in the world exports of fruits and vegetables is only about 1 per cent. And it is only about 2 per cent of the fruits and vegetables produced in the country are processed and there is considerable potential to increase it to about 10 per cent. India enjoys a comparative advantage in agriculture. Comparative advantage, in itself, is a relative concept and it depends upon the relative changes in the international market. A major difficulty faced by India in the international market is the high level of subsidies given by the developed countries for their agri-exports. Hence, it is imperative to evolve concrete strategies to make Indian agriculture competitive and enhance its efficiency. For this purpose, on the one hand, we should be seeking substantial reduction in the support given to agriculture by the developed countries, and on the other hand, Indian agriculture would also require to be supported to maintain and improve its competitiveness. This paper analyses the share of agriculture in total exports, its constraints for international trade and also list out the initiatives of the government for promoting agriculture trade.

Keywords: Agriculture, Economy, GDP, Exports, Constraints and Initiatives.

INTRODUCTION

Agriculture,the largest private enterprise in India, is the lifeline of the economy. Agriculture provides the underpinnings for our food and livelihood security and support for the economic growth and social transformation of the country. During 2008-09 the agricultural sector contributed to approximately 15.7 per cent of India's GDP (at 2004-05 prices) and 10.23 per cent (provisional) of total exports besides providing employment to around 58.2 per cent of the workforce. In the recent past, the impact of various food, financial and economic crises has been felt across the world. This has compromised the lives, livelihood and food security of the people. Therefore, there is a compelling case for increased investment in the sector. The continued high growth of agriculture is essential to meet the food and nutritional requirements of the people and provide livelihood and income in rural areas. Agriculture will continue to have the pride of place in national policies and plans, since the nation's food security depends on the performance of the agricultural sector.

India is among the 15 leading exporters of agricultural products in the world. As per International Trade Statistics, 2009, published by the World Trade Organization (WTO), India's agricultural exports amounted to US$ 21.37 billion, with a share of 1.6 per cent of world trade in agriculture in 2008. Agricultural exports have shown an increasing trend. Agricultural exports increased from Rs. 79,039.72 crore in 2007-08 to Rs. 85,961.82 crore in 2008-09, registering a growth of about 8.76 per cent. However, the share of agricultural exports in the country's total exports declined to 10.23 per cent from 12.05 per cent during 2007-08. The increase in the value of agricultural exports during 2008-09 was primarily because of higher exports of basmati rice, tobacco (un-manufactured), wheat, spices, meat and preparations, paper/wood products, other cereals, cashew nuts, castor oil, tea and coffee, dairy products, fresh and processed fruits, and vegetables and oil meals, compared to the corresponding period of the previous year. The export of non-basmati rice, sugar, molasses, and raw cotton, including waste, registered a decline as compared to the previous year. Agricultural imports increased from Rs. 29,906.24 crore in 2007-08 to Rs. 36,736.52 crore in 2008-09, registering a growth of 22.84 per cent over the corresponding period of the previous year. The share of agricultural imports in the country's total imports also declined to 2.74 per cent during 2008-09 compared to 2.95 per cent in 2007-08. The increase in the value of agricultural imports during this period was primarily due to higher imports of sugar, fixed vegetable oils (edible), raw and waste cotton, cashew nuts, other cereals, tea, and wood and wood products. However, a decrease in imports was registered in the case of raw jute and oilseeds in 2008-09.

Agricultural exports is more competitive at the new exchange rate; it also stimulates the growth of the agro-processing industry, with strong backward linkage to agriculture. A logical extension of the current programme of reforms is the elimination of all restrictions on the movement of agricultural commodities both domestically (across states) and also for export. This has been accepted as an element of the economic reforms. All central government restrictions on domestic trade have been removed, though some state governments' restrictions remain. Restrictions on agricultural exports have been reduced significantly, though not as yet fully eliminated. Some of the remaining restrictions, such as, the restriction on exports of pulses and coarse grains are not really binding in practice, but have been continued with an eye to avoid any psychological pressure on prices.

The post-Uruguay round experience has been a mixed one for agricultural trade in India. While exports in certain areas have registered a high growth, in certain other areas, the growth rate has not been satisfactory. Exports of rice (basmati and non-basmati), coffee, tobacco, dairy and poultry products, spices, groundnut, guar gum meal, oil meal, fresh fruits and vegetables, meat and its preparations, raw cotton including waste, and paper/wood products have shown significant growth. Exports of pulses, castor oil, and marine products have not shown significant growth. At the global level, average bound tariffs have been reduced in the Uruguay round. However, measures like, tariff escalation, variable tariffs, complex tariffs and also certain nontechnical barriers still persist. Domestic support and export subsidies continue to remain high in a few developed countries. For most high-value agricultural products, including fruits and vegetables, fish, beef, poultry products, and spices, many importing countries have developed new standards, besides tightening existing standards. These factors have acted as inhibiting forces in actualizing the export growth potential of the country. Other factors that have led to limited exports include inadequacies in infrastructure, poor quality awareness, and poor post-harvest management.

Globalization has led to increased competition from international markets and pressure to dismantle protectionist instruments. Since agriculture in India is more a matter of livelihood than a commercial venture, it is necessary to build capacities in the system so that it is able to withstand the forces of globalization and compete wherever possible. While there are a large number of issues to be addressed at the micro and macro levels, the "Capacity Building to Enhance the Competitiveness of Indian Agriculture and Registration of Organic Products Abroad" scheme aims to address some of the limited micro-level capacity creation issues. The capacity building under this scheme may be in the form of academic, relevant research, market surveys (domestic and international), or in the form of creation of physical assets critical to agriculture in the international context. Table 1 shows the comparison of Indian agri-exports. During the year 2009-10 exports increased by 1.7 per cent as compared to 2008-09.

SHARE OF AGRICULTURE IN TOTAL EXPORTS

An analysis of Table 2 reveals that during the period under review, agriculture and allied products export in total exports of India varied from 15.56 per cent in 1999-2000 to 9.25 per cent in

Table 1: Agri-exports from India (US$ million)

Commodity	*2008-09*	*2009-10 (P)*	*% Growth*	*% Share*
Plantation crops	1,081.77	1,053.18	-2.64	0.59
Tea	585.42	623.24	6.46	0.35
Coffee	496.34	429.94	-13.38	0.24
Agri & allied products	14,528.10	12,627.51	-13.08	7.07
Cereal	3,344.62	2,997.97	-10.36	1.68
Rice	2,454.09	2,365.46	-3.61	1.32
Wheat	0.3	0	-99.74	0
Others	890.23	632.52	-28.95	0.35
Pulses	117.68	86.75	-26.28	0.05
Tobacco	751.09	916.27	21.99	0.51
Unmanufactured	600.79	763.29	27.05	0.43
Manufactured	150.29	152.98	1.79	0.09
Spices	1,391.62	1,302.42	-6.41	0.73
Nuts & seeds	1,269.85	1,221.28	-3.82	0.68
Cashew incl. CSNL	645.82	597.29	-7.52	0.33
Sesame & Niger seed	347.89	321.87	-7.48	0.18
Groundnut	276.14	302.12	9.41	0.17
Oil meals	2,251.63	1,662.59	-26.16	0.93
Guar gum meal	294.18	240.6	-18.21	0.13
Castor oil	481.75	461.26	-4.25	0.26
Shellac	22.92	15.11	- 34.06	0.01
Sugar & molasses	1,056.70	27.32	-97.41	0.02
Processed foods	1,824.93	1,978.56	8.42	1.11
Fresh fruits & vegetables	951.53	1,093.45	14.92	0.61
Fruits/vegetable seeds	26.17	30.61	16.94	0.02
Processed & misc. processed items	847.23	854.5	0.86	0.48
Meat & preparations	1,173.34	1,332.39	13.55	0.75
Poultry & dairy products	346.61	194.73	-43.82	0.11
Floriculture products	80.93	61.85	-23.58	0.03
Spirit & beverages	120.24	128.39	6.78	0.07
Marine products	1,534.39	2,093.38	36.43	1.17

Source: DGCIS

Table 2: Agriculture and allied products export and total exports of India (Volume: Rs. crore)

Year	*Agriculture and allied products export*	*Total exports*	*Percentage share of agriculture and allied products export in total exports*
1995-1996	21138	106353	19.88
1996-1997	24239	118817	20.40
1997-1998	25419	130100	19.54
1998-1999	26104	139752	18.68
1999-2000	25016	159561	15.68
2000-2001	28535	203571	14.02
2001-2002	29312	209018	14.02
2002-2003	33691	255137	13.21
2003-2004	36247	293367	12.36
2004-2005	38079	361879	10.52
2005-2006	46703	456418	10.23
2006-2007	58959	571779	10.31
2007-2008	76006	655864	11.59
2008-2009	77783	840755	9.25

Source: Economic Survey, Government of India.

2009-09. However, after the initial increase in 1996-97, the percentage share of agriculture and allied products decreased for four consecutive years. In 2001-12, it remains stable. From the year 2002-03 to 2005-06, it again declined but again showed a marginal increase for two years. However, the share of agriculture and allied products again decreased in the subsequent year of 2008-09 and reached its lowest level.

In 1995-96, the per cent share of agriculture and allied exports stood at 19.88 per cent. For more than four decades, the industry remained highly protected and agriculture served as a source of cheap raw materials for the domestic industry, a very huge segment of which was inefficient and globally non-competitive. This led to a dampening effect on the agriculture exports and investment in agriculture. The new economic policy since 1991-92 has tried to correct this imbalance and agriculture has started to achieve some advantages through competitive exports. A number of policy changes have been introduced for making agriculture exports more feasible. Indian agriculture thus began to appear internationally competitive and two important policy changes made this possible. First, the deliberate reduction in the excessive protection earlier accorded to the manufacturing sector. This led to the improvement in the relative profitability of agriculture. Secondly, letting farming community receive market oriented prices so as to bring about a more equitable terms of trade in respect of agriculture sector.

There was also the encouraging indication of decreased level of subsidies for agriculture by the advanced industrial countries. The share of agriculture and allied exports increased slightly in 1996-97, to reach its peak of 20.40 per cent. It recorded a level of Rs. 24239 crore. Agriculture exports had been given special attention by the Government of India, since it was in the area that there appeared to be the greatest potential for raising farm incomes, tackling unemployment and earning foreign exchange. The impetus for agricultural growth in agriculture exports was visualized through enhanced infrastructure support and by building up an encouraging policy environment.

CONSTRAINTS AFFECTING EXPORT PERFORMANCE

The performance of the Indian agricultural sector in the last decade has provoked dramatically differing assessments. Some have described it as a 'golden revolution', presumably to distinguish it from the earlier 'green revolution'). Others have dismissed these views as a hyperbolic description of a fundamentally stagnant sector. India is one of the largest and lowest cost producers of high value agricultural commodities and yet has a minuscule share in global trade. It produces nearly 11 per cent of all vegetables and 15 per cent of all fruits in the world. The unit values of its exports (free on board, FOB) are nearly half the corresponding world unit values. Yet its share in global exports of vegetables is only 1.7 per cent and in fruits a meagre 0.5 per cent. At the same time, its own market is heavily protected. Finding an explanation for this strange conjunction of low costs, low exports, and high protection is vital to any assessment of the competitiveness of Indian agriculture in a liberalized global trading environment.

In a World Bank report submitted to the Agriculture Ministry, it has been highlighted that despite leading producer of fruits and vegetables in the world, India's export is poor due to high delivery costs, fragmented supply chain and poor logistics with poor quality standards. India's share in the global export of vegetables remained at 1.7 per cent and that of fruits at 0.5 per cent. The inability to compete abroad presently may lead to the inability to compete at home in future as the multinational companies will be dominating the domestic market availing quality products at competitive prices from other countries.

The country also lacks appropriate technology and infrastructure in many aspects of modern storage and shipping methods, post-harvest handling, value addition, etc. The situation is further restricted due to complicated export regulations and procedures. An exporter faces enormous difficulties to equip himself on various parameters of export like regulatory, quality standards, global export opportunities, tariffs on exports, production scenario and availability, present export trend, etc. for developing gainful strategic approach in a competitive mode.

Many economists and policy makers have, in the past, attributed India's poor export performance to an overvalued real exchange rate and the anti-export bias in its trade policy, the latter being a by-product of the Government of India's (GoI's) broader objective of achieving self-sufficiency and food security in agriculture. The gradual depreciation of the Indian currency since the mid-1980s, the large devaluations in 1991 and 1993, and the subsequent move to a flexible exchange rate regime corrected the overvaluation in the real exchange rate. During the last several years, a number of policies have been initiated to reduce the anti-export bias in India's trade policy. While these reforms have relaxed some of the constraints affecting the horticulture sector, the much anticipated surge in export is yet to materialize. While India's unit value of exports continues to be one of the lowest in the world, its share in global exports in recent years has been less than that in the early 1990s. The main constraints affecting the agriculture exports are explained in Chart 1 (Planning Commission Report on Agricultural Marketing Infrastructure and Policy Required for Internal and External Trade, 2007).

Chart 1: Constraints affecting export performance

Supply Side Issue
1. Low and volatile growth in agriculture
2. Low productivity levels
3. Limitations to expansion of acreage
4. Gross Capital Formation (GCF) in agriculture and the allied sectors
5. Disconnect between the farmer and the market—inadequate infrastructure for grading, packaging and transportation.
6. Domestic prices are high as compared to the international prices
7. Restrictions on exports of certain commodities from time to time

Factors Eroding Benefit of Low Cost Production
1. Lack of cargo space and high air freight rates
2. High sea freight rates

Non-Tariff barriers – Major Issues
1. Issues relating to pesticide residues
2. Delays in equivalence
3. Lack of harmonization with Codex
4. Capacity building issue
5. Impractical approaches to Product testing
6. Unreasonable clearance procedure
7. Traceability
8. Environment and labour issues

Source: Planning Commission, Government of India.

Supply Side Issues

Agriculture accounts for about 14.2 per cent of the GDP of the country and employs about two-thirds of its population. However, low and variable growth of output, poor and declining yields, inadequacy of capital formation and infrastructure and degradation of natural resources due to inefficient cropping patterns work as major obstacles for rapid and sustainable agricultural growth. As a result, Indian agriculture is still not prepared to face the challenges arising out of the complete phase out of the quantitative restrictions on import. Nor it is able to exploit its full potential for exports.

Low and Volatile Growth in Agriculture: Low and volatile growth rates in Indian agriculture and allied sectors was reflected in the average annual growth rate of value added in the sector declining from 2.1 per cent during the Ninth Plan to 1.7 per cent during the Tenth Plan. As against the target of annual growth rate of 4.1 per cent during the Eleventh Plan (2007-2012), agricultural growth rate in the first year (2007-08) was very impressive (4.7 per cent). But due to deficient rainfall in 2008-09 and 2009-10 it is only 1.6 per cent and 0.2 per cent respectively.

Low Productivity Levels: The Gross Domestic Product (GDP) in the country like India is experiencing a faster rate of growth in the recent years. With regard to the composition of GDP, the percentage shares of various sectors have largely changed. The percentage share of the agriculture in the total GDP has declined; on the contrary the percentage share of services in the GDP is rising faster. In the financial year 2009-10, the percentage share of services in the total GDP accounted to 56.9 per cent in total GDP. On the other hand percentage share of agriculture in the GDP declined to 14.6 per cent in 2009-10 from 22.2 per cent in the financial year 2003-04 notwithstanding the fact that the share of this sector in the GDP has been declining over the years, its role remains critical as it provides employment to around 52 per cent of the workforce. The rates of growth and share of agriculture and allied activities in the GDP of the country are given in Table 3.

Limitations to Expansion of Acreage: While there is some scope for wasteland reclamation, there are obvious limitations to the expansion of acreage in Indian agriculture. Enhancement of agricultural growth is essential for achieving an overall GDP growth rate in the range of 8 to 10 per cent, and improved productivity is critical for achieving accelerated agricultural growth.

Gross Capital Formation (GCF) in Agriculture and the Allied Sector: The GCF in agriculture and allied sectors as a proportion to the GDP in the sector stagnated at around 14 per cent during 2004-05 to 2006-07. However, there is a marked improvement in this figure during the current Five Year Plan. It increased to 16.03 per cent in 2007-08 and further to 19.67 per cent in 2008-09 (provisional) and to 20.30 per cent in 2009-10 (quick estimates [QE]). However, the GCF in agriculture and allied sectors relative to overall GDP has remained stagnant at around 2.5 to 3.0 per cent (Table 8.2). As a result the share of GCF in agriculture and allied sector in total GCF remained in the range of 6.6 to 8.2 per cent during 2004-05 to 2009- 10 (Table 4). There is need to significantly step up investment in agriculture, both by the private and public sectors to ensure sustained target growth of 4 per cent per annum.

Table 3: Sectoral growth rates of real gross domestic product (GDP)

Year	*Agriculture and allied activities*	*Industry*	*Services*	*Total GDP at factor Cost*
2003-04	10.0 (22.2)	6.6 (25.8)	9.1 (52.0)	8.5 (100)
2004-05	0.7 (20.8)	8.6 (26.0)	9.9 (53.2)	7.5 (100)
2005-06	5.2 (18.2)	9.3 (27.9	11.1 (53.9)	9.5 (100)
2006-07	3.7 (17.1)	12.7 (28.7)	10.2 (54.2)	9.7 (100)
2007-08	4.7 (16.4)	9.5 (28.8)	10.5 (54.8)	9.2 (100)
2008-09	1.6 (15.6)	3.9 (28.0)	9.8 (56.4)	6.7 (100)
2009-10	0.2 (14.6)	9.3 (28.5)	8.5 (56.9)	7.4 (100)

Source: Economic Survey (GOI) (2004-07), CSO (GOI)
(Figures in parenthese indicate percentage share in total GDP)

Table 4: GCF in agriculture and allied activities (Crore at 2004-05 prices)

Year	*GDP*	*Agriculture & allied activities*		*GCF/GDP in agriculture & allied activities*	*GCF in agriculture as per cent of total*
		GCF	*GDP*		
2004-05	29,71,464	76,096	5,65,426	13.46	2.56
2005-06	32,54,216	86,611	5,94,487	14.57	2.66
2006-07	35,66,011	90,710	6,19,190	14.65	2.54
2007-08	38,98,958	1,05,034	6,55,080	16.03	2.69
2008-09P	41,62,509	1,28,659	6,54,118	19.67	3.09
2009-10QE	44,93,743	1,33,377	6,56,975	20.3	2.97

Source: Central Statistics Office.
Notes: P–provisional. Q–quick estimates.

Disconnect between the Farmer and the Market: Inadequate Infrastructure for Grading, Packaging and Transportation: The existing marketing infrastructure is far from adequate. Nearly half of the villages are still not connected by roads. The teledensity in rural areas is only around 2.0 as against the national average of more than 11. At the level of regulated markets, there are only 1093 grading units in a total of 7557 market yards/sub-yards majority of which are for grains. The facilities for perishables are very few. The availability of scientific storage capacity is estimated to be only 30 per cent of the requirement. The cold storage facility availability is estimated to be 10 per cent only. The estimates for loss of primary produce before reaching the market due to lack of proper handling, cleaning, sorting, grading and packaging facilities at the village level are about 7 per cent for food grains, 30 per cent for fruits and vegetables and 10 per cent for spices. The unavailability of appropriate infrastructure both in terms of physical infrastructure and institutions for marketing of agriculture produce have created a disconnect between the producers and the market.

Domestic Prices are High as Compared to the International Prices: India is undoubtedly the third largest producer of agro and food products, next to USA and China. Yet, the demand in the internal markets being high, the domestic prices in the case of most of the crops/produce are higher as compared to the prices ruling in the international markets making exports a difficult proposition.

Restrictions on Exports of Certain Commodities from Time to Time: Despite a very liberal Foreign Trade Policy, there have been several restrictions on the export of agricultural products. This prevents the regular flow of restricted commodities for export and makes it difficult to cultivate a regular market for these products on a sustainable basis. Frequent restrictions on the export of onions, pulses and wheat are some of the examples. In the post-WTO era, an export growth led strategy for the Indian agriculture should be considered a preferred option for increasing the incomes of the farmers.

Non-tariff Barriers : Major Issues

Issues Relating to Pesticide Residues: The maximum residue levels (MRLs) of pesticides and other contaminants are largely based on technology development and not based on actual risk assessment. The level of protection goes beyond the ALOP (Appropriate Level of Protection) enshrined in the SPS Agreement. Further, there is no harmonization of MRLs across all countries of a customs union. This issue needs intervention.

Delays in Equivalence: Most developed countries take many years to reach a decision on equivalence on standards and processes with exporting countries. For instance, USA took 3 years on organic standards, Japan took 20 years for market access on mangoes, and EU has already taken more than 8 years to agree on equivalence in case of egg products. Australia has already taken more than 6 years to give market access for mangoes.

Lack of Harmonization with Codex: Although the reference point for standards is Codex, most developed countries establish stricter standards as is allowed under the SPS Agreement. The true purpose of establishing Codex standards is not achieved by the developing countries. Moreover, even though the Codex provides for a special and differential treatment for developing countries, it remains only on paper.

Capacity Building Issue: The SPS Agreement provides for ensuring capacity building programmes for developing countries. Under this, only seminars and conferences are organized. When it comes to organizing specific training programmes, either it takes a long time to organize it, or it is too little.

Impractical Approaches to Product Testing: Taking the example of aflatoxin in spices, processed food, groundnuts, and cereals, there is a requirement of meeting a certain MRL value of aflatoxin in these products. The sampling procedure for testing purposes is extremely complex and expensive. The procedure is technically and economically not feasible in the case of developing countries. Moreover, it is expected that the MRL should be respected on the arrival of the consignment at the port of the importing countries (e.g. EU ports). This is impractical because aflatoxins can come up at any stage after drawal of samples for testing. The voyage provides an optimum environment for growth of aflatoxins. No exporting country can absolutely guarantee this, not even the most developed countries.

Unreasonable Clearance Procedure: Certain developed countries like the EU destroy processed food consignments at their ports if the risk to human health is high. This is unreasonable. The exporting countries must have the first right to the rejected consignment and should have the option to either take it back to their country or to ship it to another country where it is acceptable according to its laws. EU laws do not apply to other countries. The unreasonable procedure needs a change.

Traceability: This is a concept that has just been defined by the Codex and its application is still to be established. However, countries like the EU have already started demanding traceability in all the products right from the farm to the consumer. This is technically and economically not feasible in many developing countries. India's view is that traceability may be considered only a risk management tool and only if no other feasible option to control that risk is available. Moreover, it should not be applicable on raw produce and should not be used as a barrier to trade.

Environment and Labour Issues: The SPS Agreement, through the Codex, allows formulation of standards and practices for ensuring food safety and fair trade practices. In the name of fair trade, most developed countries are expecting compliance with their environment and labour requirements. This is an issue, which has been under discussion at other fora, but when it comes to Codex discussions, it is difficult to oppose.

Factors Eroding Benefit of Low Cost Production

Lack of Cargo Space and High Airfreight Rates: India has a unilateral open skies policy for air cargo. According to this policy, any operator, including foreign operator, can operate any number of flights by any type of aircraft to any airport having customs and immigration facilities without any bilateral agreement. The operators are also free to charge rates according to the demand and supply situation. But according to exporters, many airlines don't offer cargo space because of one-way freight (to Europe and North America) and so only handful of airlines including Air India and Indian Airlines remain the major handlers of freight.

High Sea Freight Rates: Price competitiveness is essential in order to sustain the market. Transportation of mangoes by air is costlier by 10 times, as compared to sea, to most of our Asian markets, especially to the west Asian markets. Thus, export of fruits and vegetables in bulk by sea is the best alternative. However, in order to preserve quality and extended shelf life during sea transportation, there is need for development of protocols for management of different varieties of specific fruits and vegetables during voyage time, through use of alternative techniques of refrigeration, and controlled/modified atmosphere management.

GOVERNMENT INITIATIVES FOR INCREASING THE AGRICULTURE EXPORTS

The government is giving lot of emphasis on agriculture sector for increasing the production and productivity of agriculture commodities for achieving an impressive growth in the agriculture front under the GDP. A number of new initiatives like Technology Mission for Integrated Development of Horticulture in the North Eastern States (TMNE), National Horticulture Mission (NHM), National Food Security Mission (NFSM), Macro Management in Agriculture (MMA), Rastriya Krishi Vikash Yojana (RKVY), National Project on Organic Farming (NPOF), National Project on Management of Soil Health and Fertility (NPMSHF) etc. indicate the intensive approach in this direction. The success of these programmes will definitely lead to significant rise in agriculture production at the end of XI plan. The surplus production after meeting the domestic requirement will help to promote export and will have a great impact on Indian economy. This section presents the government's successful initiatives for promoting agriculture exports.

Public-Private Sector Initiatives in Agriculture Sector: Agri-Export Zones

The concept of food parks and agri-export zones (AEZs) has been initiated besides several incentive schemes by the Government of India. The Central Government released a food processing policy in 2001. However, the role of the State is considered vital. The concept of AEZ attempts to take a comprehensive look at a particular produce located in a contiguous area for the purpose of developing and sourcing for raw materials, their processing and packaging, and finally their export. AEZs have been approved by the Government of India with a total envisaged investment of Rs. 1,325 crore. A total number of 60 AEZs have been approved in 19 states of India. Since the AEZ was flagged off in the 2001 Export-Import (Exim) Policy, the actual investment flows from both the state governments as also private sector was only Rs. 145 crore in 2002. The concept of AEZs which aims to give fillip to agriculture exports, comprises the following: (*a*) identifying a potential zone based on agro-climatic requirements for a particular crop; (*b*) integrating various assistance programmes of Central and state government agencies and providing fiscal incentives to exporters; (*c*) implementing the same through involvement of private and public partnership and (*d*) integrating all the activities till the produce reaches the market.

Vision 2015

Given the strengths and opportunities of the food processing sector, Vision 2015 has been developed by the ministry of food processing industries, together with an appropriate strategy and implementable action plan so as to enhance farmer income, generate employment opportunities, provide choice to consumers at affordable price and contribute to overall national growth by increasing: the level of processing of perishables from six per cent to 20 per cent, value addition from 20 per cent to 35 per cent and share in global food trade from 1.5 per cent to 3 per cent. Vision 2015 aims at enhancing and stabilizing the income level of the farmers by assuring wider and better choice by enhancing dynamism, competitiveness, by ensuring safety and quality of food by introducing a transparent and scientific system of standards. To achieve these aims a transparent and industry-friendly regulatory regime is proposed to be established.

CONCLUSION

A major area where policy reforms can help agriculture is in the area of rural credit. Poor banking practices, including, especially, laxness regarding loan recovery, has greatly weakened the cooperative credit system and also rural lending by the commercial banking system. The financial sector reforms currently underway will address this problem through a combination of rationalization of interest rates to reduce the disincentive of unviable lending rates which discourage rural lending, and by the recapitalization of banks, and restructuring of cooperative credit institutions. The new economic policy since 1991-92 has tried to correct this imbalance and agriculture has started to achieve some advantages through competitive exports. A number of policy changes had been introduced for making agriculture exports more feasible. Indian agriculture thus has begun to appear internationally competitive and two important policy changes made this possible. Addressing infrastructure requirements in the agriculture sector, especially tariffs, testing procedure, freight rates, storage, communication, roads, and markets should be the priority. Public-private partnership models can be of help in ensuring faster development of these requirements which are of vital importance for the growth of agriculture exports.

REFERENCES

1. CII "Challenges and way forward for Agriculture products exports" CII seminar broacher November 10 2010, Chennai, Tamil Nadu.
2. Department of Agriculture and Cooperation, "Annual Report 2009-2010" Ministry of Agriculture, Government of India, March 2010.
3. Krishnaveni, L. and Sangita Ghosh, (2004). "India's Agricultural Exports: Some Challenges" *The IUP Journal of Agricultural Economics,* Volume I, pp. 62-71.
4. EXIM Bank, (2010). "India's Agri-export Performance – A review" *Agri Export Advantage,* Vol. XIV, Issue V.
5. EXIM Bank, (2005). "Recent Trends in India's Agricultural Exports" *Agri export Advantage,* Export –Import Bank of India Vol. IV, issue IV.
6. FICCI, (2010). "Survey on Exports", FICCI, Federation House, 1, Tansen Marg, New Delhi.
7. Government of India, "Economic Survey 2010-2011, *Government of India,* February, 2011.
8. Meijerink, G.W. and Achterbosch, T.J. (2009). "India's position in agricultural trade liberalization - The puzzle of protection" *Strategy & Policy Brief,* 14.
9. Joachim von Braun, Ashok Gulati, Peter Hazell, Mark W. Rosegrant and Marie Ruel, "Indian Agriculture and Rural Development Strategic Issues and Reform Options" *International Food Policy Research Institute,* ifpri@cgiar.org.
10. Singh, J.P. (2001). "Strategy for Effective Agriculture Marketing Extension to Meet the Challenges in 21st Century" *Manage Extension Research Review.*
11. Ravi Kumar, K.N., Sree Lakshmi, K. and Krishna Kumar, K.V. (2001). "Exploring the Agricultural Export Potential of Andhra Pradesh – A SWOT" *Manage Extension Research Review.*
12. Ministry of Commerce, "WTO Agreement on Agriculture and its Implications" Govt. of India, *India and the WTO,* May 1999, Vol. 1 No. 5.
13. Montek S. Ahluwalia, "India's Economic Reforms" *Planningcommission.nic.in*
14. Sridhar, S. (2006). "India.s Agricultural Exports: Opportunities and Challenges" *Cab Calling,* pp. 31-39.
15. Pallavi, "A Case for Boosting India's Agri Exports" www.afcindia.org.i n/april_2010/ Chapter6.pdf.

2

Resilience Strategies for Manpower Issues in the Special Economic Zone

S. Shanmugasundaram and N. Panchanatham

Assistant Professor, Department of Business Administration, Annamalai University, Annamalai Nagar. India. E-mail: 3s.shan@gmail.com.
Professor & Head, Department of Business Administration, Annamalai University, Annamalai Nagar. India. E-mail: panchanatham@gmail.com

ABSTRACT

*I*n the past ten years, Indian exports have grown at a rate of nearly 22%. Some commodities have enjoyed faster export growth than others. Some of India's main export items are cotton, textiles, jute goods, tea, coffee, cocoa products, rice, wheat, pickles, mango pulp, juices, jams, preserved vegetables etc. India exports its goods to some of the leading countries of the world such as UK, Belgium, USA, China, Russia, etc. The Special Economic Zone (SEZ) is a specially delineated duty-free enclave which shall be deemed to be foreign territory for the purpose of trade operations and duties and tariffs. The study analyses the problems disturbing the raw material in Special Economic Zone units in Chennai with the help of administering questionnaire. The study found that the non-availability of material in time is a major problem of the study units while its costs come second. Imported materials can be substituted by indigenous ones, it leads to an appreciable rise in the foreign exchange earnings. If goods are procured from the local market, proper planning and forecasting of the production schedules are to be prepared and followed strictly. It is suggested that for producing export products of the right quality for foreign buyers, an effective policy and organizational framework must be made. Another major problem is the delayed supply of material. Supply bottlenecks also tend to increase the costs in India. India has indigenous stocks on 3-4 months and imported stocks of 9 months and more. It is suggested to improve the supply of material, the study units where possible may have buffer stocks. As the country is longing for entering into developed stage from the developing stage, there is no second thought on the stimulation of exports. "Export is the engine for economic development.".

Abbreviations : EPZ — Export processing zone, EOU—Export Oriented Unit and SEZ—Special Economic Zone.

INTRODUCTION

Export means the transferring of any goods from one country to another in a legal way for the purpose of trade. Export goods are provided to the foreign consumers by the domestic producers.

The history of Indian exports is very old. During ancient times India exported spices to the other parts of the world. India was also famous for its textiles which were a chief item for export in the 16th century. Textiles and cotton were exported to the Arab countries from Gujarat. During the Mughal era India exported various precious stones such as ivory, pearls, tortoise stones, etc. But during the British era, Indian exports declined as the East India Company took control of foreign trade. Though India has seen some product diversification in its export basket, it has not expanded significantly in the two big markets—Africa and Latin America countries. India's business with South Asian countries is also negligible. This region has not been integrated with the global economy, though political and economic initiatives have been taken in the recent past in this direction.

In the past ten years, Indian exports have grown at a rate of nearly 22%. Some commodities have enjoyed faster export growth than others. Some of India's main export items are cotton, textiles, jute goods, tea, coffee, cocoa products, rice, wheat, pickles, mango pulp, juices, jams, preserved vegetables, etc. India exports its goods to some of the leading countries of the world such as UK, Belgium, USA, China, Russia, etc.

It is very clear that Indian exports have still not achieved their true potential and there exists immense opportunities for expanding the basket of India's exports. With a strategic attention to the new markets that are evolving due to free trade, India is witnessing a boom in both manufacturing and services. There are few problems which need to be solved before India makes a mark for itself in the export sector. The Indian goods have to be of superior quality. The packaging and branding should be such that countries are interested to import from India. At the same time India must look for potential markets to sell their goods. The government should frame policies which give boost to the exports.

Special Economic Zone

Export plays a very important role in the economic growth of the country. Growth in exports improves the country's position in Balance of Trade, Balance of Payments, forex reserves, etc. It also benefits by reduction in the budget deficit, increase in the country's share in exports, i.e., world trade and by providing employment opportunities across the country. The share of our country in international trade has been as low as 0.75% and it was felt necessary to increase the same by increasing the exports. A policy was introduced on 01.04.2000 for setting up of Special Economic Zones in the country with a view to provide an international competitive and hassle-free environment for exports. Accordingly the units may be set up in special economic zones for manufacturing goods and rendering of services.

The Special Economic Zone (SEZ) is a specially delineated duty-free enclave which shall be deemed to be foreign territory for the purpose of trade operations and duties and tariffs.

- No license required for imports.
- No fixed wastage norms.
- Contract farming allowed for agriculture/horticulture units.
- A designated duty-free enclave, to be treated as foreign territory.
- Manufacturing, trading and services: all types of activities allowed.
- Developed plots and ready to build space made available.
- Job work on behalf of domestic exports also allowed to direct exports.
- Support services like banking, post-offices, clearing agents would also be made available in the zone complex.
- Exemption from the Central Excise Duty on procurement of capital goods, raw materials, consumable spares. etc. from the domestic market.
- Supplies from domestic tariff Area (DTA) to SEZ units treated as deemed exports. Further, supplies from DTA to SEZ to be treated as exports under section 80 HHC of the Income Tax Act also.

Keeping in view the objective for augmenting infrastructure facilities for export production, it has been permitted to set up Special Economic Zones in the public, private, joint sector or by the state governments. Thus, the private sector has also been invited to develop the infrastructure facilities in the SEZs. Foreign companies can also set up SEZs. Hover the government has a lead role in setting up SEZs. The minimum size of a Special Economic Zone shall not be less than 1,000 hectares. Minimum area requirement shall, however not be applicable to product specific and port/airport based SEZs. This is expected to promote self-contained areas supported by world class infrastructure oriented towards production of goods for exports. It was also envisaged that some of the existing export processing zones would be converted into special economic zones.

Relevant Reviews

Cherie Marriott's study focused on the economic growth in Mauritius, driven by an expanding labour force, capital accumulation, and increased productivity. Over the past two decades, the government has turned the country around from a sugar-based economy to one supported by a labor-intensive Export Processing Zone and a niche tourist industry.

Chen Xiangming in his doctoral study titled "Some social aspects of China's special economic zones as a development strategy: Capitalist means to socialism" analyzed (a) the world-system approach and its extensions; (b) institutional and geographic diffusion; and (c) macro environments and found out that SEZs differ from China's treaty ports of the 19th century and the SEZ and coastal development strategy was associated with spatial inequality, and led to an emerging functional specialization of urban growth centres.

Tsui Kai Yuen (1987) in his thesis titled "A social cost-benefit analysis of export processing zones in some Asian countries" has examined the static welfare effects of the EPZ and found that EPZ exports are unstable than other kinds of (non-EPZ) export activities and hence EPZ does not seem to be an essential component of development strategy.

Roberts Mathew William (1991) in his doctoral dissertation "Export Processing Zones in Jhamaica and Mauritius" examined the industrial development of Jamaica and Mauritius via EPZs and found that both countries have benefited from their EPZs. However, both countries continue to face difficulties, promoting, manufacturing, diversification, utilization of local inputs, and technological transfers.

Ge wei (1993) in his doctoral study "Export Processing Zones, Multinational Firms and economic system transformation (China)" examined the EPZ's role in the utilization of domestic abundant resources, labour and the EPZ's role in the promotion of export-led economic growth in host less developed countries (LDS) and found that the establishment of an EPZ is an effective policy instrument in transforming an inward-looking, technology-backward, and labour-abundant economy to a more open and efficient structure.

Srinivasan Radhika (1997) in his thesis titled "Export processing zones in the context of trade liberalization: The salience of casualized labor in India (women factory workers)" analyzed the contours of liberalization and the importance of roofing the 1991 shifts in a broad social-political framework and what is learned from this study is that with the tacit support of the state, firms located in EPZs create a casualized labour force by adopting flexible production systems and by marginalizing trade union activity.

Objectives

1. To study the kinds of labour problems of the exporting units SEZ, Chennai metropolis.
2. To offer concrete suggestions to tackle the problems of the study units.

Methodology

The study made use of both primary and secondary data to address the issues taken up for research. Journals, reports, books, trade publications, articles, research papers and manuals are presented at appropriate places of the study. The required primary data were obtained by conducting a census study of the exporting units in the reference area. A well designed interview schedule was used for the census study. The interview schedule was finalized after pre-testing. The present researcher went through the records kept by Development Commissioner, MPEZ-Special Economic Zone. Having obtained the permission from the officer concerned, the researcher contacted all the 88 units functioning under the jurisdiction of Chennai-SEZ. As the number of study units was found to be controllable in number, it was thought to conduct a census study instead of sample survey.

Labour Problems

Labour is of different grades in the same way as materials. Inasmuch as labour cost had become a significant part of total production cost of a product, management has to focus attention on:
(a) creation of environment conducive to efficient labour performance;
(b) establishment of adequate control over labour time; and
(c) accounting properly for labour cost.

Control of labour cost presents certain practical difficulties due to the peculiarities of labour. In case of labour, neither is it possible to introduce a rigid control system nor to foresee its consequences. Any attempt on the part of management to utilize labour time effectively without recognizing the human element is bound to bring about strained relationship between them. Strained relationship results is reduced production at a higher cost. The best utilization of labour time and the consequent increased output will necessarily mean a low incidence of labour cost per unit of output.

Techno Labour

Techno labour to the zones in India is a myth. Manufacture of parts components and sub-assemblies, etc., in the zones does not lead to any acquisition of technology. Technology transfer has greater impact on exports packing and marking of goods is another sphere on which exporter should pay special attention (V.P. Gupta, 1995-96). What is the right packing and how to pack the goods properly keeps on changing with the passage of time with the advent of new packing products and technologies. Marking is required as a necessary step to facilitate identification of the goods at the time of transportation, shipment, custom clearance and storing.

Labour Productivity and Wages

Adam Smith recognized that a nation should employ its resources in a way in which it has 'some advantage'. It was left, however, to the English economist David Recardo to refine this insight into the logical principle of comparative advantage that has held pride of place in economic thought since Ricardo's 1817 formulation. In a simple illustration of what, under free trade, would determine trade between England and Portugal in wine and cloth, Ricardo focused on the relative differences in labour productivity (output per hour) in producing wine and cloth in England and Portugal. Ricardo wanted to "Pierce the monetary veil" and concentrate instead on the non-monetary real forces that determine trade. The focus is on the allocation of resources, and not on the balance of payments, which is adjusted through changes in wages or foreign exchange rates (Gerald M. Meier, 1998).

Industry-wise analysis of respondents' labour problem brought to the forefront that the problem of 31.04% of the units in the consumer products industry was the inefficiency of labour which was followed by demand of labour for higher pay, inadequate supply of techno labour, lack of trained labour and high labour turnover respectively of 27.59%, 17.24%, 13.79% and 10.34% of the units in the same groups of consumer products industry. Such details about the units in the other three groups of industry are provided in Table 1.

It is noticeable from the above table that among the consumer product industrial units, the prominent labour problem is labour inefficiency (31.04%). Among the leather and textile garments industrial units, it is high labour turnover (37.5%), among the electronics and software industrial units, it is the demand for higher pay (29.41%) and for engineering and other industrial units, it is the 'demand for higher pay'(27.78%).

Table 1: Industry-wise presentation of labour problem

Type of Industry	*Problems*					*Total*
	Demand for high pay	*Lack of techno labour*	*Lack of trained labour*	*More labour turnover*	*Poor efficiency*	
Consumer products industry	8 (27.59)	5 (17.24)	4 (13.79)	3 (10.34)	9 (31.04)	**29 (100)**
Textile and leather industry	5 (20.83)	4 (16.67)	3 (12.5)	9 (37.5)	3 (12.5)	**24 (100)**
Electronics & software industry	5 (29.41)	3 (17.65)	3 (17.65)	4 (23.53)	2 (11.76)	**17 (100)**
Engineering and others	5 (27.78)	3 (16.67)	4 (22.22)	4 (22.22)	2 (11.11)	**18 (100)**
Total	**23 (26.14)**	**15 (17.04)**	**14 (15.91)**	**20 (22.73)**	**16 (18.18)**	**88 (100)**

Figures in parenthesis denote per cent to total.
Source: Primary Data.

Hypothesis Testing

HO = There is no significant difference between the kinds of study units and the labour problems faced by them.

Table 2: Chi-square value: Kinds of study units and labour problems

Export Problems	*Chi Square value*	*P value*	*S/NS*
Labour problems	9.32	21	NS

Note : S—significant at 5% level (p value = 0.05):
NS—Not significant at 5% level (p value > 0.05)

The calculated value of X^2 (9.32) is less than the table value at 5% level (21). Hence, the hypothesis is accepted and therefore, it has been proved that there is no significant difference between the type of industry and labour problems.

Findings of the Present Study

Industry-wise analysis of the kind of material problem has disclosed that the problem of 37.94% of the units in the consumer products industry is the delayed supply of material. This is followed by high cost; inferior quality and cumbersome procedures respectively of 27.58%; 17.24% and another 17.24% of the units in the category of consumer products industry.

It is also ascertained that delayed supply of material is the problem of as large as 48% of the units under leather and textile industry group followed by high cost, sub-standard quality and tedious import procedures respectively of 28%, 16% and 8% of consumer products industrial units.

It is also found that the problem of delay in the supply of domestic material is the prevalent one for the units in all the four categories of industrial units. It is prevalent among 48.28% of consumer products industrial units; 44% of leather and textile industrial units, 47.62% of electronics and software industrial units and 44.32% of engineering and other industrial units. Among 88 study units, 44.32% face the problem of non-availability of home-grown material in time.

Suggestions

The non-availability of material in time is a major problem of the study units while its costs come second. Imported materials can be substituted by indigenous ones. It leads to an appreciable rise in the foreign exchange earnings. If goods are procured from the local market, proper planning and forecasting of the production schedules are to be prepared and followed strictly.

It is suggested that for producing export products of the right quality for foreign buyers, an effective policy and organizational framework must be made. To achieve an appropriate level of quality in export products, it is suggested to organize quality control operations in an effective way.

One of the major problems faced by the study units next to non-availability of material is high cost of material and it is an inhibiting factor. This problem has also been succinctly pointed out by Abid Hussain Committee, "India is often at a disadvantage vis-a-vis competing countries because its cost of production, hence export prices, are higher than in competing countries, not only because of the higher prices of importable and non-traded inputs, or because of time and cost over-runs implicit in managerial inefficiency, but also because of much lower levels of productivity, of all which stem from the aforesaid problems". It is suggested that the need of the hour is product development and product adaptation, research on new products and product diversification.

Another major problem as revealed by the study is delayed supply of material. Supply bottlenecks also tend to increase the costs in India. India has indigenous stocks of 3-4 months and imported stocks of 9 months and more. It is suggested to improve the supply of material, the study units where possible may have buffer stocks.

CONCLUSION

The EPZ policy in India underwent gradual relaxation of procedural and operational rigidities. The changes effected in this policy since 1991 have been far reaching and significant. It is believed that the overall and EPZ investment climate has an overwhelming bearing on the EPZ performance. In India, however, a conducive policy framework has had only a limited impact on the zone performance. Though the gross exports, foreign exchange earning and employment increased phenomenally in absolute terms, their growth rates declined substantially. Growth in exports per unit of employment also slowed down indicating deterioration in the export performance. Net value addition performance compares favourably with other Asian countries but it has not been consistent and the trend growth rate in value addition had not been statistically different from zero. Furthermore, these zones also failed to promote non-traditional exports. Traditional sectors, namely, electronics and gems and jewellery dominate. This could be due to the piecemeal nature of the policy changes. Various committees were set up to examine the performance of the zones. These committees made fa- reaching recommendations regarding incentive package, development of infrastructure and improvement in governance. However, policy changes remained slow and extremely cautious. Even the introduction of the SEZ policy did not have impact on the SEZ performance. Their performance continued to slide.

SEZs are expected to induce dynamism in the export performance of a country by eliminating distortions resulting from tariffs and other trade barriers, the corporate tax system, excessive bureaucracy, and missing infrastructure. Fall in the protective walls and reforms in the tax system reduced the gap between EPZ and other units in the wider economy in respect of tax incentives. There should have been significant improvement in the quality of infrastructure and governance to compensate them for the lost benefits. But this did not happen. Dysfunctional policies, regulations, lack of single-window clearance facilities, poor attitude of the officials, centralized governance, stringent labour laws and poor physical and financial infrastructure, all accounted for an undesirable investment climate. The study reveals that the SEZ scheme requires a complete reorientation if the hype created over SEZs is to be justified. As the country is longing for entering into developed stage from the developing stage, there is no second thought on the stimulation of exports. "Export is the engine for economic development."

REFERENCES

1. Abid Hussain Committee, Government of India, Report of the Committee on Trade Policies, p. 15.
2. Dobrydnio, Ronald, (1987). "Marketing strategies and export performance", The George Wahington University, USA.
3. Balu V. (2008). *International Trade.* Sri Venkateswara Publications, p. 381.
4. Ian Hamilton, F.E. (1987). *Industrial Change in Advanced Economics.* Billing & Sons Ltd., Creat Britain, p. 26.
5. Ge Wei, (1993). "Export Processing Zones, Multi-national firms and economic system Transformation (China)", University of Pennsylvania (USA).
6. Jay Narayan Vyas, (1990). Import of Capital Goods and Raw Materials. Ahmedabad, K. Patel & Co., Publishers, p. 169.
7. Jafer, Syed Hussain Ali, (1987). "An economic evaluation of the United States Generalized system of Tariff preferences (International Trade, Liberalization)", Ph.D. Dissertation Abstract, The University of Wisconsin – Madison (0262), DAI-A 47/09 (U.S.A), p. 3505.
8. Jeevanandam C. (2008). Foreign Exchange Practice, Concepts and Control. Sultan Chand and Sons, New Delhi, p. 332
9. Hari Shankar Singhania, (1999). Economic issues Global and National – A Business perspective, p. 91.
10. Nagendra, (2000). Quality, Productivity and compliances – The Survival kit for the future, Paper submitted in the International Conference, New Delhi.
11. Iyengar, S.P. (2004). Cost Accounting. Sultan Chand & Sons, New Delhi, Ninth Edition, p. B-1.4.
12. Srinivasan Radhika, (1997). "Export Processing Zones in the context of trade liberalization. The salience of casualized labour in India (Women factory workers)", Cornell University.
13. Chen Xiangming, (1988). "Some social aspects of China's special Economic Zones as a development strategy: Capitalist means to socialism" , Duke University, (USA).
14. Tsui Kai Yuen, (1987). "A Social Cost-Benefit analysis of export processing zones in some Asian countries", University of Toronto (Canada).
15. Marriott, Cherie, (1995). "Going up Markets", Journal of Asia Money, pp. 4-5.
16. Gerald M. Meier, (1998). The International Environment of Business, Stanford University, Oxford University Press, p. 34.

3

Ayurvedic Medicine in Indian Souk Echelon and Overseas Countries

M.A. LALITHA THIRUPURA SUNDARI AND C. KATHIRAVAN

Lecturer, Department of Business Administration),
AKD. Dharma Raja Women's College, Rajapalayam.
Assistant Professor, Department of Business Administration, Annamalai University,
Annamalai Nagar, Tamil Nadu, India.

ABSTRACT

Ayurveda is a form of holistic medicine that originated in India thousands of years ago. The central tenet to Ayurvedic treatment is a focus on preventative health, similar to most concepts of holistic medicine. This paper examines its uses, preventive maintenance of the body, mind and spirit, as one unit will prevent serious malfunction in the long run.

INTRODUCTION

Ayurveda is one of the world's oldest medical systems. It originated in India and has evolved there over thousands of years. In the United States, an Ayurvedic medicine is considered a complementary and alternative medicine. A group of diverse medical and health care systems, practices, and products that are not presently considered to be part of the conventional medicine. Complementary medicine is used together with conventional medicine, and alternative medicine is used in place of conventional medicine. (CAM)—more specifically, a CAM whole medical system. A complete system of theory and practice that has evolved over time in different cultures and apart from conventional medicine. Examples of whole medical systems include traditional Chinese medicine, Ayurvedic medicine, homoeopathy, and naturopathy. Many therapies used in Ayurvedic medicine are also used on their own as CAM—for example, herbs, massage, pressing, rubbing, and moving muscles and other soft tissues of the body, primarily by using the hands and fingers. The aim is to increase the flow of blood and oxygen to the massaged area., and specialized diets. This fact sheet provides a general overview of Ayurvedic medicine and suggests sources for additional information.

Background

Around 1500 BC, Ayurveda's fundamental and applied principles got organised and enunciated. Ayurveda traces its origins in the Vedas, *Atharvaveda* in particular, and is connected to Hindu religion. *Atharvaveda* (one of the foremost ancient books of Indian knowledge, wisdom and culture) contains 114 hymns or formulations for the treatment of diseases. Ayurveda originated in and developed from these hymns. In this sense, Ayurveda is considered by some to have divine origin. According to a later writer, the system of medicine was received by Dhanvantari from Brahma, and Dhanvantari was deified as the god of medicine. In later times his status was gradually reduced, until he was credited with having been an earthly king. The *Sushruta Samhita* of Sushruta appeared during the 1st millennium BC. Dwivedi & Dwivedi (2007) – on the work of the surgeon Sushruta – write:

The main vehicle of the transmission of knowledge during that period was by oral method. The language used was Sanskrit — the vedic language of that period (2000–500 BC). The most authentic compilation of his teachings and work is available in a treatise called *Sushruta Samhita.* This contains 184 chapters and description of 1,120 illnesses, 700 medicinal plants, 64 preparations from mineral sources and 57 preparations based on animal sources.

Cataract surgery was known to the physician Sushruta in the first millennium BC, and was performed with a special tool called the *jabamukhi salaka*, a curved needle used to loosen the lens and push the cataract out of the field of vision. The eye would later be soaked with warm butter and then bandaged.

Underwood & Rhodes (2008) hold that this early phase of traditional Indian medicine identified 'fever (*takman*), cough, consumption, diarrhea, dropsy, abscesses, seizures, tumors, and skin diseases (including leprosy)'. Treatment of complex ailments, including angina pectoris, diabetes, hypertension, and stones, also ensued during this period. Plastic surgery, cataract surgery, puncturing to release fluids in the abdomen, extraction of foreign elements, treatment of anal fistulas, treating fractures, amputations, cesarean sections, and stitching of wounds were known. The use of herbs and surgical instruments became widespread. The *Charaka Samhita* is arguably the principal classic reference. It gives emphasis to the true nature of each person: body care, mental regulation, and spiritual/consciousness refinement.

Other early works of Ayurveda include the *Charaka Samhita*, attributed to Charaka. The earliest surviving excavated written material which contains the works of Sushruta is the Bower Manuscript, dated to the 4th century AD. The Bower manuscript quotes directly from Sushruta and is of special interest to historians due to the presence of Indian medicine and its concepts in Central Asia. Vagbhata, the son of a senior doctor by the name of Simhagupta, also compiled his works on traditional medicine. Early Ayurveda had a school of physicians and a school of surgeons. Tradition holds that the text *Agnivesh Tantra*, written by the sage Agnivesh, a student of the sage Bharadwaja, influenced the writings of Ayurveda.

The Chinese pilgrim Fa Hsien (ca. 337–422 AD) wrote about the health care system of the Gupta empire (320–550) and described the institutional approach of Indian medicine, also visible in the works of Charaka, who mentions a clinic and how it should be equipped. Madhava Sarngadhara (fl. 1300), and Bhavamisra (fl. 1500) compiled works on Indian medicine The medical works of both Sushruta and Charaka were translated into the Arabic language during the Abbasid Caliphate (ca. 750). These Arabic works made their way into Europe via intermediaries. In Italy, the Branca family of Sicily and Gaspare Tagliacozzi (Bologna) became familiar with the techniques of Sushruta. British physicians travelled to India to see rhinoplasty being performed by native methods. Reports on Indian rhinoplasty were published in the *Gentleman's Magazine* in 1794. Joseph Constantine Carpue spent 20 years in India studying local plastic surgery methods. He was able to perform the first major surgery in the western world in 1815. Instruments described in the *Sushruta Samhita* were further modified in the western world.

WHAT IS AYURVEDA?

Ayurveda, known as the "science of life" in ancient Sanskrit, has been a key part of a comprehensive natural health care system in India and Sri Lanka for over 2000 years. The basic tenet of Ayurveda is that health conditions should be treated with holistic, natural therapies tailored to the needs of each individual. In addition to treating the physical body with Ayurvedic herbs, Ayurveda focuses on balancing the mind and spirit to achieve inner harmony.

Ayurveda teaches that each person is a blend of three *dosha*s, or vital energies within the body: ***Vata***, ***Pitta*** and ***Kapha***. Each person is born with an optimal balance and a unique harmony among the three *dosha*s. Later in life, negative health may arise from an imbalance in the three *dosha*s — and the science of Ayurveda is used to bring back this essential harmony.

Unlike Western medicine which is typically used as a reactive mechanism to fight disease once it occurs, Ayurveda is used to strengthen and nourish the body before the advent of negative health conditions. Ayurvedic practitioners typically recommend a natural course of herbs, diet, exercise and meditation to bring harmony back to the individual. This may be accomplished with a regimen of detoxification/purging herbs to initially rid the body of negative toxins followed by beneficial herbs which focus on bringing the three *dosha*s back into balance. In returning the mind, body and spirit back to its original *dosha* balance, Ayurvedic practitioners believe that an individual is better able to withstand future illnesses and adverse health conditions while living a more pleasant, harmonious life.

Objectives

- To facilitate availability of raw drugs which are authentic and contain essential components as required under pharmacopoeial standards to help improve quality of drugs, for domestic consumption and export.
- To gradually validate therapy and drugs to address in particular the chronic and new life-style related emerging diseases.
- To create awareness about the strengths of these systems in India and abroad and sensitize other stakeholders and providers of health.
- To provide full opportunity for the growth and development of these systems and utilization of their potential, strength and revival of their glory.

STATUS OF AYURVEDA IN INDIA

In India, 8400 Ayurvedic medicines/pharmacies are available. In India, 60% of the registered physicians are involved in non-allopathic systems of medicine. In addition to the nearly 4,00,000 Ayurvedic practitioners, there are over 1,70,000 homeopathic physicians. Reliance on Ayurvedic medicines is heavy in certain regions of India, such as Kerala in the southwest. Many Ayurvedic practitioners in small villages are not registered.

Within India

In 1970, the Indian Medical Central Council Act which aims to standardize qualifications for Ayurveda and provide accredited institutions for its study and research was passed by the Parliament of India. The state-sponsored Central Council for Research in Ayurveda and Siddha (CCRAS) is the premier institution for promoting traditional medicine in India. The studies conducted by this institution encompass clinical, drug, literary, and family welfare research. To fight biopiracy and unethical patents, the Government of India, in 2001, set up the Traditional Knowledge.

AYURVEDA AT GLOBAL LEVEL

Ayurvedic medicines are one of the most ancient systems of treatment in India and now spreading globally. Natural products are also a part of our everyday life. India has a rich heritage of using Ayurvedic and herbal medicines supported by neutraceuticals. Ayurveda and herbals have just recently started rising on the horizon of alternative system of medicine. Ayurveda and herbal have been practicsed and used all over the world for many years. But only recently they havestarted getting legal acceptance in many countries as alternative system of medicine. India is called "Botanical Garden of the world" as it is the largest producer of medicinal herbs. Out of more than 25,000 plants of medicinal value, only 10% are used for their medicinal value. Around 1800 species are systematically documented in the codified Indian systems of medicine. These herbal products are preventive, protective, nutritive and curative. Stems, roots, flowers, fruits and seeds have medicinal uses. There are thousands of herbs. As per W.H.O. report, more than 80% of the world population uses medicines made from herbal and natural products. Current global market of herbal and Ayurvedic medicines is estimated to be more than US$ 100 billion, out of this E.U. accounts for about 40%, Japan 20%, USA 10%. The Asian countries together account for 30% of the global market. During the last decade importance of alternative medicine was realized and with the inclination to this, the growth rate of Ayurvedic and herbal industry can be put to more than 30% for the last 25 years. The world, which due to technological advances, developed medicines which are quick acting, potent and capable to treat and provide symptomatic relief, has now started to feel the need for longer lasting and more fundamental cures for their problems of health. Ayurveda accounts for more than 80% of user profile of traded medicinal plants, with 719 plants being used in this sector.

The lowest number of species (49) is in the modern system of medicine. It is estimated that over 8000 units are engaged in preparation of wide range of herbal products using medicinal plants. Most of the units use the Ayurveda system of medicine. There are also licensed practitioners numbering around 5,00,000, who believe in processing the plants themselves and preparing medicines. Besides, there are also estimated one million folk healers in and around villages of India. There also medicinal plants cultivation and consumption at home level (Tulsi and Aloe vera and such others) which are beyond the estimation for commercial cultivation. Based on the current commercial consumption levels in the ISM sector (Rs. 384 crore), and export level (Rs. 463 crore only crude drugs), it is estimated that commercialization of medicinal plant cultivation was to the extent of Rs. 847 crore (2001-02) in India. Because of their uniqueness Ayurvedic products as an alternative system of medicine, and many herbal products of Indian origin, have potential to win a considerable share of the world market. Reportedly, UK, UAE, Sweden, Indonesia and USA have already recognized Ayurveda as a health care system and thirty more countries are on the verge of doing so. India with its wide variety of climatic and soil conditions has ample scope in gaining a foothold in the global plant based pharmaceutical market. But the promotional efforts by industries and government have not been sufficient to achieve the required potential presented by the markets abroad. Thus, an appropriate planning and action based on the market requirements is essential. India has 45,000 diverse plant species spread over 16 different agro-climatic zones, 10 vegetation zones, 25 biotic provinces and 426 habitats of specific spices.. Besides, India has up to 18,000 flowering plants, 2500 algae, 23,000 fungi, 1600 types of lichen and 1,800 varieties of bryophytes. Of this vast quantum around 15,000 to 20,000 are of medicinal value, but out of this only, 7,000 to 7,500 plants are used by traditional medicine systems in India. In the light of such situation, there is a need for establishing backward and forward linkages for the herbal sector and strategies for their seamless integration for a sustainable growth oriented performance of the sector, specifically on the export front.

Modern Market Developments

The SAARC (South Asia Association for Regional Cooperation) was formed in 1985; its member countries are India, Pakistan, Nepal, Bangladesh, Bhutan, Maldives, and Sri Lanka. These countries all have been influenced by Ayurvedic medicine. Trade in Ayurvedic medicines within the SAARC is mostly limited to raw materials that grow in one region (e.g., high mountains, northern climate) and are then exported to other regions (e.g., lowland southern areas). Because of the large number of small factories that try to serve the local communities, with products labelled with the local language, there is little opportunity for suppliers in one SAARC country to send finished products to another SAARC country or even abroad.

Entrepreneurs in these countries (mainly in India) seeking to break into the market for natural products have determined, rightly, that the demand for traditional style Ayurvedic medicines both inside and outside the region is limited, despite growth trends as high as 20% annually encountered in the late 1990s. They have aimed to bolster interest by carrying out scientific research into promising herbs and formulas that are based on Ayurveda but not necessarily reflecting traditional practices. Of necessity, such research eventually focuses on finding active ingredients, and this has led to the development of isolates from plants that are sold as "nutraceuticals" (substances not registered as drugs, but used like nutritional and dietary supplements, sold over the counter in various formulations with specific health benefits). For these, there is a growing worldwide demand. The main suppliers of nutraceuticals are Japan, China, and the U.S., but India stands to become a significant contributor.

India Exporters

Name	Product Exported	Foreign Country
Wws Skyshop (P) Ltd.,	AYURVEDIC MEDICINE AYU-SLIM	United Arab Emirates
Wws Skyshop (P) Ltd.,	AYURVEDIC MEDICINE AYU-SLIM	United Arab Emirates
Venus Industrial Corporation	AYURVEDIC MEDICINE DABUR'S PHUDIN HARA	Australia
Ayurvet Limited	AYURVEDIC MEDICINE SUPERLIV CONCPREMIX 20KG	South Africa
Global Influence	AYURVEDIC PROPRIETARY MEDICINE LIV 52 K DROPS	Not Available
Global Influence	AYURVEDIC PROPRIETORY MEDICINE CYSTONE UNCOATED TABS	Moldova

Ayurveda Herbal in India - Future

Ayurveda/herbal in India 2015 will be an altogether different industry but with the collective efforts from various departments. The whole Ayurveda/ herbal industry needs to be more streamlined, transparent and there should be proper linkage between the producer, processor and aggregators of Ayurveda/herbal products and medicines in order to achieve the targets.

In India the aromatic and herbal based medicinal industry in addition to health and diet supplements is growing at a fast pace and expected to grow at an average rate of more than 20% both at global as well as domestic sphere. To handle such an immense industry we need an integrated approach. For this ASSOCHAM has made a few suggestions and these are as follow.

ASSOCHAM SUGGESTION ON AYURVEDA HERBAL INDIA 2015

Popularization of Herbal Preparations to Create Awareness

According to India Ayurveda system one should always eat such food that is healthy to the body in addition to providing complete nutrition. This comes under the present-day nutraceuticals. There is a need to create an awareness of nutraceuticals for good health and rejuvenation. There are hardly any side-effects of these herbal products. As part of social marketing and awareness programmes more Ayurveda herbal spas and herbal parks should be created. In these herbal parks information on different kinds of herbs, health rejuvenation, famous herbal preparations with good Ayurveda health tips should be provided in order to popularize the Ayurveda Herbal India 2015.

Explore the Domestic and Export Market

Ayurvedic herbal products are required not only in India but also across the world.. But in the absence of integrated market segment and associated promotional activities most of these products are unable to put an impact which they are supposed to make. In order to tap the domestic and export market trade fair and exhibitions must be organized where buyers and sellers of these products can meet and explore new business opportunities. ASSOCHAM is already playing its role in this direction. ASSOCHAM has found out that trade fairs and exhibitions have the capability of tapping this industry where it will be easy both to procure the raw material and market the finished products. Electronic media should also be used for quick results.

National Medicinal Plants Board (NMPB) and its Role in Promoting Ayurvedic/ Herbal Products

Government of India set up the National Medicinal Plants Board (NMPB) in 2002 to coordinate the matters related to medicinal plants. It also supports the policies and programmes that are meant for the growth of trade, its export, cultivation and conservation. NMPB is responsible to check the growth of the medicinal plants across the country. At state and regional level the growth of medicinal plants is take care by the State Medicinal Plants Boards (SMPB). Till September 2006 there were 35 SMPBs.

Verdict

The key suppliers in Ayurveda are Dabur, Baidyanath, and Zandu, which together have about 85% of India's domestic market as well as foreign countries.

Dabur India Ltd. is India's largest Ayurvedic medicine supplier and the fourth largest producer of FMCG. It was established in 1884, and had grown to a business level in 2003 of about 650 million dollars per year, though only a fraction of that is involved with Ayurvedic medicine. Last year, about 15% of sales volume was pharmaceuticals, the remaining 85% were mostly non-medicine items such as foods and cosmetics. Dabur's Ayurvedic Specialities Division has over 260 medicines for treating a range of ailments and body conditions--from common cold to chronic paralysis. These materials constitute only 7% of Dabur's total revenue (thus, less than 50 million dollars). Dabur Chyawanprash (herbal honey) has a market share of 70% and chewable Hajmola digestive tablets has 88% share. Other major products are Dabur Amla Hair Oil, Vatika (Shampoo), and Lal Dant Manjan (Tooth Powder).

Sri Baidyanath Ayurvedic Bhawan Ltd. (Baidyanath for short) was founded in 1917 in Calcutta, and specializes in Ayurvedic medicines, though it has recently expanded into the FMCG sector with cosmetic and hair care products; one of its international products is Shikakai (soap pod) Shampoo. Baidyanath has a sales volume of about 350 million dollars, but most of the product sales are in the cosmetic range. The company reports having over 700 Ayurvedic products, made at 10 manufacturing centers, with 1,600 employees. Included items are herbal teas, patent medicines, massage oils, and chyawanprash.

Zandu Pharmaceutical Works was incorporated in Bombay in 1919, named after an 18th-century Ayurvedic. The company focuses primarily on Ayurvedic products (in 1930, pharmaceuticals were added, but the pharmaceutical division was separated off about 30 years later). However, today Zandu has a chemicals division and cosmetics division. Its total sales volume is about 45 million dollars. One of its current projects is to develop a dopamine drug from a plant extract, applying for new drug status in the U.S.

The Himalaya Drug Company, was established in 1934 in Bangalore. It currently has a business level of about 500 million dollars and has a U.S. distribution division (Himalaya USA). It is known in the U.S. for the product Liv-52, marketed as a liver protector and therapy for liver diseases like viral hepatitis; the product was first marketed in India in 1955.

Charak Pharmaceuticals was founded in 1947, and currently has three distribution centers in India; it produces liquids, tablets, and veterinary supplies. It has gained a large advantage with its new product Evanova, a preparation containing 33 herbs and minerals and non-hormonal active ingredients used as a menopause treatment alternative to HRT. Soya is one of the main ingredients in this product. The product also contains Ayurvedic herbs that act like selective estrogen receptor modulators as well as asparagus root (shatavari), which reduces the frequency and intensity of hot flashes.

Vicco Laboratories, was established in 1958. It mainly produces topical therapies based on Ayurveda and is best known internationally for its toothpaste product, Vajradanti, which has been marketed in the U.S. for more than 25 years.

The Emami Group, founded in 1974, provides a diverse range of products, doing 110 million dollars of business annually, though only a portion is involved with Ayurvedic products, through its Himani line; the company is mainly involved with toiletries and cosmetics, but also provides Chyawanprash and other health products.

Aimil Pharmaceuticals Ltd., incorporated in 1984 and engaged in manufacturing and sale of both generic and proprietary Ayurvedic medicines, with a business level of about 20 million dollars annually. Its wide range of Ayurvedic herbal formulations, covering most therapeutic segments, was honored by the Indian government's National Award for Quality Herbal Preparations and National Award for R & D in the year 2002. It is known for its proprietary formulas for hepatitis, diabetes, menstrual disorders, digestive disorders, and urinary diseases.

Implication

1. As the year 2010 drew to an end, we witnessed the Fourth World Ayurveda Congress (WAC) with its central theme 'Ayurveda for All', attracting over 4000 delegates from different parts of India, 300 foreign delegates from over 60 countries.
2. Ayurveda's growing popularity, and the increasing public curiosity towards all its aspects.
3. The year 2011 promises to be a very crucial year for the AUS (Ayurveda, Unani, and Siddha) sector, especially as the world is seeking affordable health solutions and western medicine is facing a crisis. Ayurveda is the world's most comprehensive, personalized, holistic and sustainable health system.
4. The reasons are many: Ayurveda provides much more than just a system of medicine - it offers the keys to a healthy way of life and living; better understanding of how systemic theories of Ayurveda 'shastra' can provide new insights and paradigms in the biomedical 'sciences'.

CONCLUSION

Ayurveda is the system of medicine incorporating centuries of wisdom in it. The emphasis here is on ways to promote health rather than just treat disease. The beauty of the system is that every individual is unique rather than being just another case of particular disease. It is one of the few systems of medicine taking mental, emotional and spiritual well being into account. All the suggestions and remedies prescribed are totally in conjunction with nature.

REFERENCES

1. Chopra, A. and Doiphode, V.V. (2002). Ayurvedic medicine-core concept, therapeutic principles, and current relevance. *Medical Clinics of North America.* 86(1): 75–88.
2. Courson, W.A. (2008). State licensure and Ayurvedic practice: planning for the future, managing the present. Newsletter of the National Ayurvedic Medical Association [online journal]. Autumn 2003.
3. Dodds, J.A. (2008). Know your CAM provider. Bulletin of the American Academy of Orthopaedic Surgeons/ American Association of Orthopaedic Surgeons [online journal].
4. Gogtay, N.J., Bhatt, H.A. and Dalvi, S.S. et al. (2002). The use and safety of non-allopathic Indian medicines. *Drug Safety.* 25(14): 1005–1019.
5. Lead poisoning associated with Ayurvedic Medications—Five States, 2000–2003. Morbidity and Mortality Weekly Report. Centers for Disease Control and Prevention Web site. Accessed on February 14, 2008.
6. Lodha, R. and Bagga, A. (2000). Traditional Indian systems of medicine. *Annals of the Academy of Medicine,* Singapore. 29(1): 37–41.
7. Mishra, L., Singh, B.B. and Dagenais, S. (2001). Ayurveda: A historical perspective and principles of the traditional healthcare system in India. Alternative Therapies in Health and Medicine. 7(2): 36–42.
8. Mishra, L., Singh, B.B. and Dagenais, S. (2001). Healthcare and disease management in Ayurveda. Alternative Therapies in Health and Medicine. 7(2): 44–50.
9. Saper, R.B., Kales, S.N. and Paquin, J. et al. (2004). Heavy metal content of Ayurvedic herbal medicine products. *J. Am. Medi. Asso.* 292(23): 2868–2873.
10. Shankar, K. and Liao, L.P. (2004). Traditional systems of medicine. Physical Medicine and Rehabilitation Clinics of North America. 15(4): 725–747.
11. Singh, B.B., Vinjamury, S.P. and Der-Martirosian, C. et al. (2007). Ayurvedic and collateral herbal treatments for hyperlipidemia: a systematic review of randomized controlled trials and quasi-experimental designs. Alternative Therapies in Health and Medicine. 13(4): 22–28.
12. Subbarayappa, B.V. (2001). The roots of ancient medicine: an historical outline. *J. Bioscience.* 26(2): 135–144.

4

Role of Tourism in India's Foreign Exchange Earning: A Micro Study

G. KALAISELVI, V. RAJALAKSHMI AND A. MEENAKSHI SUNDARARAJAN

Assistant Professor, Department of Commerce, S.T. Hindu College, Nagercoil–629002.
E-mail: gkssthc@gmail.com.
Associate Professor, Department of Commerce, Sarah Tucker College, Tirunelveli–627007.
Principal, S.T. Hindu College, Nagercoil–629 002.

ABSTRACT

Tourism is widely acclaimed as an important global industry offering immense employment opportunities and foreign currency. Foreign exchange is an important gain from tourism. Tourism is also referred to as 'invisible exports' as it earns foreign exchange not by exporting goods or services but by promoting foreign tourists arrivals. Tourism is one of the sources of the much required foreign exchange in India as it has vast tourism potential. It has grown substantially over the last three decades in India. Although India has progressed a lot in tourism, it is still way behind the developed even the developing countries. Tourism is India's second largest foreign exchange earner but its potential has not been exploited to the full. India's share in international tourism is insignificant considering the continental size of the country and its rich tourist resources. However, today the circumstances have improved to a great extent and the industry is being accepted as one with tremendous prospects in terms of foreign exchange earnings and employment. The present study has been undertaken to measure the contribution of tourism in India's foreign exchange earnings based on the available secondary data. It is inferred from the analysis that there is a steady growth of foreign tourist arrivals (FTAs) and foreign exchange earnings (FEEs) in India with some minor deviations in the study period. It is found that the correlation between FTAs and FEE is highly significant ($r = 0.98$, $p < 0.000$) which infers that there is a strong relationship between FTAs and FEEs. It is also found that India's share in world tourist arrivals and world tourism receipts is not significant. However, by implementing efficient marketing strategies India will become the most prefered tourist destination in the world in near future and tourism will be the first largest foreign exchange earner for India with maximal share of world tourist receipts.

Keywords: Tourism, Export industry, Foreign tourists, Foreign exchange.

INTRODUCTION

Tourism is widely acclaimed as an important global industry offering immense employment opportunities and foreign currency. Foreign exchange is an important gain from tourism. Foreign exchange receipts from international tourists are major earners of foreign currency and exceed the receipts from any other single industry. Countries are in need of foreign exchange to meet their developmental needs. Tourism is also referred to as 'invisible exports' as it earns foreign exchange not by exporting goods or services but by promoting foreign tourist arrivals. Tourism offers remarkable scope for narrowing down the gap in balance of payment by earning foreign exchange at low social cost. The major economic benefit in promoting the tourism industry has, therefore, tended to be the earning of foreign exchange. Income from foreign tourism in the form of foreign exchange earnings adds to the national income and as an invisible export may offset a loss on the visible trading account and be of critical importance in the overall financial reckoning. This is truer in the case of developing countries like India.

World Tourism

Tourism is one of the world's largest industries with an average growth rate of 5% over the past twenty years. World Tourism Organization (UNWTO) observes that tourism is the world's largest growing industry with no sign of slowing down in the 21st century (WTO, 1999). There has been a significant improvement in the international tourist arrivals and tourist receipts. The international tourist arrivals were 439 million in 1990, 698 million in 2000 and 880 million in the year 2009 (WTO 1999; WTO 2010). Another reliable indicator of the growth of world tourism is the increasing international receipts on account of tourism. The world tourism receipts increased to US $ 852 billion in the year 2009 from US $ 475.3 billion in 2000 (WTO, 2010). Tourism has emerged as the most lucrative business having tremendous potential for earning foreign exchange. Faced with problems of declining terms of trade of agricultural products and high level of protection against manufacturing, many developing countries have turned to tourism for earning much needed foreign exchange to finance development projects. In over 25 countries tourism has now become one of the top three "export" items in their national economy (Kaul and Virender, 1994).

Indian Tourism

Tourism is an upcoming and fast growing industry in developing countries like India. It has grown substantially over the last three decades in India. Till the 1980s and early 1990s, tourism in India was primarily associated with elitism. The policies were never framed with an intention to promote tourism. The potential of the industry was hugely undermined. However, today the circumstances have improved to a great extent and the industry is accepted as one with tremendous prospects in terms of foreign exchange earnings and employment. Though tourism in India gained importance belatedly, it has grown at a rapid pace and enhanced its share in international tourist arrivals as well as in foreign exchange earnings. During the period 1951 to 2001 Indian tourism achieved a compound growth rate of 16.2% in foreign exchange earnings as against world average of 13.5% (PTI, 2009). Tourism is India's second largest foreign exchange earner (Bheemaraj, 2008). It has now been recognized as an "export industry" due to its multiple advantages. According to World Travel and Tourism Council, India will be a tourism hot spot from 2009 to 2018 having the highest ten year potential. The Travel and Tourism Competitiveness Report, 2007, ranked tourism in India 6th, in terms of price competitiveness. In the year 2005, Conde Nast listed India as the 10th chosen destination in the world. Surprisingly in the year 2006, India has moved to the 4th position. Latest trends of tourism in India show India as a fast emerging and highly ranked tourist place of South East Asia. India is the leading destination in the South Asia region with a share of 41.2% of tourist arrivals to South Asia in 2007 (Ishwara, 2010). The remarkable growth in Indian tourism market has identically benefited many support industries like hotels, aviation, transport, sports and medical tourism. Now tourism is one of the largest service industries in India with a contribution of 6.23% to national GDP and 8.78% of the total employment (TTDC, 2010). The above figures may sound big from India's point of view but when compared with France (75.1 million), Spain (53.6 million), USA (46.1 million) our figure 3.5 million seems negligible (Ramakumar and Rajashree Shinde, 2008). Recognizing the benefits of tourism, Indian government has established policies and programmes to promote international travel. Many Indian travel packages are offered by Indian tourism for foreigners all over India. The international tourists' arrival to India has been on a constant rise for a while now, indicating a strong recovery in the fundamentals of tourism industry. With outlook of global tourism appearing positive, the international tourist flow into India is expected to register far better growth than earlier (KRC Research, 2003).

Statement of the Problem

Every country is ambitious to reach the economically developed status. To achieve their economic growth foreign exchange earnings by the country is one of the essential aspects. Tourism has emerged as an industry to earn foreign exchange without much problem, struggle and cost. India also requires foreign exchange to meet its developmental needs. Tourism is one of the sources of the much required foreign exchange in India as it has vast tourism potential. Tourism has become an important sector in Indian economy and is the second largest source of foreign exchange earnings. The immense potential of tourism for earning foreign exchange was recently recognized and "export house" status was given to it in 1998. In spite of India's rich cultural values, natural and artificial attractions, the number of foreign tourist arrivals to India does not seem to be satisfactory and its foreign exchange earnings are meagret. Therefore, efforts have been taken both by public and private sectors to attract and increase the length of their stay in India which has resulted in the increase of the foreign tourists and foreign exchange earnings in the last one decade. The present study has been undertaken to measure the contribution of tourism in India's foreign exchange earnings.

Objectives

- To study the growth of foreign tourist arrivals in India
- To study the progress of foreign exchange earnings from tourism in India
- To find out the share of India in the world tourism as well as in Asia and the Pacific region in terms of foreign tourist arrivals and foreign exchange earnings.

Significance of the Study

Tourism offers an opportunity for earning foreign exchange at low cost which is very much essential for the countries' economic development. The expenses incurred by the international tourist inevitably have a positive effect on the balance of payment position of the destination country. India is one of the few countries in the world blessed with tremendous variety of tourist resources and has something to offer to everyone. Tourism is India's second largest foreign exchange earner but its potential has not been exploited to the full. India's share in international tourism is insignificant considering the continental size of the country and its rich tourist resources. There still exist several hitches which need to be considered so as to exploit the true potential of tourism industry in India and make the country to register far better growth in future. Hence the study of foreign exchange earnings through tourism in India is of great importance.

Data Collection

The present study is fully dependent on the secondary data. Data required for the study are gathered from secondary sources of information such as books, government publications, journals, newspapers and websites for the period ranging from the year 2000 to 2009.

Statistical Tools

The tools applied in the study include percentage change analysis, trend by the method of Ordinary Least Square, the Karl Pearson's coefficient of correlation and graph.

In this study the percentage change analysis has been used to know the growth of foreign tourist arrivals and to know the progress in the foreign exchange earnings.

Percentage change = (Difference in figures of two years) / (Previous year's figures) * 100.

In order to project the trends of foreign tourist arrivals and foreign exchange earnings, the method of Ordinary Least Squares is fitted. The trend is represented by the equation.

$$Y = a + bx$$

Karl Pearson coefficient of correlation (r) is used to find out the relationship between foreign tourist arrivals and foreign exchange earnings.

$$r = [n\Sigma XY - \Sigma X \Sigma Y] / [Sqrt(n\Sigma X^2 - (\Sigma X)^2 . Sqrt(n\Sigma Y^2 - (\Sigma Y)^2]$$

Foreign Tourist Arrivals (FTAs) in India during the Period from 2000 to 2009

Table 1 shows the FTAs to India for ten years from 2000 to 2009 with percentage change in the arrivals over the year. To analyze foreign exchange earnings from tourism it is necessary to study about the FTAs as foreign exchange through tourism can be earned only when there are FTAs.

Table 1: Foreign tourist arrivals (FTAs) in India, 2000-2009

Year	FTAs in India *(in million)*	*Percentage change over the previous year*
2000	2.65	6.7
2001	2.54	-4.2
2002	2.38	-6
2003	2.73	14.3
2004	3.46	26.8
2005	3.92	13.3
2006	4.45	13.5
2007	5.08	14.3
2008	5.28	4
2009	5.11	-3.3

Source: Ministry of Tourism, Government of India, 2009-10.

Tourism in India has grown substantially in the last three decades. In 2000, the number of FTAs touched 2.65 million with the percentage of 6.7. In the years 2001 and 2002, the tourism industry worldwide passed through a difficult phase on account global economic downturn, high level of uncertainty due to the terrorist attacks, Iraq war and Severe Acute Respiratory Syndrome (SARS) epidemic. The Indian tourism was adversely affected after 11th September 2001 terrorist attacks on USA, Afghan war, Indo-Pak war tension and registering a decline of 4.2% in the year 2001 against the growth of 6.7% achieved in 2000. Terrorist assault on the Parliament and in some places of India had enormous detrimental effects on tourism. FTAs in India recorded a decline of 6.9% during the year 2002 as compared to 2001.

However, things started looking bright for the Indian tourism industry especially in 2003. The campaign "Incredible India" initiated by the Tourism Ministry helped to create a colourful image of India abroad and directly led to an increase in the FTAs to 14.3% in 2003. In the year 2004, India's tourism sector was thriving and it registered a rapid growth of 26.8 % in the year 2003. In 2007, the number of FTAs touched the magic 5.08 million and swelled by 12%. The FTAs during 2009 was 5.11 million which is 3.3% less compared to 5.28 million during the year 2008. Mumbai terror attacks and global economic downturn were the main causes for the decline. However, the slump in the tourism sector is showing a reversal in the trend and an improvement has been observed in the year 2010. The total FTAs between January to June 2010 was 26.3 lakh as against 23.7 lakh during the same period in 2009 (Tourism Statistics, 2010). It is inferred from the analysis that there is a steady growth of FTAs with some minor deviations in the study period. Figure 1 shows the FTAs to India from 2000 to 2009.

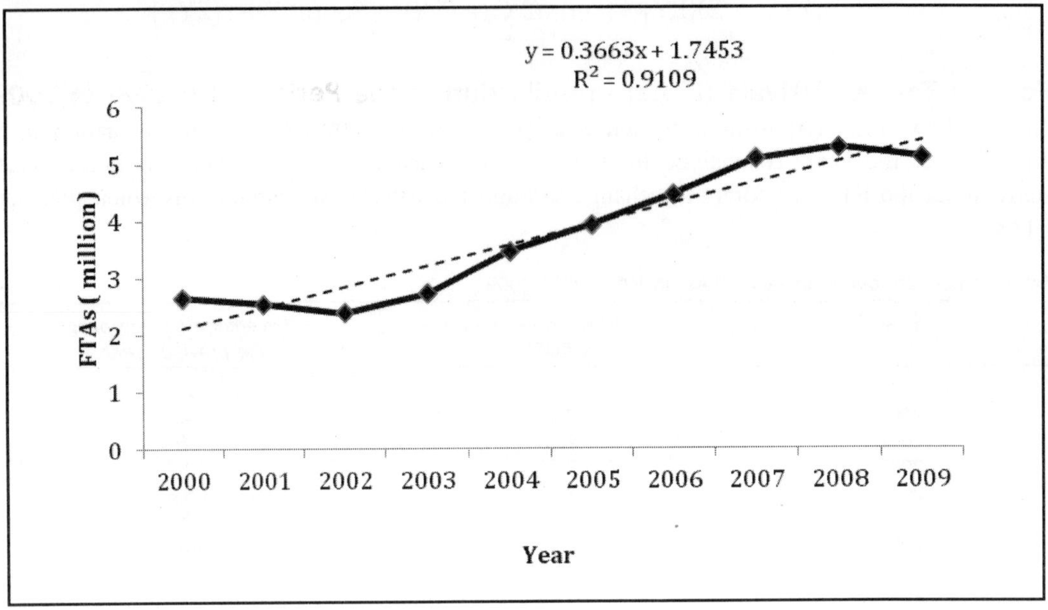

Fig. 1. Linear fit of FTAs in India. The linearly fitted trend line of FTAs shows that there is a steady growth in the tourist arrivals.

Table 2: Foreign exchange earnings (FEEs) from tourism in India, 2000-2009

Year	FEE *(in Rs. crore)*	*Percentage change over the previous year*
2000	15,626	20.7
2001	15,083	-3.5
2002	15,064	-0.1
2003	20,729	37.6
2004	27,944	34.8
2005	33,123	18.5
2006	39,025	17.8
2007	44,360	13.7
2008	50,730	14.4
2009	54,960	8.3

Source: Ministry of Tourism, Government of India, 2009-10.

Table 2 presents the FEE in India from tourism from 2000 to 2009 with a percentage change over the years. In 2000, the FEE of India from tourism was Rs.15626 crore but there was a steep decline in FEE from 20.7% in 2000 to 3.5% in 2001 and further to 0.1% in 2002. This decline was due to the decrease in the number of tourists in these years. However, from the year 2003, Indian tourism registered a steady increase in FEE and the maximum percentage change of 37.6% was observed in this year. During the year 2007, India also earned foreign exchange through tourism to the tune of Rs. 44,360 crore which is 33.8% more than the last year's earnings. In the year 2009, tourism made a significant contribution to India's foreign exchange earnings which grew to Rs. 54,960 crore. The modest increase of 0.6% of India's

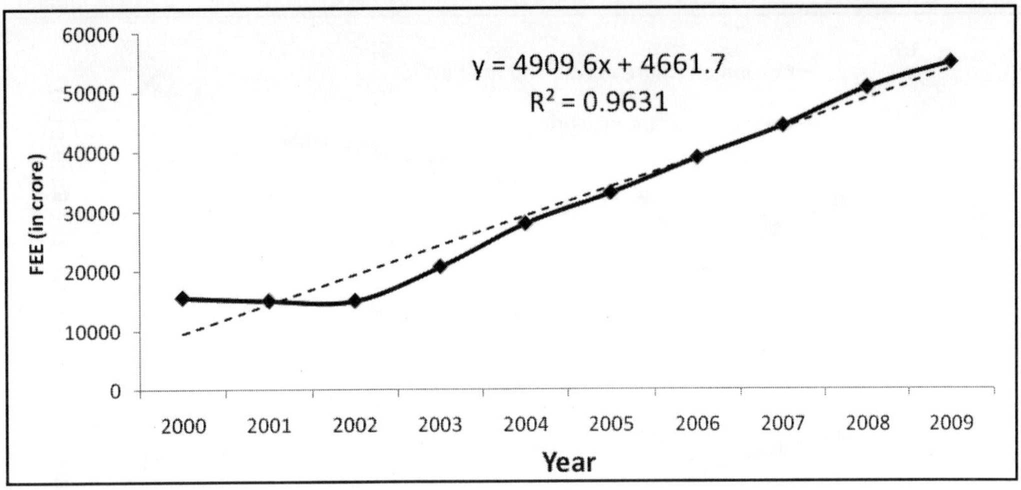

Fig. 2. Linear fit of FEEs in India.

share in the international tourist arrival in 2009 translated to the additional foreign exchange earnings. Figure 2 shows the FEE of India from tourism from 2000 to 2009.

The linearly fitted trend line of FEE shows that there is a steady progress in foreign exchange earnings through tourism in India. If the trend continues, tourism will become the topmost foreign exchange earner of India. It is found that the correlation between FTAs and FEE is highly significant ($r = 0.98$, $p < 0.000$) which infers that there is a strong relationship between FTAs and FEEs.

Table 3: Share of India in international tourist arrival in world and Asia and the Pacific region, 2000-2009

Year	International Tourist Arrivals (in million)		FTAs *in India (in million)*	*Percentage share and Rank of India in world*		*Percentage share and rank in Asia and the Pacific*	
	World	*Asia and Pacific*		*Percentage share*	*Rank*	*Percentage share*	*Rank*
2000	683.3	109.3	2.65	0.39	50	2.42	11
2001	683.4	114.5	2.54	0.37	51	2.22	12
2002	703.2	123.4	2.38	0.34	54	1.93	12
2003	691.0	111.9	2.73	0.39	51	2.44	11
2004	762.0	143.4	3.46	0.45	44	2.41	11
2005	803.4	154.6	3.92	0.49	43	2.53	11
2006	8470	166.8	4.45	0.53	44	2.67	11
2007	904.0	181.9	5.08	0.56	41	2.79	11
2008	919.0	184.0	5.28	0.57	41	2.87	11
2009	880.0	181.6	5.11	0.58	41	2.81	11

Source: UNWTO Tourism Market Trends and Barometer, June 2010.

Table 3 shows the share of India in world tourist arrivals as well as in Asia and the Pacific region. Even though the country has vast potential in tourism sector, India's share in the world tourist market during 2000 was only 0.39%. In 2002 its share declined to 0.34%. The year 2005

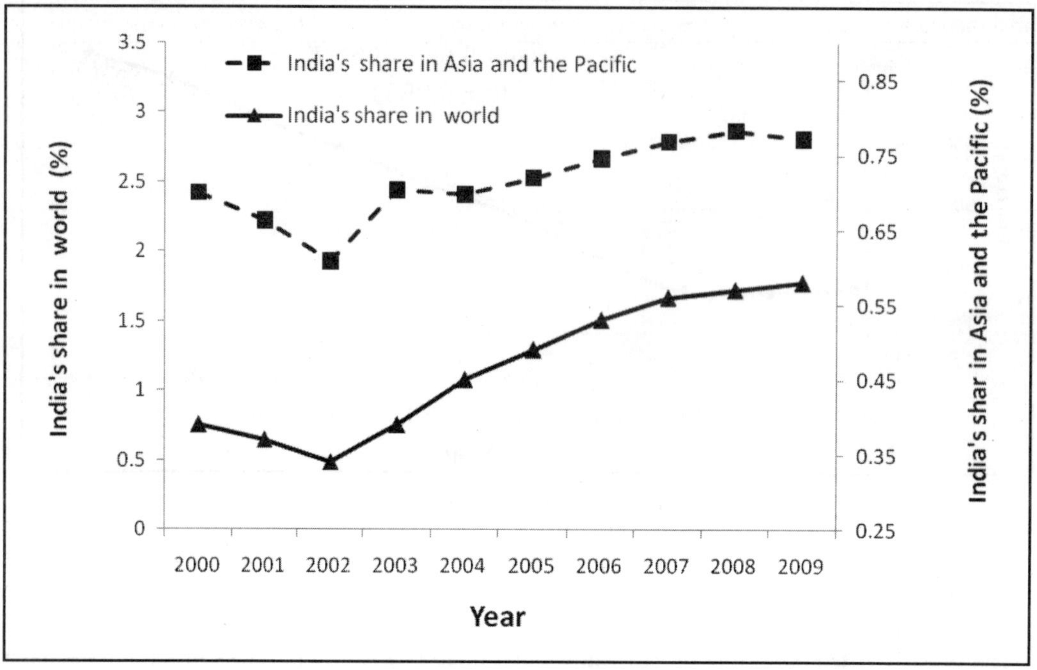

Fig. 3. Share of India in international tourism arrivals in world and Asia and the Pacific region, 2000-2009.

had been a highly successful year so far as tourism in India is concerned because the share of India in world tourism which was hovering between 0.37% and 0.39%, was 0.49% in 2005. In the year 2009, India's share in world tourist market increased to 0.58%. India ranks 41st in terms of its contribution to world tourist arrivals for the last three years. A look at the traffic figures reveals that India attracts very few international tourists and contributes less than 1% to the world tourist market. The share of India is meagre ranging from 0.34% to 0.58% in the study period. It is inferred from the analysis that India's share in international tourism is insignificant even though it has rich cultural values and natural resources.

India's share in Asia and Pacific region is also small when compared with other Asian countries. Its share ranges from 1.93% to 2.87% during the study period. India ranks 11th position for the last seven years in Asia and the Pacific region tourist arrivals.

The main reasons for the low share are:

- India's distance from affluent tourist markets of the world such as USA, Europe, Canada, Japan and Australia.
- India has developed its tourism organizations recently as compared to other countries whose tourist arrivals are much higher.
- India's neighbours are not affluent and hence tourists from neighbouring countries are less.
- Lack of promotional efforts and poor infrastructural facilities.

Table 4: Share of India in international tourism receipts in world and Asia and the Pacific region, 2000-2009

Year	International tourism receipts s (in US $ billion)		FEE in India (in US $ million)	*Percentage share and rank of India in world*		*Percentage share and rank in Asia and the Pacific*	
	World	*Asia and Pacific*		*Percentage share*	*Rank*	*Percentage share*	*Rank*
2000	475.3	85.3	3460	0.73	36	4.06	10
2001	463.8	88.3	3198	0.69	36	3.63	12
2002	481.9	96.5	3103	0.64	37	3.22	13
2003	529.3	93.7	4463	0.84	37	4.76	9
2004	633.2	124.1	6170	0.97	26	4.97	8
2005	679.6	135.0	7493	1.1	22	5.55	7
2006	744.0	156.9	8634	1.16	22	5.5	7
2007	857.0	187.0	10729	1.25	20	5.74	6
2008	942.0	208.9	11747	1.25	23	5.62	6
2009	852.0	203.2	10605	1.24	22	5.22	6

Source: UNWTO Tourism Market Trends and Barometer, June 2010.

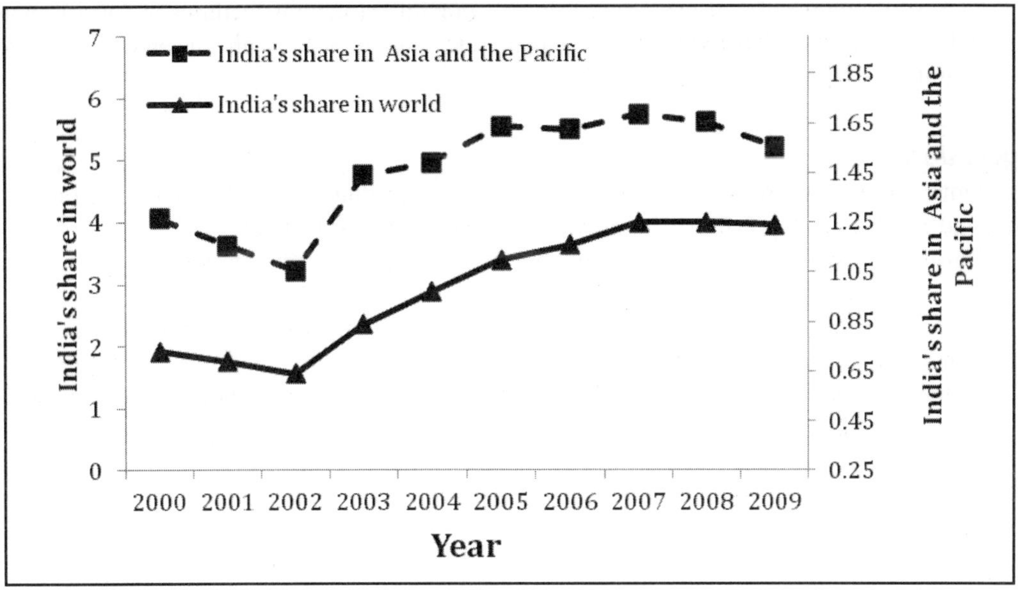

Fig. 4. Share of India in world and Asia and the Pacific region tourism receipts, 2000-2009.

Table 4 presents the share of India in world tourism receipts and in Asian and the Pacific region tourist receipts. The analysis indicates that India's share is meagre in world tourism receipts ranging from 0.64% to 0.97% during the period from 2000 to 2004. In 2005 it touched 1.10% and again rose to 1.25% in 2007. In the year 2009, its share was 1.24% and ranks 22nd in the world tourism receipts.

Regarding tourism receipts in Asia and the Pacific region, India's share has been from 3.22% to 5.74% and ranks 6th for the last three years. It is inferred that though tourism is the second largest foreign exchange earner of India, the progress of earning is very slow compared to the rest of the world.

Findings

Few findings that emerge from the study are given below:

- A steady growth in the FTAs during the study period has been discerned. The FTAs increaed from 2.65 million in 2000 to 5.11 million in the year 2009.
- It is found that there is a steady progress in FEE from tourism with some minor deviations. In 2000 India's FEE was Rs.15,626 crores which increaed to Rs. 5,49,600 crores in 2009.
- Indis's share in world tourism arrival is minimal which is ranging from 0.34% to 0.58%.
- India occupies 41st position in world and 11th position in Asia and the Pacific region in terms of toursit arrivals in the year 2009.
- India's share in world tourism receipts is also not siginificant which ranges from 0.64% to 1.25%.
- India ranks 22nd position in world and 6th position in Asia and the Pacific region in terms of tourism receipts in the year 2009.
- Lack of promotional and marketing efforts, poor infrastructural facilities at tourist spots, lack of coordination between public and private tourism sectors are the main causes for minimal FTAs and FEE.

Sugesstions

To promote safe tourism while ensuring that it remains a profitable industry, it is imperative to understand the factors that hamper its growth and check them effectively.

- Tourist infrastructure in India should be strengthened and tourists should be provided with clean hotels, reliable transfort systems and affordable shopping centres.
- All airports and railyway stations should provide information to the tourists and facilitate their travel plans.
- To make access to India easy, VISA formalities and Customs clearance procedures should be simplified.
- Private sector should be involved in providing required tourist infrastructure.
- The maintenance of tourist destinations should be taken up efficiently and their sanctity and beatuy must be restored.
- The government should frame effective marketing starategy to broaden the tourist base in the existing markets, explore new tourist markets and promote and facilitate intra-regional travel. The publicity and marketing strategies to increae the tourist traffic should be effectively implemented.
- Willingness and active involvement of local people is of importance as success in tourism depends on effective human relations. Threfore, there is an immediate need to infuse tourism awareness in our society so that the interaction between the local people and guests can be maintained.
- To earn more foreign exchange, foreign tourists should be coaxed to spend more amount of time and money in India.

CONCLUSION

Tourism perhaps the only "marketed " or "marketable" product which results in enormous transfer of fund. It plays a crucial role in the economic delvelpemnt of a country and enhances the country's capacity to earn foreign exchange. India is a country that has immense tourism potential to attract foreign tourists and thereby earn foreign exchange. Tourism is India's second largest foreign exchange earner but its potential has not been exploited to full. Although India has progressed a lot since the 1950s with respect to tourism, it is still way behind the developed even the develping countries. It is the responsibility of the state and central governments to frame and implement effective marketing polices and programmes for attracting more and more foreign tourists to India and increasing their length of stay in India by way of creating and developing tourism infrastructure, exploiting unexploited tourist spots, publicity and promotion. The current status indicates that India will become the most prefered tourist destination in the world in near future and tourism will be the first largest foreign exchange earner of India with maximal share of world tourist receipts.

REFERENCES

1. Bheemaraj, P. (2008). "Importance of Tourism in Economic development: A Micro study", *Southern Economist*, Vol. 46, pp. 35-38.
2. Kaul, Virender (1994). "Tourism and the Economy", Har Anand Publications, New Delhi, 1994, pp. 30.
3. KRC Research, "Tourism Industry sets in buoyant zone", http://www.krchoksey.com, Retrieved on Dec,12, 2009.
4. Prafulla Chandra Mohanty (2004). "Marketing of Tourism Services in India – A study with special reference to Orissa", Orissa Review, September 2004, pp. 8-10.
5. PTI (2009). "Foreign exchange earnings from Tourism" http://www.livemint.com/2009/11/06125705/foreign-exchange-earning-from.html.
6. Ramkumar, A. and Rajashree Shinde (2008), "Product development and Management in Rural tourism", Conference of Tourism in India – Challenges ahead, May 2008, IMK.
7. Tourism Statistics (2010). Ministry of Tourism, Government of India. TTDC (Tamilnadu Tourism Development Corporation) Policy Note 2009-10, and 2010-11.

Websites

- www.incredibleindia.org
- www.tamilnadutourism.org
- www.unwto.org

5

The Factors Affecting Export Performance of Tea Industry

G.S. Subashini and N. Dinesh

Asst. Professor, Department of Business Administration, Annamalai University, Chidambaram
Student, Department of Business Administration, Annamalai University, Chidambaram

ABSTRACT

Tea is indigenous to India and is an area where the country can take a lot of pride. This is mainly because of it pre-eminence as a foreign exchange earner and its contribution to the country's GDP. In all aspects of tea production, consumption and export, India has emerged to be the world leader, mainly because it accounts for 31% of global production. It is perhaps the only industry where India has retained its leadership over the last 150 years. Tea production in India has a very interesting historyt. The range of tea offered by India -- from the original orthodox to CTC and Green Tea, from the aroma and flavour of Darjeeling Tea to the strong Assam and Nilgiri Tea-remains unparalleled in the world. For the past few years there is a greater efficiency in the industry worldwide and competition from low cost producers. This paper attempts to identify the relationship between the internal and external factors to export performance of tea industry in Coonoor. The target respondents are from the tea industry in Coonoor. The questionnaires were designed and distributed to the officials and employees of tea industry in Coonoor. An interview was also conducted to gain a detail insight of the respondent. A checklist was used during the plant visit to observe the real scenario of the researcher employed ANOVA , descriptive statistics for analysis of the data. The findings of this study discuss the demographic profile of respondents as well as tea industry in general.

INTRODUCTION

The term export derives from the conceptual meaning as to ship the goods and services out of the port of a country. The seller of such goods and services is referred to as an "exporter" who is based in the country of export whereas the overseas based buyer is referred to as an "importer". In international trade, "exports" refers to selling goods and services produced in home country to other country's markets. Ownership advantages are the firm's specific assets, international experience, and the ability to develop either low-cost or differentiated products within the contacts of its value chain. The locational advantages of a particular market are a combination of market potential and investment risk. Internationalization advantages are the benefits of retaining a core competence within the company and threading it though the value chain rather than obtain to license, outsource, or sell it. In relation to the eclectic paradigm, companies that have low levels of ownership advantages do not enter foreign markets. If the company and its products are equipped with ownership advantage and internalization advantage, they enter through low-risk modes such as exporting. Exporting requires significantly lower level investment than other modes of international expansion, such as FDI.

Ways of Exporting

The exporter can decide to export directly or indirectly to a foreign country.

Direct Selling in Export Strategy

Direct selling involves sales representatives, distributors, or retailers who are located outside the exporter's home country. Direct exports are goods and services that are sold to an independent party outside of the exporter's home country. Mainly the companies are pushed by core competencies and improving their performance of value chain.

Indirect Selling

Indirect exports is simply selling goods to or through an independent domestic intermediary in their own home country. Then intermediaries export the products to foreign markets.

EVOLUTION OF TEA INDUSTRIES IN INDIA

Tea First Planted

In 1835,36,42,000 tea plants raised in Calcutta from the China seed were sent to Upper Assam, Kumaon, Sirmore and South India. C.A Bruce, now appointed Superintendent for Tea Culture in Assam, started a tea garden at Saikhawa, near Sadiya, in 1836. The first Indian owned tea estate was started in 1876. Tea was exported from the ports of Calcutta, Bombay, Karachi and Chittagong.

First Tea Auction in India

On the 27th of December, 1861, the first tea auction ever to be held in India was conducted under the instructions of Messrs. R.Thomas and Company, General Brokers, by the firm, Mackenzie Lyall, at No 2 Mission Row, Calcutta.

Import and Re-Exports of Tea

We learn from the earliest records available that at the turn of the century, India imported tea from Ceylon (Sri Lanka), China (primarily Green tea), Java and the Shan States (Burma). Much of this was re-exported as foreign tea but a portion was blended and re-exported. Imports in 1907/08 amounted to 6.5 million Ibs. By 1917, it was recorded, foreign tea was blended under bond with Indian tea, for re-exports. Waste tea, exports were known to have existed in 1915. These shipments were made to the USA and the UK for the manufacture of caffeine.

International Tea Market Expansion Board

In 1935, the International Tea Market Expansion Board was formed and a scheme adopted by which all producing countries participating in the regulation scheme were to contribute sums towards the expansion of world tea consumption.

Export Duty 1947

On 17th July, an export duty of 2 *anna*s per Ib was imposed and subsequently raised to 4 *anna*s per lb. In the same year the new Tea Board building was inaugurated with renewed powers granted to the Board under the Tea Act.

Coonoor Auctions

The Coonoor Auction Centre started functioning on 23rd March 1963.

Consultative Committee

In December 1966, a Consultative Committee of the Main Tea Trade Associations was recommended and formed to consider all matters affecting the tea trade.

Some Statistical Facts about the Indian Tea Industry

- The total turnover of the tea industry is around Rs. 10,000 crore.
- Since independent tea production has grown over 250%, while land area has just grown by 40%.
- There has been a considerable increase in export too in the past few years. Total net foreign exchange earned per annum is around Rs. 1847 crore.
- The labour-intensive tea industry directly employs over 1.1 million workers and generates income for another 10 million people approximately. Women constitute 50% of the workforce.

Literature Review

In the export performance research, the most commonly used criteria for measuring firm size are the number of employees and or total sale volume (Constantine S.K, Nigel F.P & Chris I.). The firm size is understood to have mixed effects (Aaby and Slater (1989) and Chetty & Hamilton (1993)). The positive effects are found when size is measured by total firm sales, while some negative effects are found when measured by number of employees (Kaynak and Kuan, 1993). It is found that firm experience on export has positive relationship on export performance (Madsen 1989).

The technological strengths are positively correlated to the export (Abay and Slater,1989). Almost all the research concludes that technology is best applied as standard in the market worldwide (Christensen et al., 1987). Previous studies suggest that the domestic market orientation is a major barrier to a firm's export involvement and commitment (Karafakioglu, 1986).

International trade theory suggests that export growth contributes positively to economic growth which is measured by output growth by the following; facilitate the exploitation of economic scales for small open economics (Helpman Krugman,1985). There is a disagreement among the researchers, about how quantitatively important are the growth depressing effects of inflation at what levels of inflation these effects begin to appear. Malik and Chowdhury (2001) showed the lowest inflation is positively correlated to economic growth in a particular country. Kaynak and Kua (1993) found that export market attractiveness has a positive effect on export performance whereas the other research states that there is a negative or insignificant effect on export performance.

Trade barriers, cultural differences and physical distance to export markets have been found to play an important role in the export development and success (Caavuagil, 1984; Kaynak and Erol,1989). Exporting is also defined as shipping of goods produced in the company's home country to other countries for marketing (Wheelen and Hunger, 2000).

Objectives

- To identify the factors determining the export performance of tea in tea industry, Coonoor.
- To categorise the factor according to the importance.
- To analyze the significant difference between experience and factors determining the export performance.

Problem of the Statement

Tea exporters have developed into a mature industry that has gained acceptance both domestically and internationally. Indian tea industry is playing a vital role in boosting the economy of the country. It has been observed that Coonoor tea industry is in the same line with other industries, where the low cost labour is comparatively an advantage. Therefore this study examines the factors affecting the export performance with regard to firm's characteristics, its competency factor, economic factors, market factors and contextual environment factors.

Research Design

Both quantitative and qualitative approaches were employed for this study. Operationally this research had been undertaken in two major phases, the first phase was observation and reviewing similar research conducted previously. The second phase was basically the collection of primary data through structure questionnaire.

Sample Size

The ranges of observation for this study were sampled Coonoor tea industries. We surveyed the high-level administrators and senior employees of each firm. The instruments were measured on 5-point Likert type scale. The questionnaires were distributed to 290 manufacturing managers/ senior employees from tea industries in Coonoor, and 75 usable questionnaires were returned.

Table 1: Status of questionnaires

Item	Total	Invalid	Not received	Valid/ considered for this study
Total questionnaires	200	30	95	75
Ratio	100%	5%	22.5%	72.5%

Questionnaire Design

For the quantitative questionnaire, it has two sections. Section 1 consists of personal information whereas the section 2 consists of the interview questions, which are regarding the current situation, competitive environment, future perspective of tea industries.

Data Analysis

In particular, the researcher used descriptive analysis for demographic factors like standard deviation and mean,. whereas, to draw the relationship between internal and external factors, ANOVA is performed to find the significant difference between demographic variables and internal and external factors. The five-point Likert scale is employed in this study since it is most appropriate and reliable. The interval for the range in measuring each variable has been calculated below;

(5-1)/5=0.8 it means items with scores fall between the range of:
4.21-5.00 considered very important
3.41-4.20 considered important
2.61-3.40 considered average
1.81-2.60 considered not important

1.00-1.80 considered not important at all

Measure of central tendency and ANOVA is used to find out the significant difference between independent and dependent variables.

Table 2: ANOVA for experience of respondents and economic and contextual factors
H0: There is no significant difference between experience and economic and contextual factor
H1: There is a significant difference between experience and economic and contextual factor

Factors	*Sum of squares*	*Df*	*Mean square*	*F*	*Significance*
	33.582	74			
Economic factors	3.615	4	.904	2.721	.036
	23.253	70	.332		
	26.869	74			
Contextual environment factor	5.155	4	1.289	2.935	.026
	30.733	70	.439		

Source: Primary Source

Table 3: Summary of the levels of importance of factors

Factors	*Mean*	*Std. deviation*	*Level of importance*
Firm Characteristics			
Size of firm	3.51	.844	Important
Length of firms experience	3.68	.661	Important
Importance of marketing strategy	3.85	.651	Important
Commitment of firm to export performance	3.93	.664	Important
Firm Competency Factors			
Quality of tea manufacture technology	4.35	.762	Very important
Management marketing knowledge	4.33	.759	Very important
Relationship with customer	4.31	.805	Very important
Adequacy of infrastructures in firm	4.31	.697	Very important
Cost advantage in labour and procuring raw material	4.33	.723	Very important
Economic Factors			
Role of economic growth—exporting country	3.93	.704	Important
Role of economic growth—importing country	3.81	.817	Important
Economic policy—exporting country	4.04	.829	Important
Economic policy—importing country	4.03	.870	Important
Effect of inflation—exporting country	3.89	.831	Important
Effect of inflation—importing country	3.93	.723	Important
Market factors			
Market attractiveness	4.01	.797	Important
Market competitiveness	4.27	.664	Very important
Market structures	4.33	.644	Very important
Contextual Environment Factors			
Export market barriers	4.25	.718	Very important
Cultural difference	4.20	.735	Important
Physical distance of export	4.20	.735	Important

Source: Primary Source

Findings

Table 2 shows a significant difference between experience and economic, contextual factors. Since the p value is less than <0.05 we reject the null hypothesis and accept alternate hypothesis that there is significant difference between experience and economic, contextual factors. The level of importance, mean, S.D, of firm characteristic, firm competency factor, economic factor, market factor, contextual environment factor are shown in the Table 3. Among all these firm competency factors, market competitiveness, market structure, export market barriers are considered very important while the remaining ones are considered less important.

CONCLUSION

The export performance of tea industry is analyzed by collecting the data with the help of questionnaire. This study examines the factors affecting the export performance with regard to firm characteristic, firm competency factor, economic factors, market factors and contextual environment factors. All these factors are important for export performance. Among these factors, the ANOVA table shows the significant difference between experience, contextual factors and economic factors.

REFERENCES

1. Aaby, Nila-erik and Slater, S.F. (1989). "Management Influences on Export Performance: A review of empirical literature 1978-88", International marketing review.
2. Cavugil, S.T. and Zou, S. (1994). "Marketing Strategy-performance Relationship: An investigation of the empirical link in export market ventures", *Journal of Marketing.*
3. Chetty, S.K. and Hamilton, R.T. (1993). "Firm-level Determinants of Export Performance a meta analysis" International marketing review.
4. Christensen, C.H. and Rocha, A. "Empricial Investigation of the Factors Influencing Exporting Success of Brazilian firms" *Journal of Business Studies.*
5. Helpman, et al. (1985). "Market Structure and Foreign Trade, Cambridge," MA: MIT press.
6. Hollis, (2003). "Industrial Concentration Output and Trade: An Empirical Exploration", *Review of Industrial Organization.*
7. Madsen, T.K. (1987). "Empirical Export Performance Studies: A Review of conceptualization and findings.

6

A Study of Continuous Evolution in Computing System

DEEP MALA SIHINT

B.Sc., M.A (English), MCA, Lecturer, Jayawant Institute of Management Studies, Tathwade, Pune-411033, E-mail:- deep_sihint@yahoo.com.

ABSTRACT

New computer technologies have increased the possibility for users to generate digital content at any location and time. Computing systems have become an important paradigm in today's world of networking system. Ranging from wireless laptops to cellular phones and Wi-Fi/ Bluetooth-enabled PDAs to wireless sensor networks, mobile computing has become ubiquitous in its impact on our daily lives. The debut if iPhones and the proliferation of other hand-held devices have spurred excitement and interest in this evolving field. We believe that these emerging learning objects should be enriched with contextual characteristics in a machine interoperable and interpretable manner in order to preserve the meaning, or semantics. In recent years a variety of computing devices has emerged, including portables, palmtops and PDAs. In consequence, the evolution of computing devices has imposed a clear need for evaluation methods that are specifically suited for computing devices. The more evolved is the computing market towards mobile computing systems; the more difficult becomes the human computer interface evaluators to choose among the approaches for mobile applications. In this paper, we present our thoughts related to the ability to enhance digital content that emerges when computing devices are used to support different learning activities.

Keywords: Computing, Learning, Information, Laptops, Devices.

INTRODUCTION

After a horrible year in 2009, laptops sales were back with a bang growing by 60% in 2010. The year 2011 saw laptop sales coming close to 50% of overall shipments and after that the Indian market reflects the global scene where laptop sales overhauled those of desktops PCs sometimes back. Within laptops, the notebook category saw stellar growth albeit on a small base. A lot depends on whether or not tablets take off in India in 2011.Meanwhile, netbooks are evolving into something more than cut down notebooks. AMD's fusion chips are powering a new crop of netbooks that don't choke on HD video unlike their atom powered predecessors. Between Fusion and Intel's dual core atom, netbooks are definitely going to pack more of a computing punch on 2011. [1]

A STUDY OF RETURN OF THE LAPTOPS

In the last week of December 2010, research firm IDC India was optimistic about the PC sales in the Indian market. For the last three quarters of 2010, unit shipments stood at 7.4 million pieces working out to a year-on-year growth of 31%. IDC expected overall PC sales in 2010 to also record a growth of 31% with close to 10 million PCs being shipped. Within overall PC sales, desktop sales were placed at 4.68 million units, a 19% increase. Notebook PC sales were a 2.72 million units, recording a 60% growth over the previous year. In the July-September quarter, Indian PC sales touched 2.79 million. PC shipments in India were expected to total 13.2 million units in 2011, a 24.7% rise from 2010, according to Gartner. Although that may be a tad slower, the fact is, it remains a healthy growth rate. [3]

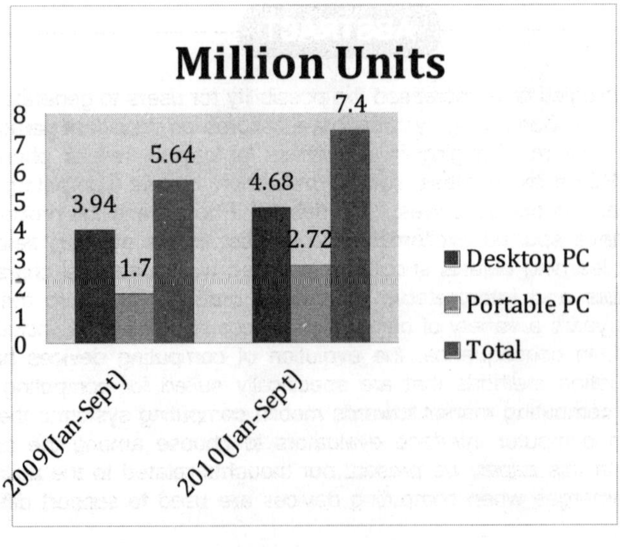

Fig. 1. A study of Indian PC market in 2009-2010(million Units).

A SURVEY OF HOW CONSUMER BRINGS CHEER

According to IDC and other industry watchers, it was the Indian consumer who made the biggest contribution to the rise in PC sales. It is interesting to note that the purchasing power of the Indian consumer in 2010 was the highest that it has been during the last 30 years. According to a World Bank report, the purchasing power parity of India stood at almost $3,000 in 2010. A number of recent studies have demonstrated that there is rapidly growing middle class in emerging countries and that India is due for huge growth in its middle class over the course of the next decade. In this overall PC (notebooks and desktops combined) market, Dell retained its market leadership with an increased market share of 16.7% while both HP with 13.7% and Acer with 10.6% retained the second and third positions respectively, albeit with reduced market share as others like Lenovo began making inroads. In terms of desktops PC sales, which even now form the bulk of PC purchases, Dell clinched the top position in the Indian PC market for the first time with a share of 9.8%; HP and Acer at second and third position respectively during 2010 according to IDC study. Similarly, for notebook PCs, Dell retained its position with the market share of 27% followed by HP and Acer the second and third respectively. [3]

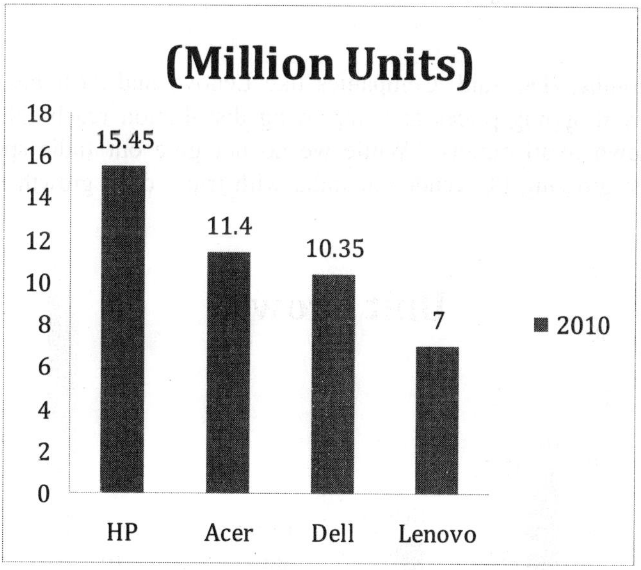

Fig. 2. Worldwide PC market in 2010.

TWEAKING BUSINESS STRATEGIES

According to Gartner in 2009, mobile PCs accounted for 55% of all PC shipments globally and by 2012, mobile PCs are expected to account for 70% of shipments. Shipment growth in 2010 was largely driven by the advent of low-priced consumer mobile PCs both in regular notebooks and mini-notebooks, according to Gartner. According to IDC between June 2008 and July 2009, 97,480 netbooks were sold. By June 2010, those numbers had shot up by 243% to 335,018 for

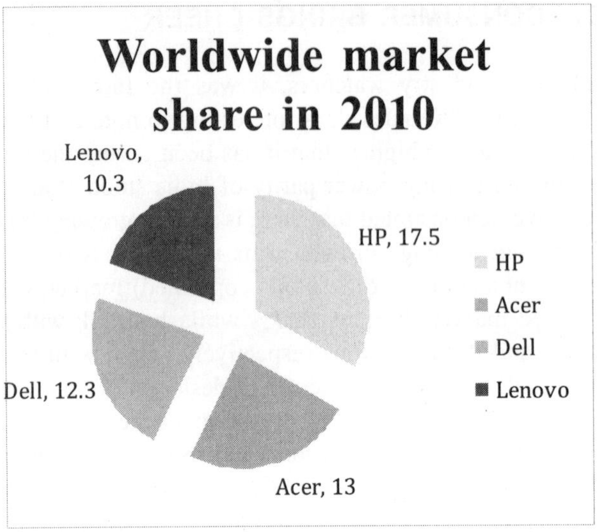

Fig. 3. Worldwide market share in 2010.

the preceding 12 months, IDC said. Companies like Lenovo and Acer became competitive in the Indian market by dropping prices and improving distribution reach-either through channel partner or through own retail outlets. "While we do not give out India specific numbers, we have been the fastest growing PC vendor in India with triple digit growth rates". [2]

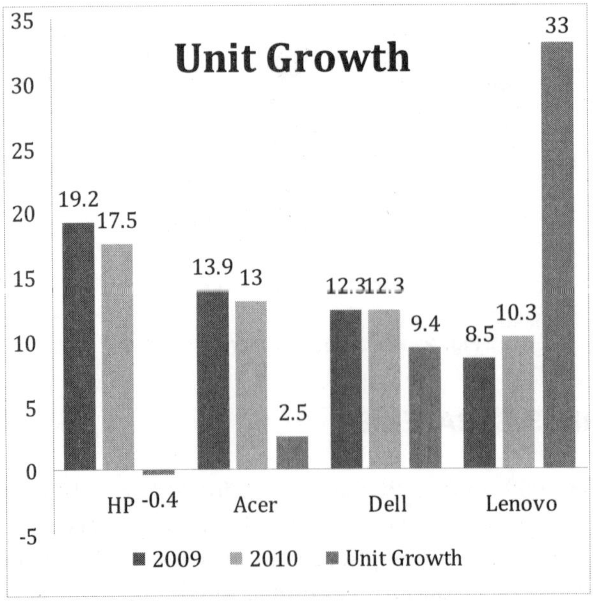

Fig. 4. Worldwide PC market share 2009 Vs 2010.

3G REBOOT

With 3G services and broadband set to take off in 2011, netbooks and other MIDs are set to enter a new growth phase. Netbooks face competitions from thin clients and smart phones. While some PC makers including Dell and Acer have already lunched their version of smart phones in India, others like Lenovo are yet to join the party. In 2011, Acer also focussed on expanding its presence in the smart phone segment, bringing in a new range of smart phones to address this market. The netbook will remain a significant part of the broader market for the Internet connected devices and the uses that the netbook and tablet are put to differ significantly. Devices such as netbooks will continue to drive demand as both enterprise and personal consumer move towards high performance, low-cost mobile computing devices.[2]

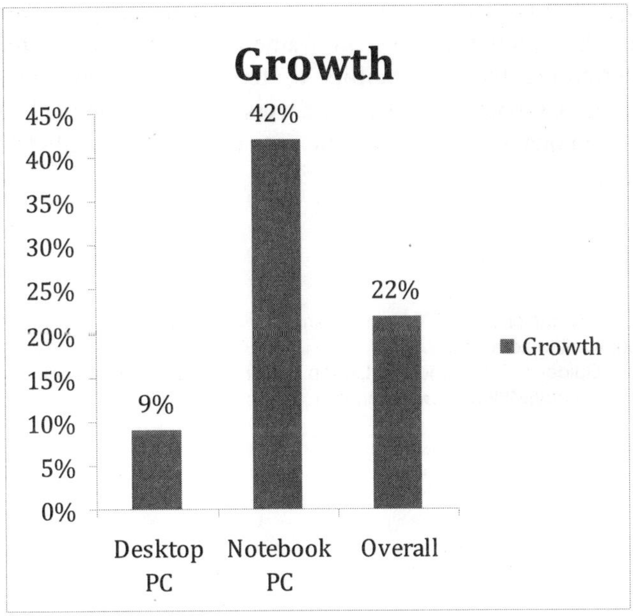

Fig. 5. Indian PC market: 2011 forecast by Form factor.

According to Gartner's PC installed base forecast, the total number of PCs in use will reach 1.78 billion units in 2013 by which time the combined installed base of smart phones and browser equipped phones will exceed 1.82 billion units. Gartner expects that by 2012, the split between desktops and notebooks would be 50% each.

THE FUTURE PROPELLERS

The growth of netbooks is increasing and vendors are going all out to drive volumes, like in 2009, when this category grew in excess of 200%. Gartner predicted that by the fourth quarter of 2011, mobile PCs would outgrow desk-based PCs in India, although the total number of desktop based shipments would be higher than that of mobile PCs for the year as a whole. In

2011, the desktop PC market would grow by 5% totaling 7.2 million units and mobile PC shipments will grow 61% to tot up 5.9 million units. PC sales have always risen from repeat buying sectors including the government, education, BFSI, etc. Considering the low penetration of PCs in India, repeat buying sectors have helped vendors expand their market share.[4]

CONCLUSION

Computing system is an important and evolving technology. It enables personnel to effectively communicate and interact with the fixed organizational information system while remaining unconstrained by physical location. It may be implemented using many combinations of hardware, software, and communications technologies. The technologies must be carefully selected and the applications designed to achieve the business needs required from the overall organizational information system. The Computing system framework can assist information technology professionals in determining the applicability of technology to an organizational problem, opportunity, or directive. Computing system is a versatile and potentially strategic technology that improves information quality and accessibility, increases operational efficiency, and enhances management effectiveness.

REFERENCES

1. http://faculty.ed.umuc.edu/~meinkej/inss690/zimmerman/INSS%20690%20CC%20-%20Mobile%20Computing.htm
2. www.expresscomputeronline.com
3. Product Comparison Guide. (2010, January). Laptop Buyer's Guide & Handbook
4. http://www.osnews.com/story/22352 (new diagrams)

7

International Business: Challenges and Opportunities

Sharda Gangwar and Preeti Yadav

Faculty of Commerce, Institute for Excellence in Higher Education, Bhopal,
E-Mail: sharda_gangwar@rediffmail.com
Research Scholar, Barkatullah University, Bhopal

ABSTRACT

International business has given a new horizon to the world with new prospects to achieve high. International business is the transaction crossing national borders and hence provides various challenges and opportunities. Challenges and opportunities facing the international business vary with the social and economic scenarios of the countries involved in cross-border trade. The process of progress is entirely different with the developed, developing and the under-developed countries. Cultural diversity (ethnicity), language, norms, rules and regulations by the government and related organizations, government stability, etc., are the various challenges faced by the business community around the globe. As a coin has two faces, in business we have opportunities to garland the business hub. The growth of foreign direct investment, emergence of commercial banks, outsourcing, revitalization of private sector, tax reforms, removal of exchange control and convertibility, infrastructure development, etc., pave the path to glorification of international business. The international business has become so interdependent that if a small change in economy of one country can mark an impact on the whole world business environment as we have seen in the past few years. So, international business has become a major and vibrant component of the present state of affairs, so as its study and research.

INTRODUCTION

The world has become a global marketplace, and all types of businesses are seeking to expand their operations across national borders and into the world. Global trade is the exchange of raw materials, goods and services across the geographical borders of countries across the globe. International business is a combination of all commercial transactions either private or government between two or more countries. For example, India exports 1000 pairs of shoes @500 per pair to Japan, this transaction will be known as international business.

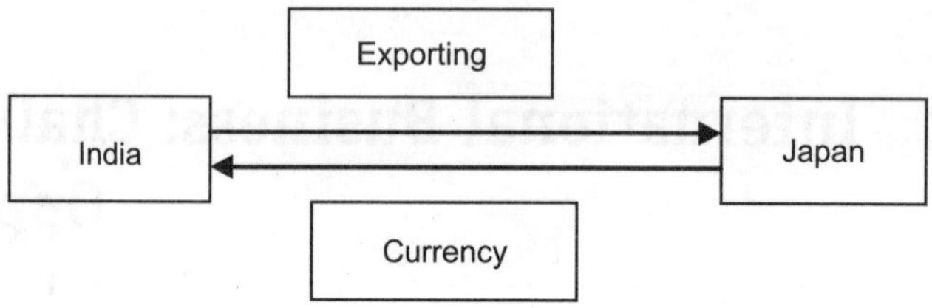

Private firms undertake such transaction for profit and business expansion, but governments may or may not do the same in their transactions *viz.,* profit, subsidies or assistance. The transaction includes sales, investment and transportation. International business has been growing rapidly in recent decades because of technological expansion; liberalization of government policies on trade and resources movement, development of institutions needed to support and facilitate international transactions and increased global competition. Because of these factors, foreign countries increase a source of both production and sales for domestic companies.

When buyers find foreign market cheaper to buy in and sellers find them more profitable to dispose of their products than the domestic market, then international marketing takes place. Thus, a more effective use of world's resources is made possible through international trade. International trade is growing faster than world output and international investment is growing much faster than the global trade. These are clear indications of the growing internationalization of business. But the conduct of international operations depends on companies' objectives and the means by which they choose to carry them out. The operations affect and are affected by the national and competitive environment that are encountered.

Foreign trade got its first impetus from the industrial revolution in the late eighteenth and early nineteenth century. Rapid development in transportation facilities resulted in a surge in international trade in the twentieth century. Today, international trade has taken the form of outsourcing and multinational companies (companies that have a presence in several countries).

HISTORY OF WORLD TRADE

World trade was prevalent much before the formation of nation states. Some important examples of ancient long distance trade are:

- The Egyptians imported spices from Arabia and the 'Land of Punt' (present- day Somalia).
- The Ptolemaic dynasty, which ruled in Egypt from 305 BC to 30 BC, traded with India.

- Arabian vessels were used to transport Indian goods to Aden.
- Chinese goods made their way to India, Persia and Rome through the silk route.

From the eighteenth century, industrialization and colonization went hand in hand. The European nations increased their political power through trade. They exploited trading opportunities in eastern countries like India.

PRESENT GLOBAL TRADE SCENARIO

There was a dramatic rise in world trade volumes in the twentieth century. While in 1928, world exports amounted to US$31.7 billion, this figure rose to US$4,215,000.2 billion by 1994. Studies conducted by the UNCTAD in 1994 show that trade in commercial services rose much faster than merchandise trade between 1970 and 1990.The G-7 group, comprising the US, France, Germany, the UK, Italy, Japan and Canada, has always commanded a dominant position in world trade. Gradually the significance of certain Asia Pacific nations, such as China, Singapore, India, Hong Kong, Taiwan and Korea, hasincreased.

Objectives of International Business

- Sales expansion
- Resources acquisition
- Diversification
- Minimise competitive risk
- Profit making
- To stand in market.

Modes of International Business

- Importing and Exporting
- Manufacturing
- Tourism and transportation
- Licensing and franchising
- Management contract
- Foreign exchange dealings
- Direct investment
- Portfolio investment

OPPORTUNITIES TO INTERNATIONAL BUSINESS

Due to globalization various opportunities have emerged which motivates the companies or firms to go international. The primary motive for going global is that there is money in the overseas markets. Those companies engaged in international business from the laid- the US, Europe and Japan, have huge assets and more than quarter of these assets are found in foreign markets. Other opportunities are as follows:

1. **Profit Advantage:** The primary motive for going global is that there is money in the overseas markets. International business could yield more earnings than the domestic. Even when international business is less profitable than the domestic, it could increase total profit if the international business enables the firm to achieve optimum capacity utilization or economies of scale.
2. **Sales Expansion:** The optimum utilization of capacity and economics of scale can be achieved through expansion of sales thereby increasing profit earnings from domestic as well as overseas markets.
3. **Growth Opportunity:** Many foreign markets have enormous growth potential that attracts foreign companies towards it. In a number of developing countries both the population and income are growing fast. It may be noted that several developing countries and the newly industrializing countries have been growing much faster than the developed countries, and therefore, providing growth opportunity in foreign markets.
4. **Domestic Market Constraints:** It is being realized that the domestic markets are no longer adequate and rich. These domestic demand constraints drive many companies to expanding the market beyond the national border. Japanese have flooded the US market with automobiles and electronics because the home market was not large enough to absorb whatever was produced. Some European companies have gone global for similar reasons. Particularly, when the domestic market is small, internationalization is the only way to achieve significant growth.
5. **Favourable Effects on Economy**

   Direct Advantage:
   - Helpful in capital formation.
   - Increase in effective demand and expansion of market.
   - Favourable utilization of factor of production.
   - Reduction in production costs.
   - Transformation of substance to monetary section.

   Indirect Advantage:
   - Exporting areas economic development.
   - Favourable effect of import on economic development.
   - Gain of Gross Domestic Production.
   - Knowledge of foreign technology.
   - Control on inefficient monopoly.
6. **Increasing Foreign Demands:** Companies that develop attractive new products, first sell them in their home markets. Sooner or later, foreign consumers may learn about these products. At this stage, most companies could export the product or service rather than produce it abroad. But the economics of foreign production changes as the foreign demand grows. Productions are carried out also in abroad keeping in view the tastes and preferences of the foreign consumers thereby increasing the quantum of earnings from both, domestic as well as foreign sales.
7. **Specialization:** International business leads to specialization and encourages production of different goods in different countries. Goods can be produced at comparatively lower cost due to advantages of division of labour.

8. **Increase in Efficiency:** Due to the global competition, the producers engaged in international business attempt to produce better quality of goods and at the minimum possible cost. This increases the efficiency of the business on one hand and benefits the consumers all over the world on the other, thereby minimizing their competitive risk.
9. **Shrinking of time and distance:** Due to faster communication, speedier transportation, growing financial flows and rapid technological changes, there has been rapid shrinking of time and distance across the globe. This facilitates as an opportunity to the producers to explore the foreign markets and expand their business activities to the largest-- leading to high earnings.
10. **Free Trade:** Trade without government interference is known as free trade that means; there is no duty on import or export as well as there is no quantitative restriction. In real world, there is hardly any example of any country following free trade policy. But specific regions of the world have made a collective attempt to create free trade areas for their economic growth. Examples include the African Free Trade Zone (AFTZ) and the European Economic Area (EEA). Free trade lowers prices in an economy by encouraging competition due to which consumer will get best quality product at lowest price thereby increasing consumer welfare. Free trade leads to international division of labour and most efficient use of productive resources of the world. This will increase world output on one hand and on the other; companies will be able to reap the benefits of economies of scale.
11. **Change the mindset of people of LDCs:** Entry of multinational companies will lead to modernization in the less developed countries. The mindset of the people will change and they will develop interest in rationalist attitude and belief in science and technology. Communal and regional ideology will take a back seat.
12. **Others:** The other opportunities available to the producers engaged in international business are the following:
    - Acquisition of raw materials from abroad often from a steadier source of supply and at lower prices.
    - Acquisition of technology and management expertise from competing in global markets.
    - Export of components and finished goods for assembly or distribution in foreign markets.
    - Inflow of income from overseas royalties, licensing fees and management contracts.

GAINS FROM INTERNATIONAL TRADE

Gains from international trade have to be studied from three angles, namely:

(i) **Gains to the world:** There is no doubt that trade will increase global production. Country, which can produce the products more efficiently will not only produce for its consumption, but will also export it. Country, which can't produce a product efficiently, will import it by exchanging it with products, which it can produce efficiently. In this way global production (and thus global welfare) may increase.

(ii) **Gains to the country:** If a country does not enter into international trade, then its social welfare function can reach up to the point where it is tangent to production possibility curve. If it enters international trade, then although it produces at the same point on production possibility curve, but it will lead consumers at a point where social welfare will be higher than in the former case.

(iii) Gains to the citizen: In case of India, where labour is abundant it can export labour-intensive products. This will increase the demand for labour on one hand and on the other income of labourers will increase. Hence, international trade can help in filling up the income disparities gap and will lead to more equality in income distribution.

Main Constituents of International Business

International trade transactions are broadly classified under three categories.

WTO report (2008): Major importing nations

Country	Worth of Goods
United States	$2.17 trillion
Germany	$1.21 trillion
China	$1.13 trillion
Japan	$762 billion
France	$708 billion
Britain	$632 billion
Netherlands	$574 billion
Italy	$556 billion
Belgium	$470 billion
South Korea	$435 billion

1. **Import Trade:** Import trade refers to the purchase of goods from a foreign country. Countries import goods, which are not produced by them either because of cost disadvantage or because of physical difficulties, or even those goods, which are not produced in sufficient quantities so as to meet their requirements.

   The main import-oriented ports of the world are:
   - Port of Shanghai
   - Port of New York
   - Port of Rotterdam
   - Le Havre
   - Toronto Harbor
2. **Export Trade:** Export trade refers to the sale of goods to a foreign country.

   Highlights on Export Trade: In 2008, the World Trade Organization (WTO) indicated that Germany is the world's largest exporter, followed by China and the US. Germany's world class engineering sector comprises small and medium enterprises that operate throughout the world. About 40% of the country's GDP comes from exports alone. Germany's contribution to total global exports amounts to about 9.5%. The top three exporting countries provide one-fourth of the world's total global exports. The top 10 exporting nations are:
   - Germany
   - China
   - US
   - Japan
   - France
   - Netherlands
   - Italy
   - UK
   - Belgium
   - Canada

3. **Enter pot Trade:** Sometimes goods are purchased or imported from one country with the objective of selling or exporting them to some other countries. It is called enter pot trade.

Major Economies Involved in International Business

S.No.	Country	Major Exports	Major Imports
1.	China	Home appliances, itchenware, sea food and other food products, shoes, clothes, toys, bags	Electrical machinery, petroleum and related products, professional and scientific instruments, metalliferous ores and scrap, office machines and data processing equipment.
2.	India	Engineering and textile products, precious stones, petroleum products, jewellry, sugar, agricultural processed products, steel, chemicals, zinc and leather products	Crude oil, machinery, military products, fertilizers, chemicals, gems, antiques and artworks.
3.	USA	Industrial supplies, including electrical machinery, transport equipment and power generating machinery, non-auto consumer goods like organic chemicals, motor vehicles and their parts, food and beverages, aircraft and parts.	Export road vehicles, petroleum, petroleum products, apparels, clothing accessories, non-metallic minerals.
4.	UK	Petroleum and petroleum products, Road vehicles, Pharmaceutical products.	Petroleum and petroleum products, Road vehicles, manufactured articles.
5.	Canada	Zinc, sugar, copper, nickel, lobsters, shrimps, snow crabs, scallops and farmed Atlantic salmons; petrol and petroleum products; energy; wheat and grain.	Electronics, clothing toys, furnishings, crude petroleum plastics and automobiles and its parts.
6.	Australia	Wheat, grain, liquefied natural gas, meat, wool, coal, iron, and diamonds.	Machinery, crude oil, petroleum products, and transport equipment.
7.	Singapore	Machinery and equipment (including electronics), consumer goods, chemicals, mineral fuels.	Aircraft, crude oil and petroleum products, electronic components, motor vehicles, iron/steel, textile yarns/fabrics, radio and television receivers/parts.
8.	Mexico	Tin, gold, silver, mercury, zinc, Natural gas, zinc, food products such as sea food, cheese, coffee, sugar, oranges, and corn.	Paper, repair parts for motor vehicles, aircraft, industrial machines, tobacco, lumber.
9.	Japan	Automobiles, electronic machinery, automotive parts, chemical and semiconductors.	Crude oil, LNG, textiles, electronic components, fishes, audio and visual apparatus, optical instruments, metals.

CHALLENGES FACED BY INTERNATIONAL BUSINESS

International business is more complicated as compared to home trade of a country. There are many difficulties, which are faced by a trader engaged in international business. The following are the special problems and difficulties in the form of challenges faced by international business.

1. **Distance:** Usually international business involves long distances. Distance between various countries is a great difficulty in carrying out international business. Due to long distances, it becomes difficult to establish close relationship between the buyers and the sellers.
2. **Diversity of Languages:** Different languages are spoken and written in different countries of the world. The difference of language creates another problem in foreign trade. It becomes difficult to understand the language of traders in other countries. All correspondence has to be done in foreign language.
3. **Transport and Communication:** Long distances in foreign trade create difficulties of proper and quick transport and communication. Both of these involve considerable delay as well as cost. The high cost of transport is a great hindrance in international business.
4. **Risk and Uncertainty:** International business is subject to greater risk and uncertainties as compared to home trade. As the goods have to be transported to long distance they are exposed to many risks. Goods in transit overseas are susceptible to the perils of the sea. These risks may be covered through marine insurance but this involves extra cost in international business transactions.
5. **Lack of information about Foreign Traders:** In foreign trade since there is no direct and close relationship between the buyers and the sellers, the sellers have to take special steps to verify the creditworthiness of the buyer. It is difficult to obtain information regarding creditworthiness, business standing and financial position of persons living in foreign countries.
6. **Dumping and Anti-Dumping Measures:** When a country floods the market of another country with products that are sold at very low prices, it is called 'dumping.' Dumping benefits the buyers but impacts a country in other ways. Nations dump products to eliminate competition, secure monopolies and increase their share of international exports. Subsidies (in the exporting country) can lead to aggressive dumping, since goods can be sold profitably at a price that is cheaper than the cost of manufacture.

   Dumping results in the following:
   - Hurts a country's domestic industry and producers.
   - Impacts the sales volume.
   - Hurts the market shares.
   - Triggers decline in profitability.
   - Leads to job losses

   Due to the above-mentioned reasons, countries have incorporated strict anti-dumping measures. The very purpose of anti-dumping measures is to protect domestic producers.

   Its advantages are:
   - Re-establishes fair trade and fair competition.
   - Provides protection to the domestic producers and the industry.
   - Rectifies unfair trade practices pertaining to dumping.

   Though many measures have been taken out to have control on dumping activities through anti-dumping measures, but on the other hand both create hindrances in international business. Dumping activity creates threats to the local producers whereas anti-dumping measures restrict the foreign exporters while making entry into the other country only for export business.

7. **Trade Barriers:** Trade barriers refer to government-imposed policies to restrict international trade. Most commonly, a country's government employs tariffs, duties, embargoes and subsidies as trade barriers. In times of flourishing international trade, imposing trade barriers prevents the nation from fully realizing the economic benefits of such globalized trade. A protectionism regime causes over-allocation of resources in the protected sector and exploitation or under-allocation of resources in free trade sectors. This usually leads the country into economic disequilibria, which hampers growth. Import restrictions affect international trade relations, which in turn leads to a decline in exports. Thus, the protectionism regime that is employed to protect certain sectors actually tends to retard the growth of the entire economy. Free trade environments offer greater and better choices in the market, leading to enhanced consumer satisfaction. With trade barriers in place, the government curbs consumer rights to enjoy competition in the market.
8. **Difficulties in Payment:** Foreign trade involves the exchange of currencies because the currency of one country is not the legal tender in the other country. Exchange rates are determined for different currencies for this purpose. But exchange rates go on fluctuating. Moreover there is a wide gap between the times when the goods are dispatched and the time when the goods are received and paid for. Thus, there is a greater risk of bad debts also in international trade. Also, remittances of moneys for payments in international business are time consuming and expensive. Hence, payments in international business create complications.
9. **Large amount of Documentation:** International business involves the preparation of a large number of documents both by the importer and the exporter. These documents may be required either under law or under customs of trade of the two countries. This creates an extra time consuming exercise while dealing in the international business.
10. **Knowledge of Foreign Markets:** Every foreign market has its own characteristics. It has its own requirements, customs, traditions, weights and measures, marketing methods, etc. An extensive study of foreign markets is required to be successful in foreign trade, which may not be possessed by an ordinary trader.
11. **Relative Effects on Economy:** The recent fall in the US stock markets is largely due to expectations of a future downturn in the economy. Lower growth leads to lower profits, therefore dividends decline and shares become less attractive. If the US enters into recession, firms will experience a decline in profitability. This is because of the :
    (a) Tendency for price wars to develop in a recession. Low sales encourage firms to cut prices
    (b) Falling sales will lead to lower revenues.

Some firms will be affected more by the downturn. Firms producing luxury goods will experience the biggest percentage fall in demand. During this time, firms producing basic necessities will be more insulated from the effects of a recession. Thus, the downfall of one economy can also mark an adverse impact on the whole world business environment creating the international business more challenging.

Strategies to Overcome Challenges

In the field of business development strategies, sustainability acquires more importance in view of the growing concept of globalisation. In this era of globalisation where the interdependence amongst the countries is growing rapidly requiring industries and enterprises to develop strategies to cope with the challenge, the companies of small economies will have to face a greater challenge than others.

A developed and powerful country, which has monopoly over technology of producing goods, can corner all the gains for itself at the cost of poor and underdeveloped countries. Usually, products produced by developed countries are highly elastic while products produced by underdeveloped countries are inelastic. Hence, terms of trade adversely affect underdeveloped countries. Price fluctuations of agricultural products, which are exported by underdeveloped countries, vary widely. Whereas price fluctuations of industrial goods exported by developed countries remain stable. Hence, international trade increases instability in the economy of underdeveloped countries. Developed countries also corner benefit of trade because terms of trade move in their favour.

Thus, these challenges focusing on sustaining international business and pursuing it further to the state of constant excellence, can be achieved by opting:

- **Organic growth activities:** By increasing sales volume, achieving economies of scale, thereby gaining synergies, or introducing any new products.
- **Inorganic growth activities:** Through M&A
- **External growth activities:** Through diversifications, joint ventures, franchising, licensing, etc.

STRATEGIC PLANNING

Strategy involves continued reassessment of the firm's political, economic, financial, and technological environments. These must be related to the changing characteristics of the firm's industry and its competitive environment. This can be clearly understood by studying elements of strategic planning, which can be followed in any of the above three strategies.

Essential Elements in Strategic Planning

1. Assessment of changes in the environments.
2. Evaluation of company capabilities and limitations.
3. Assessment of expectations of stakeholders.
4. Analysis of company, competitors, industry, domestic economy, and international economies.
5. Formulation of the missions, goals and policies for the master strategy.
6. Development of sensitivity to critical environment changes.
7. Formulation of internal organization performance measurements.
8. Formulation of long-run strategy programmes.
9. Formulation of mid-range programmes and short-run plans.
10. Organization, funding, and other methods to implement all the above elements.
11. Information flow and feedback system for continued repetition of all essential elements and for adjustments and changes at each stage.
12. Review and evaluation of all processes.

The above elements act as tools for making strategic visions that guided firms to success. They are helpful in important innovations in thinking and implementation. There are no simple formulas for innovation and creativity that suggests a firm to carry its business at international level, but the strategy literature has developed a number of approaches for achieving competitive superiority leading towards international business. This can be seen under strategy formulation.

Strategy Formulation

The strategic challenges faced by a firm cannot be solved by mathematical formulas. A deep understanding of the firm and its industry is the foundation for strategic planning. There are number of approaches laid down by various analysts for formulating strategies, but the best suited to international business are:

(a) Competitive analysis, and
(b) Strength-Country Attractiveness Matrix

COMPETITIVE ANALYSIS

A firm's competitive position can be evaluated by conducting competitive analysis of 11 factors reflecting demand and supply conditions as shown in the Fig.1. As on the demand side, the

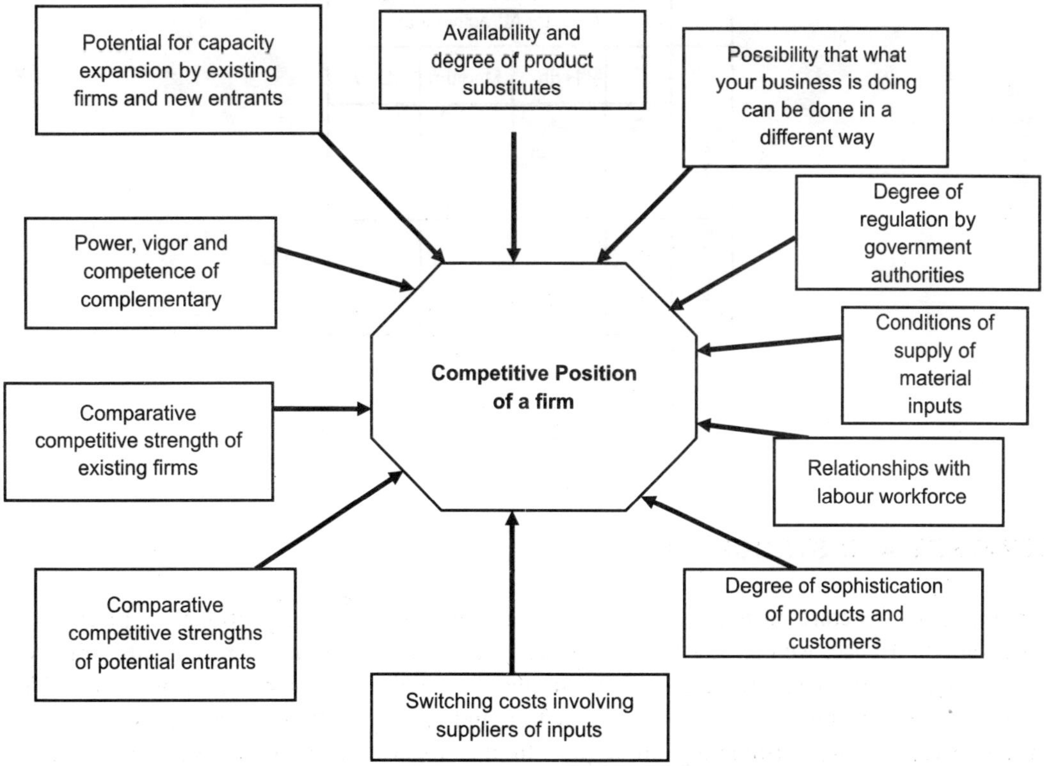

Fig. 1. Competitive analysis.

degree of feasible product substitutability is critically important, whereas, on the supply side nature and structure of costs are critical. The ability to switch among suppliers of inputs is also important as the costs involved in shifting from one supplier to another may be critically affected. Supply competition from existing firms including their potentials for capacity expansion is also a major influence on the competitive position of the firm. Complementary firms are also important. Is there a threat that your business can be carried out in another way by other firms? Answer of all these questions can be found out by this analysis, thereby leading to effective strategic planning.

STRENGTH-COUNTRY ATTRACTIVE MATRIX

After determining firm's competitive position, a firm with the help of this matrix as shown in the Fig. 2, can decide that to which country it should go for international business. In the international setting the most attractive countries, in terms of growth or political stability, in which the firm has competitive strengths offer the most favourable growth opportunities. On the contrary, there will be less or no growth opportunities in the countries of low attractiveness where the firm's competitive strengths are low.

Fig. Strength – Country Attractiveness Matrix

		Country Attractiveness		
		High	Medium	Low
Business Strengths	High	Invest / Growth		
	Medium			
	Low			Harvest / Divest

Fig. 2.

STRATEGY AND STRUCTURE

The impact of structure on the strategy is especially important in multinational or transnational organizations. Hence, we can say that the structure of an organization determines its strategy. It implies that the firm can only access those strategies, which it is organized to undertake. Thus, there is a feedback relationship between structure and strategy, which a transnational company must consider before formulating strategies. In this regard three alternative approaches are illustrated.

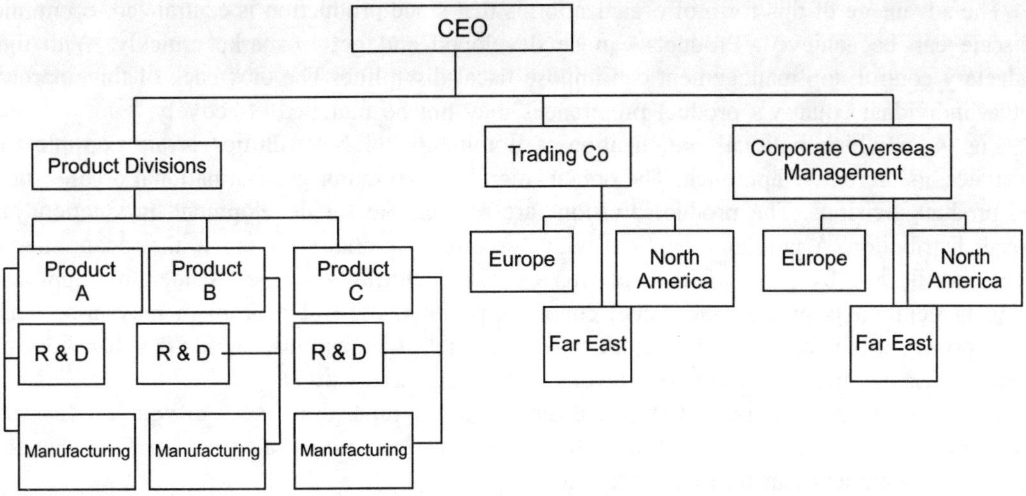

Fig. 3. Product division dominant.

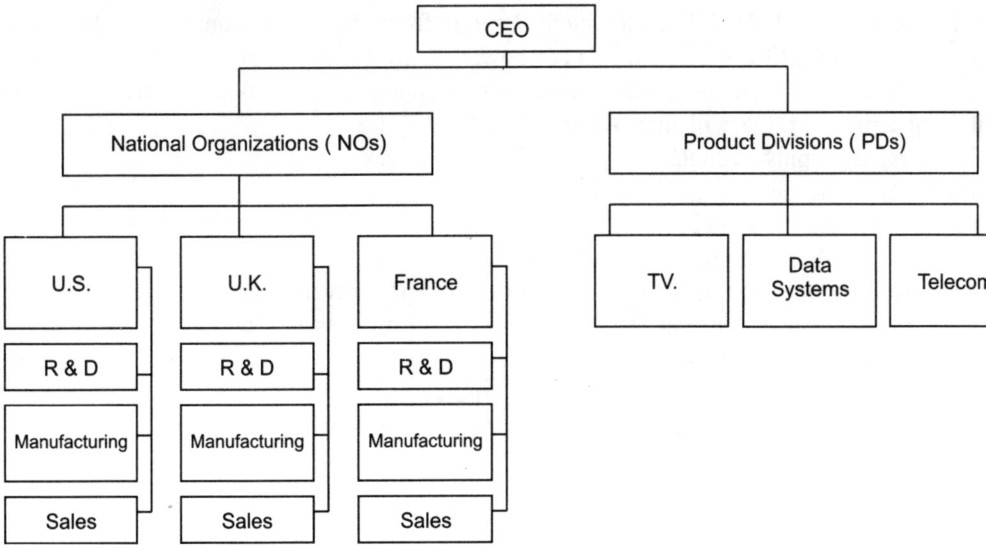

Fig. 4. National organizations dominant.

In Fig. 3 a product division basis is dominant and represents about Matsushita Electric Industrial Company. Product groups such as radios or tape-recorders report directly to the executive level. Each product has its own functional activities such as R&D and manufacturing. Matsushita Electric Trading Company is organized geographically, representing the sales arm of the product segments. The diagram shows a third group of overseas management activities also organized geographically.

The advantage of this form of organization is that since production is centralized, economies of scale can be achieved. Products can be developed and get to market quickly. With tight budgetary control, top management can impose fiscal discipline. The drawback of this approach is that individual country's product preferences may not be matched effectively.

Fig. 4 in which national organization is dominant and N.V. Philips is an example that illustrates an alternative approach. The organization has two major groups: national organizations and product divisions. The product divisions are responsible for development, production, and global distribution. A potential problem with this organizational structure is that economies of scale may be lost by geographic dispersion of manufacturing activities. Under this approach, due consideration is paid to individual country's preferences. But a problem may arise under this approach that because of the autonomy of national organizations, brands developed by the product divisions may be rejected in favour of those of competitors.

Hence, in every organization structure there appears some drawbacks to which a firm can overcome from it, if the structure is made flexible so that changing strategies as per the changing business environment can be easily fitted to it.

CONCLUSION

Although world as a whole will undoubtedly benefit from the international trade, how much does each country benefit depends on relative power of the countries. If some measures can be made to improve the terms of the international trade, definitely every country would be benefited from it. And terms of trade will improve if:

1. Elasticity of supply is high.
2. Elasticity of demand is high.
3. Country concentrates on industrial products rather than agricultural products.
4. Rate of growth of national income is high
5. Country does not depend on few items to earn export revenue.
6. Country does not depend on few non-substitutable imports like petrol.
7. Continuous technological growth.
8. High level of economic flexibility in the corporate sector to take benefit of relative price changes between imported products and indigenous products.
9. Slow population growth.

REFERENCES

1. Cheltenham: Edward Elgar, 1999. Multinationals, Technology and National Competitiveness.
2. Rosy Joshi and Sangam Kapoor, 2003. Business Environment, Kalyani Publishers.
3. Economic Times,2007. Funds no bar for shophalic India Inc, Special Report, New Delhi, Nov.
4. J. Fred Weston and Samuel C. Weaver, 2007. Merger And Acquisitions, Tata McGraw-Hill Edition.
5. Dr. Parveen Kataria, Anshu Kataria & M. Shivani, 2006. UGC- NET/SLET, Commerce, Trueman's Specific series.

8

Indian Export Trends, Issues and Challenges in Aloe Vera Leaves

N. SUMATHI[1] AND J. KAVITHA[2]

[1&2]*Assistant Professors, Adaikalamatha Institute of Management, Adaikalamatha College, Vallam, Thanjavur.*

ABSTRACT

For over three thousand years millions of people all over the world have been using aloe vera as a home remedy. Today it is being used in ayurveda, siddha and homeopathy. It is also used in Chinese and Arabian medicine in the treatment of certain skin problems such as eczema and psoriasis. Among other substances this herbal healer contains several antiseptic agents which make it effective in many internal and external infections. In ayurvedic medicine aloe is used internally as a laxative, homorrid remedy and menstrual regulator. Aloe products for internal views have been also promoted for colstipation, coughs and wounds, ulcers, diabetes, cancer, headaches, immune system deficiencies and many other ailments. The aloe leaf contains over 75 nutrients and 200 active compounds including 20 minerals, 18 amino acids and 12 vitamins including A, B1, B2, B6, B12, C and E. Many pharmaceutical companies are preparing its different products like aloe vera juice, aloe vera jelly, jams, etc. The derivative products of aloe vera as raw materials, cosmetic and personal care products, nutritional care products, aroma care products, medicinal products, and general purpose products. The aloe vera plants can be harvested in every 6 to 8 weeks by removing 3 to 4 leaves per plant yield 10 tonnes of whole plant for 12 to 15 months per hectare aloe has a high enzyme content (about 92 enzymes) which makes it a rare and valuable resource because enzymes help the body to absorb basic nutrients while also purifying it. The future Indian prospects of the aloe vera industry, the opportunities can be import and export possibilities exploited by sustained marketing growth to globally.

INTRODUCTION

Aloe vera is a popular house plant which can be snapped off and placed on cuts and burns for immediate relief. In India it is grown commercially for its high demand in cosmetic as well as in Indian system of medicine. The succulent leaves are economic part of this plant the commercial cultivation in many parts they get produced from its mature leaves used in cosmetic industry for preparation of shampoo, face creams and moisturising agents. Aloe barbadensis is native to warm, dry regions especially in southern Europe, Asia and Africa. Habitats include the areas surrounding the mediterranean sea in the eastern and southern parts of Africa. Aloe vera comprises about 200 speices, indigenous to east and South Africa. In India the plant is mainly found in Rajasthan and other dry belts. It also grows in coasts of Mumbai, Gujarat and south India. Aloe vera plants are easy to rise requiring no special care and only the occasional watering, they do best in bright sun light and do not tolerate temperature bellow 45°. It is a popular remedy for sun burn and skin rahes. The studies have shown aloe vera can help promote healing of the skins.

Common varieties and uses

Common Varieties	Uses
Aloe Barbadensis miller	Aloe vera helps heal wounds
Aloe saponaria	Aloe gel sooth burburns
Aloe chinensis	It minimize force by damage
Aloe Variegata	It screens out radiations
Aloe forex	Aloe protects from lung cancer
Aloe lalifolia	It eases in intestinal problems
Curacao Aloe	It also reduce blood sugar in diabe patients

Benefits of Aloe Vera

1. Body building blocks
2. Antifungal / anti- bacterial supplements
3. Daily dose of vitamins
4. Daily dose of minerals
5. Diabetes prevention
6. Immune support and functions
7. Regulate weight and energy level
8. Wound treatment
9. Heart burnt preventions
10. Dental health
11. Sun screen
12. Hair grower substitutes

Demand for Aloe Vera in Indian Market

In India aloe vera is largely used in cosmetic applications such as skin moisturiser, skin cream and hair tonic. Today's consumers in cosmetic, food are increasingly interested in healthy life styles, a trend which has produced a high demand for health oriented products.

Factors Influencing the Capacity Creation

Innovative marketing capability in marketing agency both in Indian and global market. The marketing strategy should be able to take "replacements share" in the existing and emerging market into justify capacity creation. In Indian market there is threat of aloe based imported cosmetics taking 3 to 5 per cent of the cosmetics ingredient market seems to be feasible.

Supply Scenario

At present aloe vera jellies largely are produced in the small scale and unorganized sector. The demand growth for aloe vera gel is taking place by the way of substitution in the existing synthetic cosmetic market and also taking proportional share in the emerging/ growing market for cosmetic products. The trend is likely to continue, paving way for increased demand for aloe vera based cosmetic products and consequently aloe vera gel.

Global Scenario and Export Opportunities

Now, aloe bulk as well as extracts are widely used in food, cosmetic, healthcare, skin care and medicinal industry as active ingredients for extra therapeutic, hygienically, rejuvenating, health enhance effectives. Aloe vera was the highlighted ingredient in 1557 new products launches worldwide, Grape seed extract was the second most popular ingredient with 350 new products launches during the same period of time, 2001- 2002. Global industry with aloe included 27000 companies, whose turnover exceeded 33 billion USD in 2001.

Research Study under Aloe Vera Products

A few developed countries like the USA are doing medical research on the uses of aloe products. Foods and Drug Administration of USA has already approved the developmental study of aloe vera in the treatment of cancer and AIDS.

Current Market Scenario and Export Potential

The current global turnover of raw aloe leaves amounts up to 70-80 million US dollars, which is expected to grow at the rate of 35% in the next five years. For processed derivatives and value added products, current global trade is estimated at around 1 billion and 25 billion US dollars respectively. USA supplies the major bulk of aloe in the world market having a share of 60-65%, where as Latin American countries supply 20-25% and Australia, Vhina and India combined together have a market share only 10%. The government target of medical plant export was to the tune of Rs. 10000 crore by the end of 2010. American consumers are most familiar with aloe's skin-care products and there have been dramatic increase in aloe vera sales in the United States. Korea is the largest international marketplace for aloe, with Japan running a close second. Both these countries have a long and respected tradition of herbal medicine. Aloe beverages are also very popular in Korea, Singapore, and Malaysia. In Australia, market for skin and hair products containing aloe is increasing. The use of aloe in cosmetic products is growing in Switzerland, Italy, and Spain and in several African nations. Aloe produced in Zanzibar, West Indies, Cape Colone, Bonaire, etc, is shipped to the United States and Europe. In India, aloe juice produced at the farms in Vidharbha region are marketed to Mumbai and Bangalore.

CONCLUSION

An aloe product is largely used in a variety of applications both internal and external. In India aloe vera is produced in small scale and unorganized sector. They should encourage to cultivate the Aloe vera in rural areas. In particularly rural areas people do not have proper knowledge about the aloe vera. So the aloe vera market should create awareness about the aloe vera by the way of using school and colleges. Proper cultivation will increase our export supply of aloe vera raw material products worldwide and increase our GDP and also utilize this medicinal plant to the society.

REFERENCES

1. Article 2(5)(b) of the REACH regulations for details.
2. Guidance for Annex V, Exemptions from the obligation to register, Version: 1, March 2010.
3. Regulated by Directive 2001/83/EC, relating to medicinal products for human use.
4. Regulated by the Food Safety Regulation 178/2002/EC.
5. 8630 Fenton Street, Suite 918|Silver Spring, MD 20910| info@iasc.org|www.iasc.org

9

Challenges and Strategies for Indian Medical Tourism Industry

BEENA JOHN

B.Sc., MBA (Mktg), M.Phil.,
JSPM'S, Jayawant Institute of Management Studies (affiliated to Pune University),
Tathawade, Pune, E-mail: beenajohnbeena@gmail.com

ABSTRACT

The growing trend of travelling outside of one's country for medical services, commonly known as "medical tourism", is expected to continue to grow exponentially in the next ten years (Keckley, 2008). Medical tourism has captured the interest of the media. It is being published and produced with increasing frequency as health and medical tourism is perceived as one of the fastest growing segments in marketing 'Destination India' today. While this area has so far been relatively unexplored, we now find that not only the ministry of tourism, government of India, but also the various state tourism boards and even the private sector consisting of travel agents, tour operators, hotel companies and other accommodation providers are eying health and medical tourism as a segment with tremendous potential for future growth. India's picture in the eyes of the world has transitioned over time from temples, colourful villagers, elephants and bullock carts to one of IT, outsourcing, call centres and talented English speaking professionals. India has entered the global age. The new portrait emerging now is that of high-tech hospitals, state-of-the art healthcare facilities, and highly competent doctors, surgeons and support staff treating people from all corners of the world. Healthcare, like food and shelter, is a basic need of humanity. Given the potential India holds as a healthcare destination, the medical tourism sector can be a major source of foreign exchange earning for the country. This study presents an analysis of the opportunities offered by the sector to our country and strategies that can help to overcome the challenges.

Keywords: Medical tourism, Challenges, Strategies.

INTRODUCTION

Medical tourism is one of the major sectors amongst the trade in services that has been growing significantly the world over particularly with the establishment of General Agreement of Trade in Services (GATS) under WTO. This sector falls under Mode II - known as "Consumption Abroad" of GATS. India is the cynosure of medical tourists (MTs) amongst its competing countries, such as Thailand, Malaysia, Singapore, South Africa, Hong Kong, Philippines, Cuba, Hungary, Israel, Jordan, Lithuania, etc. India's medical tourism sector is a growing source of foreign exchange as well as prestige and goodwill outside the country. Medical tourists have been coming for treatment in growing numbers in Ahmedabad, Mumbai, Chennai, Bangalore, Delhi, Kolkata, etc.

India's healthcare sector has made impressive strides in recent years. Several features have positioned India as an ideal healthcare destination, like cost-effective healthcare solutions, availability of skilled professionals, reputation for successful treatment in advanced healthcare segments, increasing popularity of India's traditional wellness systems and rapid strides made in information technology. India now hosts and treats an estimated of 50,000 medical tourists a year and the catalytic CII-McKinsey report projected that medical tourism could contribute up to Rs. 10,000 crore in revenue by the year 2012.

Indian efforts to promote medical tourism took off in 2002, when the confederation of Indian industry produced a study on the country's medical tourism sector, in collaboration with international management consultants, Mc Kinsey & company which outlined immense potential for the sector. Today,the Indian ministry of tourism overseas those intending to travel to India as medical tourists with M-visas.

Foreigners in increasing numbers are now coming to India for private healthcare. They come from the Middle East, Africa, Pakistan, and Bangladesh, for complex pediatric cardiac surgery or liver transplants—procedures that are not done in their home countries. They also come from the United Kingdom, Europe, and North America for quick, efficient, and cheap coronary bypasses or orthopaedic procedures. A shoulder operation in the UK would cost £10 000 ($17 460; •14 560) done privately or entail several months wait under the NHS. In India, the same operation can be done for £1700 and within 10 days of a first email contact.

Objectives of the Study

1) To recognize the advantages of India as a medical tourist destination.
2) To identify the opportunities available in medical tourism
3) To identify the strategy to attract medical tourists.

Research Problem

While the tourism department comes out with facts and figures every year, still India lags behind in medical tourism scenario. As per the World Economic Forum 2008 report, India ranks 65th thus, there is a great need of improvement in this area.

Research Methodology

Secondary data were accumulated through various sources like the internet, books, newspaper articles, etc.

Literature Review

Though the concept of 'healthcare tourism' is thousands of years old, it has got its prominence rather recently. Medical tourism is a growing sector in India. India's medical tourism sector is expected to experience an annual growth rate of 30%, making it a Rs. 9,500 crore industry by 2015.

According to the study conducted by the Confederation of Indian Industry and McKinsey consultants, last year some 1,50,000 foreigners visited India for treatment, with the number rising by 15 per cent a year.

RNCOS in its market research report, "Opportunities in Indian Healthcare Sector" finds that 1,20,000 overseas patients came to India in 2005 for medical treatment and this is expected to expand by 30%. The healthcare industry overview shows that the medical infrastructure and technology in this country is at par with those in the USA, UK and Europe. India can vie with some of its best hospitals and treatment centres in the world, and therefore make it a favourable destination.

SWOT of Indian Medical Tourism Sector

Strengths

- Medical tourism is attracting people from all over the industrialized world, from countries with relatively poor healthcare infrastructure and, in case of the US, places with exorbitantly expensive healthcare systems. Many surgical procedures are available at one-tenth the cost of those in developed countries and "there is no waiting period for elective surgery".
- Patients are offered services ranging from complex heart and orthopaedic procedures, cardiology and cardiac surgery (angioplasty, bypass, valve replacement), to oncology and onco-surgery, organ transplants (liver and kidney), bone marrow transplants, joint replacements, eye surgery and *in vitro* fertilization. The cost differential is significant compared to US and UK and other countries.
- The lower cost structure of our hospitals allows them to be more generous with resources for their well paying clients. Nurse-to-patient ratios are higher, private rooms are readily available and family members are often included in the trip and made comfortable in luxury facilities that resemble five-star hotels.

Weakness

- Indian medical care service providers need to prove quality consciousness and get international accreditation. The negative perceptions about India, with regard to public sanitation / hygiene standards or prevalence of contagious diseases, counter the positive vibes created by the cost competitiveness of Indian healthcare systems.
- In the major states, health departments issue guidelines to private hospitals specifying their obligation to provide beds, treatment and services to the public patient, and to return a portion of revenues from medical tourism into serving the public health overburden, but neither are these hospital held to account on these points by their respective state governments, nor does a standard countrywide regulatory system exist to ensure such compliance.

Opportunity

- Well equipped hospitals and availability of skilled doctors is a strength.
- Quality is a concern for potential medical tourists and 'offshore hospitals' address this concern by seeking and obtaining accreditation from bodies such as Joint Commission International (JCI), a subsidiary of the Joint Commission on Accreditation of Healthcare Organizations (JCAHO), which offers accreditation to hospitals in the US. Already 13 Indian hospitals have been accredited by the Joint Commission International (JCI) in India.
- Some advantage in availing this service accreditation is it will make tie-ups with overseas health insurance agencies such as BUPA and CHUBS who route patients to India. With these initiatives there is huge opportunity for medical tourism sector which is still untapped.

Threats to the Industry

- Some threats that the country has to overcome to become a tourist destination with competent healthcare industry are infrastructural facilities relating to:
  - Roads
  - Sanitation
  - Power backups
  - Rest/guest houses
  - Public utility services
- The biggest challenge that the Indian hospitals face is assuring the foreign patients that they will receive quality care with no hidden costs. The basic expectations that the industry feels are important to be concerned about are related to:
  - Hygiene
  - Staff (trained technically as well as in soft skills)
  - Customization
  - Insurance cover
  - Stability
  - Connectivity
  - International standard certification
  - Para-medical ambulance facilities (to and fro from Airport).

Recent Trends

In the recent past, there have been major changes in Indian healthcare delivery mechanism. India is gradually moving from conventional stand-alone set-ups to hospitals chains with well integrated networks. There is increasing penetration of information technology (IT) applications in healthcare institution. It enhances the quality of care and helps to provide one-stop-solution to the patient's need. India is also at the forefront to adopt innovative solutions such as usage of telemedicine services. There is a continuous increase in the number of healthcare institutions offering telemedicine services. Telemedicine is in infancy, but it is making inroads at a fast pace and India is expected to emerge as a country with a high penetration rate for telemedicine which can be helpful during post-operative treatments.

The Indian healthcare delivery market is also making its presence felt in the global market by providing high class quality services and focusing on medical tourism. An estimated 50 per cent of tertiary level hospitals focus on providing services to the medical tourism sector. Some big industry players have changed the face of the industry by providing world-class healthcare facilities. They already have hospital chains covering all geographic regions of India however; the current healthcare infrastructure in India is inadequate to meet the future needs and to meet the current rate of demand. This infrastructure would need an investment of approximately US$30-40 million. To meet this demand, a new paradigm in healthcare is the concept of health city township with integrated healthcare facilities have started operations across India.

Health insurance medical tourism and corporate hospitals have resulted in higher demand of quality services. This has resulted in the formation of regulatory and accreditation bodies to define standards and regulations for various healthcare facilities. This initiative will definitely improve the quality of services provided by the Indian healthcare industry. The major healthcare chains on expansion spree are APOLLO HOSPITALS, FORTIS HEALTHCARE, WOCKHARDT HOSPITALS, CARE HOSPITAL, MAX HEALTHCARE, etc., to name a few many major hospitals have already achieved the highest level of quality certification from JCI (Joint Commission International) for their healthcare services.

Initiatives Taken

India is a recent entrant into medical tourism. According to a study by McKinsey and the Confederation of Indian Industry, medical tourism in India could become a $1billion business by 2012. The report predicts that: "By 2012, if medical tourism were to reach 25 per cent of revenues of private up-market players, up to Rs 10,000 crore will be added to the revenues of these players". The Indian government predicts that India's $17-billion-a-year healthcare industry could grow 13 per cent in each of the next six years, boosted by medical tourism, which industry watchers say is growing at 30 per cent annually. India has seen a rush of healthcare providers setting up super specialty hospitals with facilities like air ambulance and shopping plazas. Hospitals are seeking recognition from insurance companies abroad, so that the patients can avail health insurance, as they would in their own country. Hospitals are also teaming up with hotels and travel agencies to offer treatment and tourism packages to interested patients and their families.

Ministry of Tourism India (MoT) is planning to extend its Market Development Assistance (MDA) scheme to cover Joint Commission International (JCI) and National Accreditation Board of Hospitals (NABH) certified hospitals. Hospital groups like The Global Hospitals Group, MIOT Hospitals, Fortis Healthcare, Apollo hospitals, Max Hospitals, Dharamshila Cancer Hospital and Research Centre have increased their presence in international market for medical tourism. The south Indian city of Chennai has been declared India's health capital, as it nets in 45% of health tourists from abroad and 30–40% of domestic health tourists. The hospitals in Chennai are equipped with state-of-the-art medical equipment and Chennai is relatively a less expensive city compared to the other metropolitan cities like Mumbai and Delhi.

The State of Maharashtra and the Federation of Indian Chamber of Commerce and Industry (FICCI) have collaborated to form the Medical Tourism Council of Maharashtra (MTCM). Their mission is "to deliver 'value for money' healthcare with a human touch." These all is immense steps & a positive trend each state is taking to promote medical tourism in a major way.

Strategies to Promote Indian Medical Tourism

- As this is a product which needs international tie-ups and international marketing, the state governments should help more. State tourism offices in India and abroad can help the companies, hospitals and states in promoting health tourism abroad so that we can tap a wider range of customers. International websites on Indian tourism with true attractive perceptions has to be created for successful branding.
- Indian hospitals must create exclusive infrastructure for corporate medical tourism, need of chartered flight services, attractive tourism packages could be part of infrastructure as there's growing pressure to reduce expenditure on healthcare.
- Neighbouring countries that actively promote medical tourism include Cuba, Costa Rica, Hungary, India, Israel, Jordan, Lithuania, Malaysia and Thailand. Belgium, Poland and Singapore. Thus, India has enough competition from the international market. This will be one of the our major threats in bringing up and developing the health tourism industry. Globalization of marketing activities by Indian tour & travel agents. Tie-ups with foreign travel agents for promotion to target customers will increase the number of persons visiting our country as medical tourists.
- Tapping the foreign customers by tying up with insurance companies abroad who could provide a genuine database of target customers. They can benefit from us by our services. Thus, this would become a way of mutual marketing tacit between the Indian health tourism industry and the foreign insurance agencies.
- In case of hospitals like Apollo and Escorts that the local demand it to be catered to is vast. Hospitals should have the facilities enough to manage the foreign customers not neglecting the local markets. Thus, it is a challenge for both the alternate therapy industry and corporate healthcare service providers to cater to this vast market efficiently without compromises in quality on either side. Doctors of India may also visiting foreign countries for pre- and post-treatment.
- Need of an identical agency like NAASCOM for medical tourism to periodically come out with realistic reports for bettering the services in the days to come.
- Our foreign consulate offices also can act as ambassadors for promoting medical tourism to give this business a big boost.
- Innovative schemes, targeting medical tourists so that they return back with great feeling of comfort, satisfaction and joy.
- More and more infrastructure avenues opened up so that consultants can join the fray for bringing in world class quality treatment facilities, all under one roof.

CONCLUSION

There is a huge opportunity in this sector as Indian healthcare institutions are in a position to offer quality medical services at one-tenth of the cost compared to many countries in the west. The biggest challenge is to position India as a favourable healthcare centre destination by providing high medical standards. Now the Indian Healthcare Federation is also working with different industry chambers to promote medical tourism in the country. Today India is projecting itself as a vibrant, colourful image of its diversity in terms of its customs, heritage sites, cultures, etc. through its campaigns and websites but it is time now of committed efforts by the government authorities, along with participation of private players and coordination among various entities related to tourism to make India become a top priority for medical tourists.

REFERENCES

1. Babu, P. George, (2009). Medical tourism in India: A case study of Apollo Hospitals, *Health and Wellness Tourism*, Pages 367-372
2. Indian Medical Tourism To Touch Rs 9,500 Crore By 2015, The Economic Times, posted on Indian Health Care. in
3. Zeenat Nazir, (2006). Just what the hospital ordered: Global accreditations", Indian Express.
4. Swamis to Surgeries, (2011). medicaltourismmag.com
5. "Indian medical care goes global", (2006). Aljazeera.Net, Laurie Goering.
6. "For big surgery, Delhi is dealing," (2008). The Chicago Tribune.
7. "MoT plans to extend MDA scheme to cover JCI and NABH to boost Medical Tourism" (2009). travelbizmonitor.com
8. Macguire, Suzanne (2007). "India - The Emerging Global Health Destination". EzineArticles. http://www.indiainbusiness.nic.in/know- india/states/tamilnadu.htm.
9. Chennai Medicare Tourism". chennaimedicaretourism.com. http://www.chennaimedicaretourism.com/whychennai.html. Retrieved 2011-01-17.
10. "India Turning Affordable, Quality Option for Medical Tourists" Indianhealthcare.in.
11. "Indian Healthcare: The Growth Story". Indianhealthcare.in. "Accreditation of Hospitals". Indianhealthcare.in
12. Chandrasekhar, P. (2006), Taj-Apollo to Tie Up For Medical Tourism, *Business Standard* July 12, p5
13. McKinsey CII Study, (2003), Healthcare in India-The Road Ahead.
14. Medical Tourism: India is the Favorable Destination in the World - RNCOS Market Report India's cost-effective and efficient medical sector has made it a favored destination for healthcare - India's Health Minister Dr. Anbumani Ramadoss

Websites

- www.medical-tourism-india.com
- http://indiamedicaltourism.co.in/
- www.health-tourism-india.com
- http://www.medinetindia.com/news.

10

Exploring Different Dimensions of Recession in Indian Scenario

Ashish Gadekar and Rimalini Gadekar

HOD (MBA), Hindustan Institute of Management and Computer Studies Mathura, E-mail: avgadekar@gmail.com

Assistant Professor, Department of Mechanical Engineering, St.Vincent Pallotti College of Engineering Technology, Nagpur, E-mail: rimalini@yahoo.com

ABSTRACT

This study explores the different dimensions of recession in the Indian scenario. This paper analyzes the factors and problems which are affecting the performance of Indian exports. This study deals with the problems the exporters face in the recession. The study also makes some findings on how the problems and disputes are settled.

INTRODUCTION

Globalization and liberalization, undoubtedly, brought benefits of advancement. Globalization compressed the world, intensified the consciousness of the world as a whole, and deepened the worldwide social relations which link distinct localities in such a way that local happenings are shaped by events occurring many miles away and vice versa. The international financial crisis that erupted in the US has started spreading ripples of troubles worldwide. The world saw the abject failure of the US Government to find a solution. The solution must be consistent with justice and social solidarity for all countries, reflect an understanding of the necessary balance between government and markets, more global cooperation in setting macroeconomic policies, rebuilding trust in the financial markets and respect the principles of democratic due process, including full transparency. America's housing collapse is often cited as having caused the crisis but the financial system was vulnerable due to the intricate and overleveraged financial contracts and operations. But the crisis was not confined to the banking and credit system. It had a domino effect on financial markets (stock exchanges and derivative markets notably), equity funds, hedge funds, insurance activities, pension funds, public finance, Forex, etc.

Beginning with bankruptcy of Lehman Brothers in September 2008, the financial crisis entered an acute phase marked by failures of prominent American and European banks and efforts by the American and European governments to rescue distressed financial institutions, in the United States by passage of the Emergency Economic Stabilization Act of 2008 and in European countries by infusion of capital into major banks. Afterwards, Iceland almost claimed to go bankrupt. Many financial institutions in Europe also faced the liquidity problem that they needed to raise their capital adequacy ratio. As the crisis developed, stock markets fell worldwide, and global financial regulators attempted to coordinate efforts to contain the crisis. The US government threw the $700 billion plan which was attempted to purchase the unperforming collaterals and assets. However, the plan was criticized by the US Congress members and they rejected the idea that the tax payers' money is used to bail out the Wall Street's investment bankers. This bailout package was controversial because it was unpopular with the public, seen as a bailout for the culprits while the ordinary person would be left to pay for their folly; "socialising the costs while privatising the profits." The bailouts appear to help the financial institutions that got into trouble (many of whom pushed for the kind of lax policies that allowed this to happen in the first place).

The initial rejection at the US House of Representatives, because of this, sent shock waves around the world. It took a second attempt to pass the plan, but with add-ons to the bill to get the additional congressmen and women to accept the plan. The stock market plunged as a result, the US Congress amended the $700 billion bailout plan and finally passed the legislation. Unfortunately, the market sentiment continuously deteriorated and the global financial system almost collapsed. While the market turned extremely pessimistic, the British government launched a 500 billion pound bailout plan aimed to injecting capital into the financial system. The British government nationalized most of the financial institutions in trouble. Many European governments followed as well as the US government. Stock markets appeared to have stabilized as October ended. In addition, the falling prices due to reduced demand for oil, coupled with projections of a global recession, brought the 2000s energy crisis to temporary resolution. In the Eastern European economies of Poland, Hungary, Romania, and Ukraine, the economic crisis has been characterised by difficulties with loans made in hard currencies such as the Swiss franc. As local currencies in those countries lost value, making payment on such loans became progressively difficult.

Table 1: Jobs cut of financial sectors

Company	Jobs cut	Percentage of headcount
Citigroup	23,500	6.3
Lehman Brothers	13,390	46.8
Bank of America	11,150	5.3
Bear Stearns	9,159	64.7
UBS	9,000	10.8
Commerzbank	9,000	24.5
Wachovia	8,393	6.9
Royal Bank of Scotland	7,200	3.2
Merrill Lynch	5,220	8.1
Morgan Stanley	4,440	9.2
Washington Mutual	4,200	NA
JPMorgan	4,100	2.3
Other US banks	2,914	NA
IndyMac	2,800	28.3
HSBC	2,780	0.9
Other European banks	2,370	NA
Credit Suisse	1,565	3.3
West LB	1,530	24.9
Goldman Sachs	1,500	4.9
National City	900	2.8
Total	125,111	

Source: Bloomberg, 9 October, 2008

As the financial panic developed during September and October, 2008, there was a "flight to quality" as investors sought safety in U.S. treasury bonds, gold, and strong currencies such as the dollar and the yen. This currency crisis threatened to disrupt international trade and produced strong pressure on all world currencies. The International Monetary Fund had limited resources relative to the needs of the many nations with currency under pressure or near collapse. Investment bank UBS stated on October 6 that the year 2009 would see a clear global recession, with recovery unlikely for at least two years. UBS quantified their expected recession durations on October 16: the Eurozone's would last two quarters, the United States' would last three quarters, and the United Kingdom's would last four quarters. Nouriel Roubini, professor of economics at New York University and chairman of RGE Monitor, predicted a recession of up to 2 years, unemployment of up to 9 per cent, and another 15 per cent drop in home prices. Given the nature of the global meltdown, it is widely feared that the crisis would deepen and threaten the economies of the Third World countries. Obviously, the implications for India will be far-reaching and reverse the process of reforms.

1. Greed of some Woes of Billions

If you think about this with a cool mind, you will find that the underlying cause of this depression is the greed of those who failed to anticipate the consequences of their actions. On a more ideological front, it is high time to have a rethink on the very idea of free markets and capitalism. I think the time has come to evolve a capitalism where everything works under a broad regulatory framework and we do not see a repeat of this condition where greed of some people can affect the lives of billions. So here concludes my attempt to explain the current economic crisis which has started to affect the lives of all of us. The above explanation is very simple and by no means it presents an accurate picture (i.e., the one that includes all the micro/macro factors) of the crisis. However, I hope that it must have given you a broad idea of the reasons behind current economic depression.

2. Past Recessions

The US economy has suffered 10 recessions since the end of World War II. The Great Depression in the United was an economic slowdown, from 1930 to 1939. It was a decade of high unemployment, low profits, low prices of goods, and high poverty. The trade market was brought to a standstill, which consequently affected the world markets in the 1930s. Industries that suffered the most included agriculture, mining, and logging. In 1937, the American economy unexpectedly fell, lasting through most of 1938. Production declined sharply, as did profits and employment. Unemployment jumped from 14.3 per cent in 1937 to 19.0 per cent in 1938. The US saw a recession during 1982-83 due to a tight monetary policy to control inflation and sharp correction to overproduction of the previous decade. This was followed by Black Monday in October 1987, when a stock market collapse saw the Dow Jones Industrial Average plunge by 22.6 per cent affecting the lives of millions of Americans. The early 1990s saw a collapse of junk bonds and a financial crisis. The US saw one of its biggest recessions in 2001, ending ten years of growth, the longest expansion on record. From March to November 2001, employment dropped by almost 1.7 million. In the 1990-91 recession, the GDP fell 1.5 per cent from its peak in the second quarter of 1990. The 2001 recession saw a 0.6 per cent decline from the peak in the fourth quarter of 2000. The dot-com burst hit the US economy and many developing countries as well. The economy also suffered after the 9/11 attacks. In 2001, investors' wealth dwindled as technology stock prices crashed.

3. Impact of a US Recession on India

A slowdown in the US economy is a bad news for India. Indian companies have major outsourcing deals from the US. India's exports to the US have also grown substantially over the years. The Indian economy is likely to lose between 1 to 2 percentage points in GDP growth in the next fiscal year. Indian companies with big tickets deals in the US would see their profit margins shrinking. The worries for exporters will grow as rupee strengthens further against the dollar. But experts note that the long-term prospects for India are stable. A weak dollar could bring more foreign money to Indian markets. Oil may get cheaper brining down inflation. A recession could bring down oil prices to $70. Between January 2001 and December 2002, the Dow Jones Industrial Average went down by 22.7 per cent, while the Sensex fell by 14.6 per cent. If the fall from the record highs reached is taken, the DJIA was down 30 per cent in December 2002 from the highs it hit in January 2000. In contrast, the Sensex was down 45 per cent. The whole of Asia would be hit by a recession as it depends on the US economy. Asia is yet to totally decouple itself (or be independent) from the rest of the world, say experts.

4. What about India?

How bad will it get for us? The official estimates of GDP growth for the first two quarters of 2008/9 stayed above 7.5 per cent. However, industry-wide indications after September are uniformly gloomy. There are reports of significant declines in output of automobiles, commercial vehicles, steel, textiles, petrochemicals, construction, real estate, finance, retail activity and many other sectors. Exports fell by 12 per cent in dollar terms in October and advance information points to a similar decline in November. After September, the economy seems almost to have gone over a cliff. When available, the official data are likely to record a sharp slowdown in the second half of the year, possibly steep enough to drag full year growth in 2008/9 to below 7 per cent. Wha's more, given the strong recessionary conditions expected to prevail in the world economy in 2009, there is no prospect of a quick turn-around in India. Indeed, on a tentative basis, I would suggest that we might be lucky to achieve GDP growth of even 6 per cent in 2009/10. What about economic policy? Can we not deploy monetary, fiscal and exchange rate policies to insulate our growth momentum from adverse external conditions? The short answer is: only to a limited degree. I outlined the main arguments last fortnight (BS, November 27). Monetary policy had already been aggressively loosened by early November and the RBI provided a further, well-balanced package last Saturday, notably including a 1 percent cut in the repo and reverse repo rates. Given the continued high rate of CPI inflation through October (latest data) and, perhaps more significantly, recent pressures on the exchange rate, the present scope for further policy rate reductions appears limited. That situation might change if external imbalances improve if a falling oil import bill and slowing non-oil imports outweigh the drop in export earnings and if capital flows stabilize. On the fiscal front, the government had pretty much exhausted the available fiscal space through its record Rs 2,37,000 crore (4.5 percent of GDP) supplementary demand in October. Though undertaken for quite different reasons, its timing may turn out to be quite fortunate. Against this background the government was wise to limit last Sunday's "fiscal stimulus" to a modest affair, totaling only about Rs. 30,000 crore (Rs 300 billion), out of which two-thirds was for "additional plan expenditure", which may not be fully spent this fiscal year. It may be far more important to actually spend the already budgeted plan expenditure effectively. If international oil and fertilizer prices stay at present levels, implying low or negligible subsidy rates (looking ahead) on price-controlled domestic sales, then there may be a case for a larger stimulus next year. Much will depend on the trajectory of revenues and other expenditures in a slowing economy. While such unprecedented monetary loosening and massive supplementary expenditures will definitely help, they will not fully neutralize the negative impact of the severe global financial and economic crisis on India's exports, investment and consumption. With over 60 per cent of global GDP having toppled into recession, a significant deceleration of India's economic growth is simply unavoidable. After all, we share the same planet as America, Europe and Japan (and a rapidly slowing China). In this context a 6 per cent economic growth in 2009/10 will be pretty good...if we achieve it.

5. How it Has Affected India?

In the age of globalization, no country can remain isolated from the fluctuations of world economy. Heavy losses suffered by major international banks are going to affect all countries of the world as these financial institutes have their investment interest in almost all countries. As of now India is facing heat on three grounds: (1) Our share markets are falling everyday, (2) rupee is weakening against dollars and (3) our banks are facing severe crash crunch resulting in shortage of liquidity in the market. Actually all the above three problems are interconnected and have their roots in the above-mentioned global crisis.

For the last two years, our stock market was touching new heights thanks to heavy investments by Foreign Institutional Investors (FIIs). However, when the parent companies of these investors (based mainly in US and Europe) found themselves in a severe credit crunch as a result of sub-prime mess, the only option left with these investors were to withdraw their money from Indian stock markets to meet liabilities at home. FIIs were the main buyers of Indian stocks and their exit from the market is certain to wreak havoc in the market. FIIs who were on a buying spree last year, are now in the mood of selling their stocks in India. As a result our share markets are touching new lows every day.

Since, the money, which FIIs get after selling their stocks, needs to be converted into dollars before they can send it home, the demands for dollars has suddenly increased. As more and more FIIs are buying dollars, the rupee is losing its strength against dollar. As long as demands for dollars remain high, the rupee will keep losing its strength against dollar. The current financial crisis has also started directly affecting Indian industries. For the past few years, the two most preferred methods of raising money by the companies were stock markets and external borrowings on low interest rates. Stock markets are bleeding everyday and it is not possible to raise money there. Regarding external borrowing from world markets, this option has also become difficult. In the last fiscal year alone, India borrowed $29 billion from foreign lenders and got $34 billion of foreign direct investment. A global recession has hurt external demand. International lenders who have become extremely risk aversive can limit access to international capital. If that happens, both India's financial markets and the real economy will be hurt in the process. Suddenly, the 9% growth target does not seem that 'doable' any more; we should be happy to clock 7% this fiscal year and the next.

However, one positive point in favour of India is the fact that Indian banks are more or less secured from the ill-effects of sub-prime mess. A glance at Indian banks' balance sheets would show that their exposure to complex instruments like CDOs is almost nil. In India, still the major banking operations are in the hands of public sector banks who exercise extreme caution in disbursing loans to needy people/companies. As a result, we are not likely to see a repeat of sub-prime crisis in India. Though there have been a presence of big US/European banks in India and even some Indian banks (like ICICI) have some foreign subsidiary with stake in the sub-prime losses, their presence is miniscule as compared to the overall size of Indian banking industry. So at least on this major front we need not worry much.

However, a global depression is likely to result in a fall in demand of all types of consumer goods. In 2007-08, India sold 13.5% of its goods to foreign buyers. A fall in demand is likely to affect the growth rate this year. Our export may get affected badly. A negative atmosphere, shortage of cash, fall in demands, reducing growth rate and uncertainties in the market are some of the most visible aspects of an economic depression. What started as a small matter of sub-prime loan defaulters has now become a subject of global discussion and has engulfed the global economy scenario.

6. Consequences of US Recession on India Job Market

Worst affected because of US recession will be the service industry of India....under service industries come BPO, KPO, IT, ITeS, etc. Service industry contributes about 52% to India's GDP growth now if that is going to get hurt then it will also hurt India's overall growth. But very slightly, India is not going to face a major impact due to US recession. People may say that there is going to be a huge job loss due to recession and will cite the example of TCS firing about 500 employees. But these were employees who didn't perform. Apart from this India's travel, tourism and power industry is going to grow at a better rate, which is again a good sign. India has a huge population so a huge consumer base so we don't have to always depend on US for our growth. India's GDP is expected to grow @8.5-8.9 % which is again way above the growth rate of US and only second highest in the world after China.

This recession gives us opportunity to be innovative and to think out of box so that the US directly don't affect our robust growth. Due to increasing rupee exporters are having a hard time and they are crying foul for cut in key lending rates. But it has been noted that our exporters are not that efficient and in past they got the benefit of depreciating rupee.

7. How to Fight Recession

Tax cuts are the first step that a government fighting recessionary trends or a full-fledged recession proposes to do. In the current case, the Bush government has proposed a $150-billion bailout package in tax cuts. The government also hikes its spending to create more jobs and boost the manufacturing and services sectors and to prop up the economy. The government also takes steps to help the private sector come out of the crisis.

7.1 Food Grain Led Growth: The way out from the crisis

The need of the hour is not just the injection of liquidity into the world economy but also in addition the injection of demand. This can occur only through direct fiscal action by governments across the world. The sectors where government spending will go up will, of course, vary from country to country, but the general objective of such spending must be the reversal of the squeeze on the living standards of the ordinary people everywhere in the world that has been a feature of the world economy in the last several years. The new paradigm must entail a food grain-led growth strategy, sustained through larger government spending towards this end, which simultaneously rids the world of both depression and financial and food crises. The trade and financial arrangements of the world economy have to be oriented towards achieving this rather than being made to conform to some a priori free market principles that have the effect of pushing the world economy into financial crises and slumps, and the peasantry and small producers of the world into destitution both during the booms and also, additionally, during the slumps.

The lessons from the ongoing financial crisis make clear that the accumulation of risk and the manufacture of crisis are inevitable in a private-led, deregulated financial system that makes short-term profits the prime objective. Limited intervention cannot fundamentally alter financial behaviour to avoid such an outcome. When financial markets are left unfettered, the system goes through a sequence of events that inevitably generate a financial and real economy boom that soon goes bust. Setting up Chinese Walls separating various segments of the financial sector may not be the best option. Nor could investment banks and hedge funds be abolished. What could however be done is to monitor investment banks and hedge funds and subject them to regulation, while seeking an institutional solution that would protect the core of the financial structure: the banking system. Fortunately, the current bailout has provided the basis for such a transformation by opting for state ownership and influence over decision making.

The twentieth century capitalist experience has been one of oscillations between state-capitalism and market-oriented capitalism, with neither solution achieving long-term systemic stability. Marxian prescriptions would, therefore, go beyond the market vis-à-vis state debate to focus on the very institutional structures that perpetuate capitalism of one kind or the other.

The financial crisis has so many ramifications mainly because it is occurring in the very core of capitalism, and originated in the US, the country that had the global power and influence to impose its own economic model on almost all of the rest of the world. And the depth and severity of the crisis are likely to signal global political economy changes that will shape the world for the next few decades. Geopolitical shifts are likely to result from such glaring exposure of economic vulnerability in the global hegemony. Large bailouts and the planned Obama fiscal stimulus in the US will lead to a big increase in the US public debt. It will also make it harder for the US to maintain its military dominance, which has been a major source of the strength of the US dollar. The changes in the world, in the next decade, will not be linear or unidirectional, and there are bound to be savage conflicts over resources and much else, but the recent pattern of global imperialism has been severely disturbed. But even more than the geopolitical or economic shift, a bigger shift may come about from the clear failure of the economic model of neo liberalism. The notions that markets know best, and that self-regulation is the best form of financial regulation, have now been completely exposed as fraudulent.

8. Reasons why Recession is Good for Starting Out

1. **Good ideas wont survive, only the best ones will:** Now with apparent crunch with the liquidity, it will no longer be a ride to wonderland. Good idea and not so good ideas won't even see the light of the day. It's only the best ones who will survive. The same old mom and pop services oriented start-ups will find it extremely difficult to cope. Remarkable tech or amazing services startups will only wade through this muck. This in itself is a weeding ground for the economy in the days ahead and your company in the years ahead.
2. **Dont flip but stay put:** Dot Coms like Pyra Labs, Mingle2, etc., are looking forward to actually flip through. That is get acquired by the Google's of the world. Remember, a good company is not to be sold but kept. So once the acquisition counter gets cooled, the competition of starting up will cool down making it a tiny winy bit easy for real people to get started.
3. **Grab the attention:** Did you know that grabbing the attention in a receding economy is easy to get, if you have a good thing in your hand. Your competition is literally busy packing off, go for the kill.
4. **Nonexistent competition:** When the declining competition is busy licking their financial wounds and sticking out their neck above the waters, you can bother less about the competition and concentrate more on the remark ability of your product.
5. **Moral Strength:** Running a company is anything but easy. So when you are able to actually reflect back on days like these when you were grappling with a recession of this magnitude, you can always give yourself a pat on your back and dig in to fight another day. It can give an entrepreneur an amazing sense of pride that he led his team out of those dark days.

6. **Fail if you must, but fail fast:** A recession is an apt laboratory for your idea. Good or bad jump in. In a green economy, a good idea is celebrated and a bad idea is tried. The pittances which keep on flowing for a bad idea, can give false assurances to founders that they just need to stick out. A receding economy nods at a brilliant idea and scoffs away at a bad idea. That way you don't have any cushions between the market and yourself to think otherwise.
7. **Recessions create great companies:** Yes, it does. Google came up when there was a tremor in economy post dot com bust. GE understood its position in the global scheme of things after the 1920s bust.
8. **Talent comes in droves not in herds:** When a recession strikes, God knows it gets dirty. Bloodbath in the stocks, layoff in the business. Yet the cost mindful founders should take a welcome relief, as talent becomes available after the IBM and GE behemoths of the world start culling talent.
9. **Thousand hungry minds, million hungry hearts:** The mantra to wade through a recession is not to listen to your banker, not even to your VC (check you may not even get one), but listening to your already dwindling customers. So when you actually hardwire it to listen to your customers, you build not good, but great businesses. Companies, in economy booms, give what customers say they want, potential winning companies at times of recession give customers what they need and don't know.
10. **VCs are out, bootstrapping is in:** You will not be riding on the stock market wave like now, VCs will see red everywhere and angels will trade their souls with devils so it seems. So what? You have got another way, bootstrapping, yes it's tough. You get pittances for things otherwise worth riches, friends run away from you and family has already been 'alienized'. Yet, this will teach you the very core of finance management. You will be using Indian *jugaad,* to actually do a thing worth millions in ways which will cost you no more than hundreds. You will be innovative while doing things and ruthless while cutting costs. That means no more of that swanky plush carpets for your office and no more of that 2 hour lunch breaks. But in the long run its good right?
11. **How to face the challenges during recession:** Due to global economic low down, many companies either weed out their employees or reduce the fringe benefits to avert the situation out of the recession. All the industrial and software sectors are reeling under the impact of the global financial crisis. On account of the global recession, large corporates worldwide downsize their staff, production and expenses. Even some of the biggest companies in India, have laid off several employees. With a result of the declination of the inflation, the satiations leading to further cuts in interest rates as a result the personal financial position of almost all the individual employees affect badly.

Many of the employees, job holders are not in a position to bear the mental agony that has developed on account of the recession and could not cope with the present situations arising out of the crisis and getting mental agony, stress, pressure, and distress.

Notwithstanding the situation of global economic slowdown, it has to be kept in mind that great opportunities exist for the individuals either employees facing retrenchment or freshers go in search for placements in job market.. Now it is the time for them to bend upon their mind for exploring the possibilities:

- To surmount from the difficult situations by sustaining equanimity.
- To take up new ideas, new dimensions, new ways and means.
- To restore the old relations, connections, friendships that were ignored due to efflux of time.
- To take into account the family relations that were neglected previously.
- To build up strong human relations with all the people who are around their life.
- To prosecute higher studies to get additional qualifications.
- To improve soft skills to get expertise.
- To enrich character, personality, individuality, behaviour, that are additionally required for future prospects.

It is an established fact that though the global economic crisis cause effects on all the industrial and manufacturing sectors, there may not be any effect in the fields of education and health throughout the world, because of the fact that these sectors are required to be developed day by day by the respective countries/governments in the interest of people. It is obvious on the part of the professionals, engineers, techies, etc., to turn their faces to search for careers in the field of education and health to take up opportunities not only for their continuance but also for the service of the needy in that sector. This gives self-satisfaction and bearing social responsibility to serve the nation.

Not only the above, but also there are so many items of work before you to take up. When you are having qualifications in one sector/line, adjoin another qualification in the co-related sector/line. For example, if you have MBA (HRM), it is also necessary for you to learn the aspects of Financial Management, Marketing Management, Information Systems Management, Banking Management, or Retail Operations Management etc. Naturally all the software employees are sedentary. It is quite necessary for them to undertake the public relations, social work, rural development, etc. They have to learn many qualities to obtain working knowledge in all corners of life to attain expertise in all the sections. Nowadays, many universities in the country and abroad, are offering a very number of academic programmes, degrees, diplomas, certificate courses tailored to suit to the present-day market set-up, for the convenience of the job aspirants. It is better to utilize all the opportunities to enrich our knowledge and expertise for better prospects.

It is now time for building their relations and evincing interest in family, relatives, friends, in all corners of the circle, to evolve affectionate understandings between the old companions, fellow workers, classmates in order to organize communion. Individuals who have been residing distantly from their parents have to return back to their parents for a while to make them happy with their presence and to give utmost satisfaction to the elders that they have been closely associated with their kith and kin. The pleasure and joy reflected in the eyes of the elders at the moment is really untold. They will feel happy with the association of their sons, daughters, sons-in-law and daughters-in-law. All the other relatives will feel happy with them. This type of association will definitely give major satisfaction and reduce mental agony and stress.

Developing old relations with friends and neighbours, moving with close contacts with utmost fervour and affection, maintaining good harmonious relations, contacts, showing interest on them on their matters of importance, will give adequate satisfaction and mental relief to those who feel strain and stress during recession. People around us will feel happy due to immensity of your combination for strengthening and build up relations for larger interests and regular interactions. The initiative and enthusiasm created for developing internal and external relations with friends and relatives around us, may reduce the painful thoughts in our mind and create a sense of happiness and joy to forget about the demerits arising out of the feeling of recession.

Instead of thinking about the continuance of your job or otherwise, it is always better to get your thoughts diverted from that point of view and make your mind to work out for a strategic plan and programmes for the development and enrichment of your personal relations with friends and relatives to build up confidence on you in the matters of social importance and support for family life. This will give ample satisfaction and joy in your day-to-day life, irrespective of the fact that you are going to be affected due to recession.

CONCLUSION

Although financial crisis is at its boom and different companies are taking various measures to control cost and in turn increase profits. Some are going for downsizing, job cuts which they call as right sizing or some other measures like salary cut, restriction on issue of bonus, incentives, etc. The companies are also planning to replace financial rewards to other actions like one employer is replacing bonuses with extra time off between Christmas and the New Year, while another is giving an allowance to be spent on wellness items such as gym memberships or toward the employee's contribution of health insurance premiums. Some employers are still giving end-of-year bonuses, although the amounts are smaller than in previous years.

Virtual teams may be created or help of service firms can be taken. These services firms are restructuring their operations by gathering specialists with diverse skills, placing them into customized teams that tackle a host of problems for their clients, then disbanding the units until they are needed again.

These may be few options, but if we think about future some other aspects must be considered. Transparent system should be made in the organization. Feasible goals should be set for the employees rather than setting highest target. It would help employees to maintain ethics in the organization.

REFERENCES

1. World Bank (2001): Globalization, Growth and Poverty: Building and Inclusive World Economy. New York. Oxford University Press.
2. Singh, Pratima (1999): "A Report on Subcontracted units and Women Workers in the Garment Industry," SEWA Academy, Ahmedabad.
3. Unni, Jeemol (1999): "Urban Informal Sector: Size and Income Generation Process in Gujarat", Gujarat Institute for Development Research.
4. www.sewa.org
5. Unni, Jeemol, Namrat Balu and Jignasa Vyas (1999): "Subcontracted Women Workers in the Global Economy: Case Study of Garment Industry in India," SEWA Academy, Ahmedabad.
6. World Bank (2000): World Development Report 2000/2001: Attacking Poverty. New York. Oxford University Press.
7. Ahluwalia, I.J. (1991), Productivity and Growth in Indian Manufacturing, Oxford University Press, Delhi.

8. Akrsasanee, N. and P. Wiboonchutikula (1994), 'Trade and Industrialization Policy and Productivity Growth in Thailand' in Helleiner, G.K (ed.) Trade Policy and Industrialization in Turbulent Times, Routledge, London and New York.
9. Alam Semenick, M. I. and A.R. Morrison (2000), 'Trade Reform Dynamics and Technical Effiicieny: The Peruvian Experience', The World Bank Economic Review, Vol. 14, No.3, 309-330.
10. Athukorala, P.C. and S.Rajapatirana (2000), Liberalization and Industrial Transformation: Sri Lanka in International Perspective, Oxford University Press, Delhi.
11. Balakrishnan, P., K.Pushpangadan and M. Suresh Babu (2000), 'Trade Liberalization and Productivity growth in Manufacturing: Evidence from Firm Level Panel Data' Economic and Political Weekly, October 7, 3679-3682.
12. Baldwin, R. (1989) 'Measuring Non-tariff Trade Policies' Working Paper # 2978, NBER, Cambridge MA, 34-39.
13. Barro, R. (1991), 'Economic Growth in a Cross Section of Countries', Quarterly Journal of Economics, 106, 401-44.
14. Barro, R. and X, Salai-Martin (1995), Economic Growth, McGraw Hill, New York.
15. Balassa, B. (1985), 'Exports, Policy Choices and Economic Growth in Developing Countries after the 1973 Oil Shock,' Journal of Development Economics, 18(2), May/June, 23-35.
16. Bhagwati, J.N. and T.N.Srinivasan (1973), 'The General Equilibrium Theory of Effective Protection and Resource Allocation,' Journal of International Economics, Vol.3, 259-281.
17. Bhagwati, J.N. and T.N.Srinivasan (1975), Foreign Trade Regimes and Economic Development: India, NBER, NewYork.
18. Bhalla S and L.J Lau (1992), 'Openness, Technological Progress and Economic Growth in Developing Countries,' Working Paper, The World Bank, Washington DC.
19. Ben-David, D. (1993), 'Equalizing Exchange: Trade Liberalization and Income Convergence,' Quarterly Journal of Economics, 108, 3, 653-679.
20. Bonelli. R. (1992), 'Growth and Productivity in Brazilian Industries: Impacts of Trade Orientation,' Journal of Development Economics, 39,85-109.
21. Cameron, G., J. Proudman and S. Reading (1999), 'Openness and its Association with Productivity growth in UK Manufacturing Industry,' Working Paper, Bank of England.
22. Celasun, M.(1994), 'Trade and Industrialization in Turkey: Initial Conditions, Policy and Performance in the 1980s' in Helleiner, G.K (ed.)Trade Policy and Industrialization in Turbulent Times, Routledge, London and New York.
23. Chand, S and K.Sen (2002), 'Trade Liberalization and Productivity Growth: Evidence from Indian Manufacturing,' Review of Development Economics, Vol.6, No 1, February.
24. Corbo, V. (1985), 'Chilean Economic Policy and International Economic Relations Since 1970' in G.Walton. (ed.) The National Economic Policy of Chile, JAI Press, London.
25. Corden, W. M. (1974), Trade Policy and Economic Welfare, Clarendon Press, Oxford.
26. Das, D.K. (2001), Some Aspects of Productivity Growth and Trade in Indian Industry, Unpublished Ph.D.Dissertation, Delhi School of Economics, University of Delhi, November.
27. Dean, J., S. Desai and J. Reidel (1994), 'Trade Policy Reform in Developing Countries since 1985,' World Bank Discussion Paper, The World Bank, Washington DC.

11

An Analytical Study of Foreign Direct Investment in Retail Sector

MANISHA N. PALIWAL AND DEEPA RANGANATHAN

Associate Professor, Sinhgad Institute of Management, Pune-41
Student- MBA (IB-IV sem), Sinhgad Institute of Management, Pune-41

ABSTRACT

In this era of globalization, with national boundaries becoming irrelevant to business conglomerates, Foreign Direct Investment (FDI) is one of the most preferred modes of entry into foreign markets. FDI can be in the form of an acquisition, joint venture or purchase of more than 10% equity stake in an Indian company. This paper is an attempt to understand the concept of foreign direct investment and its impact on an economy. It also tries to understand the Indian perspective to FDI and the broad rules governing it. Indian retail sector is very attractive as it is touted to see multifold growth in the coming years due to changing consumer behaviour and lifestyle and rising incomes. This paper thus, lays special emphasis on FDI in Indian retail. It also attempts to throw some light on the arguments for and against FDI in multi-brand retail.

Keywords: Foreign direct investment, Globalization, Retail sector, Economy.

INTRODUCTION

Foreign Direct Investment is any form of investment that earns interest in enterprises which function outside of the domestic territory of the investor. FDIs require a business relationship between a parent company and its foreign subsidiary. Foreign direct business relationships give rise to multinational corporations. For an investment to be regarded as an FDI, the parent firm needs to have at least 10% of the ordinary shares of its foreign affiliates. The investing firm may also qualify for an FDI if it owns voting power in a business enterprise operating in a foreign country. International Monetary Fund (IMF) and Organization for Economic Cooperation and Development (OECD) define FDI similarly as 'a category of cross-border investment made by a resident in one economy (the direct investor) with the objective of establishing a 'lasting interest' in an enterprise (the direct investment enterprise) that is resident in an economy other than that of the direct investor.' The motivation of the direct investor is a strategic long term relationship with the direct investment enterprise to ensure the significant degree of influence by the direct investor in the management of the direct investment enterprise. Direct investment allows the direct investor to gain access to the direct investment enterprise which it might otherwise be unable to do. The objectives of direct investment are different from those of portfolio investment whereby investors do not generally expect to influence the management of the enterprise.

Objective of the Study

- To take an overview of FDI in general.
- To study the impact of FDI to any economy.
- To understand the role of FDI in Indian economy with special reference to retail sector.

Research Methodology

The paper is conceptual and based on the data collected from secondary sources such as reference books, journals, newspapers, and websites.

Foreign Direct Investment: An Overview

FDIs can be broadly classified into two types: outward FDIs and inward FDIs. This classification is based on the types of restrictions imposed, and the various prerequisites required for these investments. An outward-bound FDI is backed by the government against all types of associated risks. This form of FDI is subject to tax incentives as well as disincentives of various forms. Risk coverage provided to the domestic industries and subsidies granted to the local firms stand in the way of outward FDIs, which are also known as 'direct investments abroad'.

- Different economic factors encourage inward FDIs. These include interest loans, tax breaks, grants, subsidies, and the removal of restrictions and limitations. Factors detrimental to the growth of FDIs include necessities of differential performance and limitations related with ownership patterns.
- Other categorizations of FDI exist as well. Vertical Foreign Direct Investment takes place when a multinational corporation owns some shares of a foreign enterprise, which supplies input for it or uses the output produced by the MNC.

- Horizontal foreign direct investments happen when a multinational company carries out a similar business operation in different nations.

Foreign Direct Investment is guided by various motives. FDIs that are undertaken to strengthen the existing market structure or to explore the opportunities of new markets can be called 'market-seeking FDIs'. 'Resource-seeking FDIs' are aimed at factors of production which have more operational efficiency than those available in the home country of the investor. Some foreign direct investments involve the transfer of strategic assets. FDI activities may also be carried out to ensure optimization of available opportunities and economies of scale. In this case, the foreign direct investment is called 'efficiency-seeking'.

FDI is considered less prone to crisis because direct investors, typically, have a longer-term perspective when engaging in a host country. In addition to the risk-sharing properties of FDI, it is widely believed that FDI provides a stronger stimulus to economic growth in host countries than other types of capital inflows. The underlying argument is that FDI is more than just capital, as it offers access to internationally available technologies and management knowhow (*The Economist* 2001).

Determinants of Foreign Direct Investment

1. Avoiding foreign government pressure for local production.
2. Circumventing trade barriers, hidden and otherwise.
3. Making the move from domestic export sales to a locally-based national sales office.
4. Capability to increase total production capacity.
5. Opportunities for co-production, joint ventures with local partners, joint marketing arrangements, licensing, etc.
6. The size as well as the growth prospects of the economy of the country where the foreign direct investment is being made is an important factor.
7. The population of a country plays an important role in attracting foreign direct investors to a country. In such cases the investors are lured by the prospects of a huge customer base.
8. If the country has a high per capita income or if the citizens have reasonably good spending capabilities, then it would offer the foreign direct investors with the scope of excellent performances.
9. The status of the human resources in a country is also instrumental in attracting direct investment from overseas.
10. If a particular country has plenty of natural resources it always finds investors willing to put their money in them. A good example would be Saudi Arabia and other oil rich countries that have had overseas companies investing in them in order to tap the unlimited oil resources at their disposal.
11. Inexpensive labour force is also an important determinant of attracting foreign direct investment. The BPO revolution, as well as the boom of the IT companies in countries like India is a proof of the fact that inexpensive labour force has played an important part in attracting overseas direct investment.
12. Infrastructural factors like the status of telecommunications and railways play an important part in having the foreign direct investors come into a particular country.

Benefits of Foreign Direct Investment

1. It helps in the economic development of the particular country where the investment is made. This is especially applicable to the developing countries. During the decade of the 90s, foreign direct investment was one of the major external sources of financing for most of the countries that were growing from an economic perspective. It has also been observed that foreign direct investment has helped several countries when they faced economic hardships.

   An example of this could be seen in some countries of the East Asian region. It was observed during the financial problems of 1997-98 that the amount of foreign direct investment made in these countries was pretty steady. The other forms of cash inflows in a country like debt flows and portfolio equity had suffered major setbacks. Similar observations were made in Latin America in the 1980s and in Mexico in 1994-95.
2. Foreign direct investment also permits the transfer of technologies. This is done basically in the way of provision of capital inputs. The importance of this factor lies in the fact that this transfer of technologies cannot be accomplished by way of trading of goods and services as well as investment of financial resources. It also assists in the promotion of the competition within the local input market of a country.
3. The countries that get foreign direct investment from another country can also develop the human capital resources by getting their employees to receive training on the operations of a particular business. The profits that are generated by the foreign direct investments that are made in that country can be used for the purpose of making contributions to the revenues of corporate taxes of the recipient country.
4. Foreign direct investment helps in the creation of new jobs in a particular country. It also helps in increasing the income of the workers. This enables them to get access to a better lifestyle and more facilities in life. It has normally been observed that foreign direct investment allows for the development of the manufacturing sector of the recipient country. Foreign direct investment can also bring in advanced technology and skill set in a country. There is also some scope for new research activities being undertaken.
5. Foreign direct investment assists in increasing the income that is generated through revenues realized through taxation. It also plays a crucial role in the context of rise in the productivity of the host countries. In case of countries that make foreign direct investment in other countries this process has positive impact as well. In case of these countries, their companies get an opportunity to explore newer markets and thereby generate more income and profits.
6. It also opens up the export window that allows these countries the opportunity to cash in on their superior technological resources. It has also been observed that as a result of receiving foreign direct investment from other countries, it has been possible for the recipient countries to keep their rates of interest at a lower level.
7. It becomes easier for the business entities to borrow finance at lesser rates of interest. The biggest beneficiaries of these facilities are the small and medium-sized business enterprises.

Disadvantages of Foreign Direct Investment

The disadvantages of foreign direct investment occur mostly in case of matters related to operation, distribution of the profits made on the investment and the personnel.

1. One of the most indirect disadvantages of foreign direct investment is that the economically backward section of the host country is always inconvenienced when the stream of foreign direct investment is negatively affected.

   The situations in countries like Ireland, Singapore, Chile and China corroborate such an opinion. It is normally the responsibility of the host country to limit the extent of impact that may be made by the foreign direct investment. They should be making sure that the entities that are making the foreign direct investment in their country adhere to the environmental, governance and social regulations that have been laid down in the country.
2. The various disadvantages of foreign direct investment are understood where the host country has some sort of national secret – something that is not meant to be disclosed to the rest of the world. It has been observed that the defense of a country has faced risks as a result of the foreign direct investment in the country.
3. At times it has been observed that certain foreign policies are adopted that are not appreciated by the workers of the recipient country. Foreign direct investment, at times, is also disadvantageous for the ones who are making the investment themselves.
4. Foreign direct investment may entail high travel and communications expenses. The differences of language and culture that exist between the country of the investor and the host country could also pose problems in case of foreign direct investment.
5. Yet another major disadvantage of foreign direct investment is that there is a chance that a company may lose out on its ownership to an overseas company. This has often caused many companies to approach foreign direct investment with a certain amount of caution.
6. At times it has been observed that there is considerable instability in a particular geographical region. This causes a lot of inconvenience to the investor.
7. The size of the market, as well as, the condition of the host country could be important factors in the case of the foreign direct investment. In case the host country is not well connected with its more advanced neighbours, it poses a lot of challenges for the investors.
8. It has been observed that some governments of the host country face problems with foreign direct investment, because of the less control over the functioning of the company that functions as the wholly owned subsidiary of an overseas company. This leads to serious issues. The investors do not have to be completely obedient to the economic policies of the country where they have invested the money.
9. There have been adverse effects of foreign direct investment on the balance of payments of a country.

5. FDI IN INDIA

According to the Government of India, FDI means investment by non-resident entity/person resident outside India in the capital of the Indian company under Schedule 1 of FEMA (Transfer or Issue of Security by a Person Resident Outside India) Regulations 2000.' All FDI in India is subject to the rules of 'FIPB' (Foreign Investment Promotion Board) constituted by the Government of India. The key Indian regulatory authorities in the context of FDI are:

- The Foreign Investment and Promotion Board (FIPB), which formulates foreign investment policy.

- The Reserve Bank of India (RBI), India's central bank with primary responsibility for implementing and enforcing foreign exchange regulations and government policies. Under the present rules, foreign investment up to 100% is permitted in almost all industry sectors. There remain only a handful of industry sectors in which no FDI or limited FDI is permitted – these tend to be "sensitive" sectors, either for security reasons, such as defense or telecommunications, or for political reasons, such as agriculture, retail, real estate, banking and insurance. In addition, the government has been simplifying procedural aspects such as the approval process in respect of FDI. FDI is permitted through either the "automatic" route or the "approval" route. Generally speaking, investments which fall within the percentage caps specified for an industry can be made under the "automatic route", which means that no prior regulatory approval is needed although the company is required to make a post-fact filing. For all other investments, the"approval" route applies, which means that prior approval of the FIPB is required before making the investment. The FIPB approval process typically takes 6 to 8 weeks, and barring exceptional circumstances, is relatively straightforward. Large-scale business activity with FDI is usually conducted through a company incorporated in India. The company can be a wholly-owned subsidiary of the foreign investor in sectors where 100% FDI is permitted or, where limits apply or for strategic reasons, a joint venture with an Indian counterparty. Incorporating a company in India is a fairly straightforward process (although occasionally time-consuming). The investment in the company can be through the holding of shares and/or equity linked instruments. If an exit is contemplated through the public markets in India, careful consideration should be given to the public offering guidelines of the Securities and Exchange Board of India—which is the country's primary securities market regulator. These guidelines contain a number of provisions and potential pitfalls affecting an investor's exit options.

Indian law recognizes the freedom of parties in an international contract to choose both the governing law, the forum (arbitration/courts) and the jurisdiction for settling disputes. However, the FIPB often requires as a condition of its approval that investment agreements be governed by Indian law. Litigation in India is an onerous and time-consuming process. Arbitration is therefore a popular dispute resolution option. India is signatory to the New York Convention, which aids enforcement of arbitral awards in India.

Table 1: Statement on sector-wise FDI inflows from April 2000 to January 2011

Sr. No.	Sector	Amount of FDI in Rs Crore in USD million		% with total FDI Inflows
1.	Services Sector	118,923.46	26,597.42	20.88
2.	Computer Software & Hardware	47,340.34	10,643.83	8.36
3.	Telecommunications	46,746.29	10,262.19	8.06
4.	Housing & Real Estate	42,162.77	9,405.20	7.38
5.	Construction Activities	40,233.46	9,059.07	7.11
6.	Automobile Industry	26,197.64	5,787.72	4.54
7.	Power	25,714.51	5,680.08	4.46
8.	Metallurgical Industries	18,072.87	4,141.18	3.25
9.	Petroleum & Natural Gas	13,584.83	3,119.76	2.45
10.	Chemicals	13,007.39	2,876.41	2.26

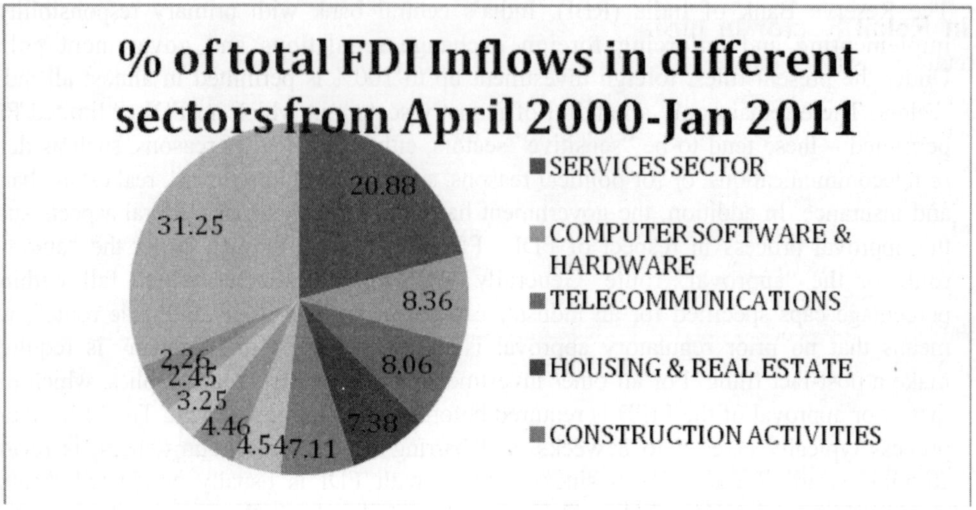

Table 2: Statement on country-wise FDI inflows from April 2000 to January 2011

Sr. No.	Country	Amount of Foreign Direct Investment Inflows		% with total FDI Inflows
		INR Crores	USD million	
1.	MAURITIUS	238,876.20	53,368.91	41.9
2.	SINGAPORE	51,963.99	11,693.83	9.18
3.	U.S.A.	42,190.39	9,370.69	7.36
4.	UNITED KINGDOM	28,298.45	6,387.08	5.01
5.	NETHERLANDS	24,877.41	5,534.70	4.35
6.	JAPAN	23,074.84	5,081.56	3.99

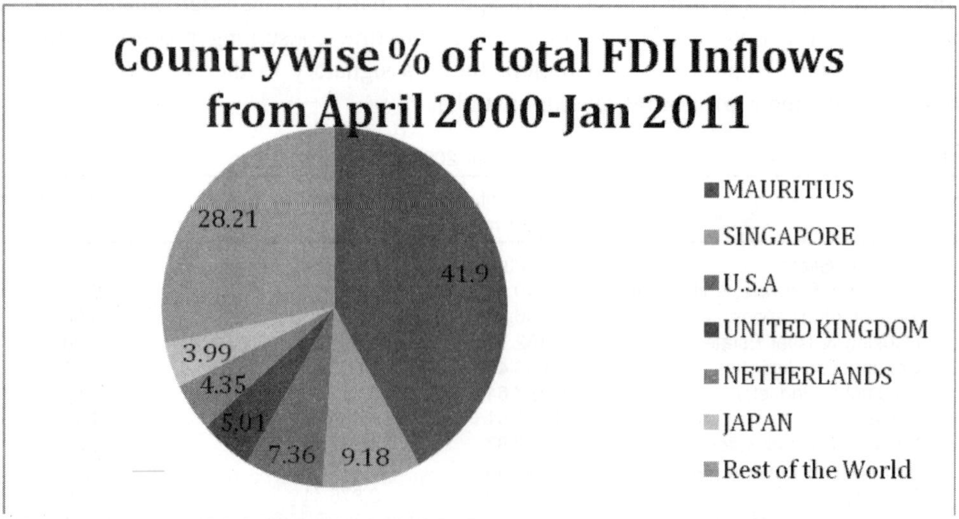

FDI in Retail Sector in India

The retail industry in India is of late often hailed as one of the sunrise sectors in the economy. AT Kearney, the well-known international management consultancy, recently identified India as the 'second most attractive retail destination' globally from among the thirty emergent markets. It has made India the cause of a good deal of excitement and the cynosure of many foreign eyes. Retail sector is one of the largest contributors to Indian GDP. It provides 15% of employment through world's largest retail network with 12 million outlets which makes it second largest employment provider in India after agriculture. The organized retail sector is growing at a rapid pace of 28% p.a. Hence, India is sometimes referred to as "nation of shopkeepers".

Starbucks, the world's largest coffee-shop operator, has taken what can be called the first step towards the entry into the Indian market. Starbucks has signed an agreement with Tata Coffee Ltd. to source beans and explore the opening of stores.

In the past few years, India has become one of the most attractive destinations for retailers across the world. The retail space in the country has seen multifold growth backed by the entry of the corporate into the sector, changing consumer behavior and lifestyle and rising incomes. The sector has witnessed exponential growth since 2001, with a clear distinction now visible between organized retail and unorganized retail.

Western retail giants like Wal-Mart and Tesco are also eyeing entry into developing markets like India and China on the back of saturation in the developed western retail markets. The BMI India Retail Report for Q3 2010, forecasts the total retail sales to grow to USD 543.2 billion by 2014 from USD 353 billion in 2010. There are multiple new malls, supermarkets and departmental stores coming up in not only Tier I but also Tier II and Tier III cities, to tap in the demand. In addition, China and India are believed to account for more than 92% of regional retail sales by 2014.

Growth Potential for Organized Retail

The retail business in the country is estimated to grow at the rate of 13% per annum to USD 590 billion in 2011-12 from USD 322 billion in 2006-07, according to a study by the Indian Council for Research on International Economic Relations (ICRIER). Additionally, the unorganized retail sector is expected to grow at about 10% per annum to USD 496 billion in 2011-12 from USD 309 billion 2006-07. The retail industry is divided into organised and unorganised sectors:

(a) Organised retailing refers to trading activities undertaken by licensed retailers, that is, those who are registered for sales tax, income tax, etc. These include the corporate-backed hypermarkets and retail chains, and also the privately owned large retail businesses.

(b) Unorganised retailing, on the other hand, refers to the traditional formats of low-cost retailing, for example, the local kirana shops, owner manned general stores, paan/beedi shops, convenience stores, hand cart and pavement vendors, etc.

Organised retail makes for 75-80% of total retail in the developed countries, whereas the unorganized retail enjoys the dominating share in the developing countries. In the past few years developing countries have witnessed the opening and spreading of the modern retail outlets like hypermarkets, superstores, supermarkets, discount and convenience stores, etc., which have a wide presence in the developed world.

However, the unorganized retail outlets continue to dominate the overall retail scene in the developing countries. This in turn implies that the wholesalers and distributors who carry products from industrial suppliers and agricultural producers to these markets remain a critical part of the supply chain.

One of the principal reasons behind the explosion of retail and its fragmented nature in the country is the fact that retailing is probably the primary form of disguised unemployment or underemployment in the country.

The given already over-crowded agriculture sector, and the stagnating manufacturing sector, and the hard nature and relatively low wages of jobs in both, many million Indians are virtually forced into the services sector. Here, given the lack of opportunities, it is almost a natural decision for an individual to set up a small shop or store, depending on his or her means and capital. And thus, a retailer is born, seemingly out of circumstances rather than choice. This phenomenon quite aptly explains the millions of kirana shops and small stores. The explosion of retail outlets in the more busy streets of Indian villages and towns is a visible testimony of this. The presence of more than one retailer for every hundred person is indicative of the lack of economic opportunities that is forcing people into this form of self-employment, even though much of it is marginal. Because of this fragmentation, the Indian retail sector typically suffers from limited access to capital, labour and real estate options. The typical traditional retailer follows the low-cost-and-size format, functioning at a small-scale level, rarely eligible for tax and following a cheap model of operations.

The Question of Foreign Direct Investment (FDI) in Retail

Given this backdrop, FDI in the retail sector becomes a very sensitive issue, with arguments to support both sides of the debate. It is widely acknowledged that FDI can have some positive results on the economy, triggering a series of reactions that in the long run can lead to greater efficiency and improvement of living standards, apart from greater integration into the global economy.

Supporters of FDI in retail trade talk of how ultimately the consumer is benefited by both price reductions and improved selection, brought about by the technology and know-how of foreign players in the market. This in turn can lead to greater output and domestic consumption.

It is believed that foreign direct investment (FDI) can prove to be a powerful catalyst which can spur competition in the retail industry. Foreign investment in retail will enhance India's retail sector through augmented investment in the cold storage, reducing the wastage immensely. It is this lack of investment in logistics of retail chains leading to inefficient market mechanism. Though India is the second largest producer of fruits and vegetables, it's battling double digit supply-side food inflation for the past 2 years. Wastage due to lack of cold storage is the prime factor. FDI will lead to supply chain improvement, development of skill and manpower, betterment in the agricultural segment as well as improved efficiencies in small and medium scale industries. A 100% FDI will draw a lot of foreign players in the market leading to employment generation and increase in competition, much to the advantage of the consumers.

Increasing FDI in the retail segment is also believed to help expand the market size, which in turn will help enhanced productivity. As a result the government also stands to gain by way of increased GDP, tax income and employment generation.

But the most important factor against FDI driven "modern retailing" is that it is labour displacing to the extent that it can only expand by destroying the traditional retail sector. Till such time we are in a position to create jobs on a large scale in manufacturing, it would make eminent sense that any policy that results in the elimination of jobs in the unorganised retail sector should be kept on hold. Entry of foreign players now will most definitely disrupt the current balance of the economy; will render millions of small retailers jobless by closing the small slit of opportunity available to them. Given their economies of scale and huge resources, a big domestic retailer or any new foreign player will be able to provide their merchandise at cheaper rates than a smaller retailer. It is true that it is in the consumer's best interest to obtain his goods and services at the lowest possible price. But this is a privilege for the individual consumer and it cannot, in any circumstance, override the responsibility of any society to provide economic security for its population. Clearly collective well-being must take precedence over individual benefits.

FDI and Retail Sector – Current Scenario

According to the Government of India [Ministry of Commerce & Industry, Department of Industrial Policy & Promotion (FC Section)] Circular 2 of 2010 Dated 30th September, 2010,Foreign Investment in Single Brand product trading is aimed at attracting investments in production and marketing, improving the availability of such goods for the consumer, encouraging increased sourcing of goods from India, and enhancing competitiveness of Indian enterprises through access to global designs, technologies and management practices. FDI in Single Brand products retail trade would be subject to the following conditions:

(a) Products to be sold should be of a 'Single Brand' only.

(b) Products should be sold under the same brand internationally, i.e., products should be sold under the same brand in one or more countries other than India.

(c) 'Single Brand' product-retailing would cover only products which are branded during manufacturing.

Government has permitted FDI in single brand retail upto 51% in joint venture for the retail of branded products. This 51% FDI is allowed through the government route,i.e., it needs the prior approval of the Government of India by submitting an application to the FIPB. Brands like Adidas, Nokia; Amway, Samsung, Sony, etc., are the examples of single brand products which are an outcome of FDI. Though 100 per cent FDI is permitted in cold chain through the automatic route in the absence of FDI in retail, the flow of such funds to the sector has been insignificant. The present FDI regime allows 51 per cent foreign investment in single brand retail and 100 per cent in wholesale cash and carry. The Ministry of Consumer Affairs and Public Distribution initially suggested a cap of 49 per cent FDI in multi-brand retail, while the Micro, Small and Medium Enterprises Ministry's recommendation is for 18 per cent FDI. But the recent skyrocketing of food prices and the declining inflow of FDI have opened a door for the Government to take a more ambitious decision on the prickly issue. But it has its meaning confined to single brand because multi-brand retail sector is one of the few sectors where FDI is not allowed. It is because there have been protests by trading associations and other stakeholders against allowing FDI in multi- brand retail.

CONCLUSION

Foreign Direct Investment (FDI) plays a major role in global business. It can provide a firm with new markets and marketing channels, cheaper production facilities, access to new technology, products, skills and financing. For a host country or the foreign firm which receives the investment, it can provide a source of new technologies, capital, processes, products, organizational technologies and management skills, and as such can provide a strong impetus to economic development.

In India, FDI is permitted up to 100% in almost all industry sectors. There remain only a handful of industry sectors in which no FDI or limited FDI is permitted – these tend to be "sensitive" sectors, either for security reasons, such as defense or telecommunications, or for political reasons, such as agriculture, retail, real estate, banking and insurance. One among the above-mentioned sectors is retail. In India, FDI of 51% through the government route is permitted only in single brand retail. FDI in Indian multi-brand retail is widely debated as there are fears that foreign players will impact the livelihood of millions of people employed in the unorganized retail sector in India. Though a cap of 49% has been suggested by the concerned ministry, there is still a long way to go before the fate of multi-brand retail is known.

REFERENCES

1. Sandeep Katwala and Scott Sonnenblick, "Foreign Direct Investment in India: A Few Key Issues", www.law.com.
2. Determinants, benefits and disadvantages of FDI,www.EconomyWatch.com.
3. Fact Sheet On Foreign Direct Investment (FDI) (From August 1991 To January 2011) (india_FDI_January2011 govt stats.pdf)
4. Mohan Guruswamy, Kamal Sharma, Jeevan Prakash, Mohanty Thomas and J. Korah (CPAS Centre for Policy Alternatives): 'FDI in India's Retail Sector: More Bad than Good?'
5. 'FOCUS: FDI and Retail Sector in India (www.religareonline.com).
6. Government of India [Ministry of Commerce & Industry, Department of Industrial Policy & Promotion (FC Section)] Circular 2 of 2010 Dated 30th September, 2010.

12

Worldwide Competitiveness of the Dyeing and Printing Industry of Jetpur

Vijay Pithadia

Director, Shri H.D. Gardi MBA College – Nyara Jamnagar Road, Opposite Garden Dinner Club, Rajkot – 360110 GJ, E-mail: drvijaypithadia@yahoo.com

ABSTRACT

The present paper discusses the worldwide competitiveness of the dyeing and printing industry of Jetpur. In the current era, every country, economy and industry is influenced by globalization. The fast-paced economic and political changes across the world are forcing India to be more globally competitive. The paper gives a bird's- eye view of globalization, its impacts on the world and Indian economy and on the domestic textile industry. The paper presents the global competitiveness of the industry of Jetpur and suggests the areas through which it can globally compete. These areas are global orientation, quality reputation, to export in the most demanding global markets, adoption of modern technology and new marketing strategies, productivity through infrastructure, value-addition of labours through leadership and motivation, establishment of the organizations on a large scale in the company form of business organization and to create brand image by providing better products at lower prices.

INTRODUCTION

Globalization broadly refers to the expansion of global linkages, the organization of social life on a global scale and the growth of a global consciousness, hence to the consolidation of world society. The impact of globalization has undoubtedly led to the economic growth. Of course, there have also been the negative effects of globalization on the world economy. The major effect of globalization is that the global economy is becoming more integrated day by day. The volume of world trade has grown at a faster rate than the volume of world output. There has been a trend of lowering the barriers of the flow of goods, services and capital among countries. In order to become competitive, companies have started investing in overseas operations. The growth of world trade, foreign direct investment and import leads to more foreign competition in the domestic markets and domestic firms are required to enhance the production and distribution capabilities. Companies have started looking at the world as a market for their products. In the whole world, there is no country or economy which is free from the effects of globalization. India is also largely influenced by the process of globalization. As India integrates into the world economy, there is a need to reposition itself as a country. From the domestic-oriented, self-sufficient licence, it has come a long way to become a globally-oriented economy focusing on those key sectors of the economy where it has a resource advantage over other nations. India has a large textile industry and is the second largest producer of textiles in the world next to China. Textile industry includes various processes like cotton picking, ginning, spinning and weaving, processing, dyeing, printing and finishing. Thus, the dyeing and printing industry of Jetpur is a part of the textile industry. It mainly deals with the dyeing and printing processes and products like cotton sarees, dress materials, khangas, kitangas, bandhani and bedsheets. The industry of Jetpur also has entered into the process of globalization through export business. But a decline in the demand of its products does not give much scope for future expansion of the industry at global level.

History and Development of the Dyeing and Printing Industry in Jetpur

As stated earlier, the dyeing and printing industry is one of the parts of the textile industry. So, it is very necessary to know about the textile industry. The Indian textile industry has been very famous for its textile products since ancient times. The decentralized textile industry of India is spread over the states of the country like Gujarat, Maharashtra, Rajasthan and West Bengal. It is also true that Gujarat, a leading state in the country has also been famous for its textiles and especially for dyeing and printing crafts. Various modes of dyeing and printing had been developed in Gujarat from the beginning of the 19th century. Ahmedabad, Rajkot, Jetpur and Kutch are the places where the dyeing and printing industries were developed in cotton materials. At that time, various trades from different places of Saurashtra had been called upon to promote the economic expansion of Jetpur. As a result, many Khatri artisans coming from Kalawad, Junagadh, Amreli, Kuthiyana, Bhesan, Majevadi and Bagasara came to Jetpur to develop printing crafts and trade and they were followed by the artisans of other castes considering the success of the industry. Many factors play an important role in the development of the industry like the quality of water, favourable approach of local government, infrastructural facilities etc.

Before 1947, a block printing method, one of the methods of dyeing and printing was used in Jetpur. Then Bachubhai, the promoter of "Jagadish Textile Dyeing and Printing Works" launched the screen printing method in the industry which had given a new outlook not only to his industrial group but also to the whole industry of Jetpur. Other block printing units also shifted gradually from block printing to screen printing and in the seventies, block printing method completely disappeared from Jetpur. Several ancillary manufacturing activities like the trade of cloth, dyes, chemicals, packaging materials, roll finishing, pressing and folding of sarees, washing ghats and transports, etc., have been promoted by the development of the industry in Jetpur.

The best period for an expansion of the industry in Jetpur took place from 1970 to 1983. Then the industry faced an economic crisis mainly due to cut-throat competition with synthetic cloth, depression of demand and a pollution case at the Honourable High Court of Gujarat state. So, Gujarat State Water Pollution Control Board stopped issuing a 'No Objection Certificate' for new units and as a result, in 1992, a "Common Effluent Treatment Plant" (CETP) was constructed to filter the polluted water. But the problem of the chemical pollution created by the washing places scattered along rivers and in agriculture fields has not been solved yet. In the past, only sarees were printed in Jetpur and sold at national-wide. Then around 1991, the entrepreneurs of the industry tried a lot to overcome the above-discussed problems. They created the demand of their printed cotton materials in the African countries and started to print khangas and kitangas (dress materials of the African people) by semiautomatic felt belt printing machines. At present, 65% of the total production is related to exports. Thus, the industry earns a lot of foreign exchange from exports.

Future Prospectus of the Dyeing and Printing Industry of Jetpur City

During the golden years of the industry, Jetpur was known as "The Little Dubai" of Saurashtra. But the decline in the demand does not give much scope for future expansion of Jetpur industry at the global level. The rising domestic demand along with opening up the world market has led to the recent growth for Indian textile and apparel industries. At this juncture, it is necessary to know our competitiveness and understand the key success factors in this quota-free regime. It is now well accepted that India and China are the two biggest beneficiaries from the phase out of the quotas. India's share in the global textile market is still around 4% against 17% share held by China. But India is well equipped to provide fashion driven products on a small sector and Indian textile products are known for their striking and rich designs and excellent finishing in West Europe and North America. With the dismantling of multi-fiber agreement since January 2005, India can now export to any country.

Besides all these, Gujarat has a leading textile sector and also the largest producer of cotton in our country. Gujarat accounts for 12% of India's textile exports, 24 to 28 % of fixed investment, production value and employment in SSI sector of the state is from textiles. The state government has announced and implemented many schemes for assisting the entrepreneurs such as subsidy for existing units for technology upgradation and setting up industrial parks. With the on-going industrial development, environmental issues have become one of the major concerns for the state administrations. Therefore, CETP for textile processing is also assisted in different places of the state. In addition to these, 25% capital subsidy provided by Ministry of Environment & Forest, state government also extends 25% capital subsidy for setting up CETP in Gujarat.

All of this discussion is about national and global scenario of the textile industry which is directly connected with the dyeing and printing industry. Jetpur industry also gets the benefits of the government schemes to increase the business and compete globally which shows that the industry is not free from the effects of globalization. But the main problem which prevents the development of the industry is the pollution of water and agricultural land because it is very harmful and dangerous to the health of people and animals and also to the agricultural crops. If the industrialists follow the government rules, they can expand their business not only at national but also at global level. Thus, the future of the of Jetpur industry is very bright.

Global Competitiveness of the Dyeing and Printing Industry of Jetpur City

Global competitiveness means better products and services at lower prices. It is a simple model. If you offer superior products at lower prices, the world comes to you. To compete globally, there should be a global orientation. There should be no export quality versus domestic quality; it should all be the same quality. It means that the industry of Jetpur must follow high quality standards not only for global market but also for domestic market so that it can expand the business successfully in foreign countries and also in India over the competitors.

The managers of the industry of Jetpur should keep in mind location, age, sex, income level, buying habits, buying trends and habits of their customers which are geographically scattered in all over the country and the world. The industry has also a cut-throat competition with the synthetic cloth. In order to gain a competitive advantage, the industry must give customers a reason to choose its products over the competitors' products of synthetic cloth. Through R&D, new features like durability of colour and fabric can be added and new uses of existing products can be identified so that the industry can achieve new customers and maintain the existing customers. For this purpose, new marketing strategies must be adopted. Another aspect is productivity through infrastructural facilities like finance, raw materials, transports, labours and textile zone. All the facilities except textile zone are available in Jetpur. If the textile zone is established near the city, all the processes of the textile industry can be undertaken before dyeing and printing. Thus, the quality of cotton fabric can be improved and the cost can be minimized. Accordingly, profit will be maximized. All of these will be very helpful to the dyeing and printing industry of Jetpur city to compete globally.

Leveraging human capital is another aspect. To compete on a global level, value-addition is indeed needed on the part of the labours. Their potential needs can be realized through leadership and motivation and productivity per labour can be increased. To compete globally, the industry of Jetpur should export to those global markets where the demand of its products is high as compared to other markets and to succeed in the most demanding markets, they must be globally competitive, not domestically competitive. All the units in the dyeing and printing industry of Jetpur are sole proprietorship or as partnership firms on a small scale. If they are established as a company form of business organization on a large scale, they can get enough financial resources, knowledge of highly qualified persons, the advantage of mass production and other benefits. To become globally competitive, the last thing is needed to create brand equity and it will emerge only if better products are offered at lower prices to the customers. Therefore, the industrialists of Jetpur should offer high quality goods but at lower prices to create brand image at global level.

CONCLUSION

The dyeing and printing industry is an identity of Jetpur. It is famous for its cheap cotton sarees at international level. It has the history of more than 60 years. The main factor which prevents the development of the industry is environmental issues. To compete globally, the managers of the industry should keep in mind certain factors such as global orientation, quality reputation of the products, to export in the most demanding global markets, adoption of modern technology and new marketing strategies, productivity through infrastructure, value-addition of labours through leadership and motivation, establishment of the organizations on a large scale in the company form of business organization and to create brand image by providing better products at lower prices.

REFERENCES

1. Jagadish Sheth, (2004). "Making India Globally Competitive", Vikalpa.
2. Manju Nair, (2005). "Creating Global Competitive Advantage: Challenge and Strategies", Management Trends.
3. Textile Review, (2006). Saket Publication, vol.1.
4. Rajubhai Patel, (2001). "Jetpur Textile Industry ni Gaikal, Aaj ane Avatikal", Business Sovenieer, Jetpur Junior.
5. Sampatram, B. (1968). "Saurashtra Deshno Itihas", Ganpat Krishnajina Chohapkan, Bombay.

13

Lack of Strategic Export Orientation and Internationalization Barriers of Indian Industries with Special Reference to SMEs in India

Saji Kuriakose and Hareesh N. Ramnathan

Associate Professor & Head, Department of Management Science, MES College of Engineering, Kuttipuram, Kerala
Associate Professor, Department of Management Studies, Sree Narayana Gurukulam College of Engineering, Kolenchery, Kerala

ABSTRACT

This paper attempts to look into the aspects that stop Indian organizations in going international and being successful in international business. There are many problems faced by an exporter in Indian scenario which include resource constraints, knowledge barriers, corruption, lack of export assistance, and poor infrastructure etc. However, researchers of this paper are of the opinion that those are the common repetitions of problems mentioned by everyone every time. The actual problem is the attitudinal problems of business promoters and their lack of seriousness or proper orientation that really stop them from being successful exporters. Authors of this paper are of the opinion that the attitudinal corrections and strategic orientation can take Indian exporters a long way to international business. The paper also narrates some of the practical experience of one of the authors which he had to face while he was handling the international business of a company in India.

Keywords: Export orientation, Internationalization, SMEs, Export barriers.

INTRODUCTION

The history of Indian exports is very old. During ancient times India exported spices to the other parts of the world. India was also famous for its textiles which were a chief item for export in the 16th century. Textiles and cotton were exported to the Arab countries from Gujarat. During the Mughal era India exported various precious stones such as ivory, pearls, tortoise stones, etc. But during the British era, Indian exports declined as the East India Company took control of foreign trade.

It is clear that Indian exports, especially from SMEs have still not achieved their true potential and there exist immense opportunities for expanding the basket of India's exports. With a strategic attention on the new markets that are evolving due to free trade, India is witnessing a boom in both manufacturing and services sectors.

PROBLEMS OF THE INDIAN EXPORT SECTOR

There are many problems faced by an exporter in Indian scenario which include resource constraints, knowledge barriers, corruption, lack of export assistance, and poor infrastructure. There are few more problems which need to be solved before India makes a mark for itself in the export sector. The Indian goods have to be of superior quality.

The packaging and branding should be such that countries are interested to export from India. At the same time India must look for potential markets to sell its goods. The government should frame policies which give boost to the exports. Coming back to the problems in India, many have discovered that corrupt government departments is the biggest problem that the nation faces. Some people worry about the infrastructure problems in India. Above all how do we deal with an nternational client in terms of response and the pace of response, service, commitment, etc., are even more important.

Indian SMEs in Export

In most developing countries, small and medium enterprises (SMEs) constitute the bulk of the industrial base and contribute significantly to their GDP. For instance, India has nearly three million SMEs, which account for almost 50 per cent of industrial output. It is an essential employment-generating sector with 50% of the private sector employment and 30–40% of value-addition in manufacturing. It produces a diverse range of products (over 8000), including consumer items, capital and intermediate goods. SMEs however in India, which constitute more than 80% of the total number of industrial enterprises and form the backbone of industrial development, even now are not export competitive and contribute only about 34% of exports. It is this feature of the SMEs that makes it an ideal target to realize its potential and become export competitive.

Literature Review

While undergoing internationalization process, most of the SMEs in India face numerous problems. It is the SMEs that constitute the major chunk of production and export in the case of many of the nations. The benefits of SMEs to any economy are easily noticeable, they include: creation of jobs at relatively low capital cost, a vehicle for reducing income disparities, and development of a pool of skilled and semi-skilled workers. Researchers have argued that promoting SMEs has been described as one of the best strategies for achieving national development goals such as economic and industrial growth (Kazem & Van der Heijden, 2006).

The literature reviewed in this paper reveals that there is substantial importance for the strategic measures for promoting exports of products by the SMEs. Several researchers have asserted that strategic orientation has a powerful influence on both management expectations and organizational performance (Kohli & Jaworski, 1990). Strategic orientation includes many traits including managers'/owners' attitude towards risk-taking, towards the style of doing business especially in the area of customer handling, entrepreneurship, objectivity, assertiveness, and information use (Wood & Robertson, 1997). They argued that an emotional state of a manager's strategic orientation is believed to influence his/her strategy formulation and subsequent decisions. They argued that a manager's strategic orientation affects which specific strategies that he or she would use, value, and bring to fruition. Strategic orientation helps to determine future strategies other organizational strategies such as financial resources, product characteristics, and technological capabilities. In essence, the strategic orientation which managers adopt has a profound effect on what an organization can do and will do, and is associated with the ultimate level of an organization's success (Allison, 1971).

Export-entrepreneurial orientation has been recognized to influence a firm's choice of internationalization and export involvement. For example, Ibeh & Young (2001) found that high export-entrepreneurial firms tend to be more innovative and proactive for exporting. They also found that export entrepreneurial firms are able to adapt and develop a higher penchant to initiate exporting. Kazem & Van der Heijden (2006) also found that there is a strong association between owners' degree of entrepreneurial orientation and the firm's competitive export performance. They concluded that exporters are likely to be proactive and to take risks in their business and operational decisions than non-exporters. Additionally, Francis and Collins-Dodd (2000) argued for the effectiveness of a proactive export orientation and caution against a traditional approach in the unstable environment. They also indicted that the most export-successful firms are those that use more proactive as well as less traditional approaches. They concluded that a stronger proactive orientation is associated with export success and that greater use of conservative strategies was associated with poor export performance. The negative association between conservative strategies and performance may be detrimental to export success (Francis & Collins-Dodd, 2000). In another study Wood and Robertson (1997) also found that a proactive orientation was associated with export success. Several other studies have also concluded that a positive correlation exists between high entrepreneurial orientation and export performance (Ibeh, 2004; Marino & Weaver, 2002). The entrepreneurial orientation of the owner/manager has also been found to have a sustainable positive relationship with performance and competitiveness (Hult, Snow & Kandemir, 2003; Ibeh, 2004; Kickul & Gundry, 2002).

Knowledge Barriers

Previous studies have shown that export barriers have a major influence on a firm's internationalization process. Aharoni's (1966) study was one of the first studies to explore export barriers. He found, among other things, that lack of knowledge is a major barrier for entry into a foreign market. In another landmark study by Bilkey & Tesar (1977), they found that firms starting export activity face difficulties in identifying opportunities in export markets, also Suarez-Ortega (2003) identified the following as knowledge barriers: lack of awareness of export assistance available to the exporters, lack of awareness of economic and non-economic benefits of export markets, lack of knowledge of potential markets, lack of qualified staff for export markets, and overall lack of knowledge of how to enter the export market (Suarez-Ortega 2003, p. 409). Also, a study of Saudi Arabian exporters of non-oil products by Crick, Al Obadidi, & Chaudhry (1998) indicated that lack of information and lack of export experience as barriers that hinder export development. In a study of non-exporters perceptions of export barriers in Cyprus, Leonidou (1995) also found that limited information to locate/analyze foreign markets and inadequate/untrained staff are barriers to export (Leonidou, 1995, p.13).The first author of this paper, before joining academics had the opportunity to handle the international business of a leading corporate in India for several years. The experiences of the author go in hands with the finding of the above studies with respect to export barriers. In most of the organizations especially in SMEs the export business is handled by non-professionals. They lack knowledge in terms of exploring new export business and maintain the existing one. Many of them fail to think from the point of view of the buyer (importer) while handling the business transactions.

Resource Barriers

According to Suarez-Ortega (2003), internal resource constraints refer to the need for a firm to possess resources in order for it to be able to commence export activity. The following factors have been recognized as internal resource barriers: lack of financial resources such as the difficulty in obtaining the necessary funds needed to start export operations (Bilkey, 1978; Keng & Jiuan, 1989; Suarez-Ortega 2003). For example, in a study of export barriers in Cyprus, Leonidou (1995) found that one of the barriers facing firms who want to export is how to get the necessary funding to finance export operations. Other researchers have also identified additional barriers as internal constraints that hamper export activity. These include how to obtain and use letters of credit for international transactions, (Barker & Kaynak, 1992; Rabino, 1980); the lack of experienced personnel to devote time to export activities (Rabino, 1980), and banks willing to support firms' international activities (Groke and Kriedle, 1967). A study by Crick et a. (1998) shows that resource factors such as lack of production capacity, high costs of labour, lack of suitable personnel with export knowledge and experience hinder firm's capability to enter the export market. In sum, this literature base leads to the hypothesis that an organization's strategic export choice is related to the export.

Strategic Initiatives : Pricing

Apart from the above-mentioned problems, there are many other mistakes generally done by the export marketer with reference to marketing functions and service functions. There could be a number of strategic orientations that can be practised by exporters in terms of marketing and the most important one is the pricing aspect. The pricing aspects are directed by the following aspects:

- The physical location of production plants might influence price.
- Fluctuations in foreign currencies affect pricing.
- The price that the international consumer is willing to pay for your product.
- The price that competitors in international markets are already charging.
- Business environment factors such as government policy and taxation.

Although all these factors play a vital role in the pricing strategy, none is as important as your business objective. In international business the first consideration while negotiating the deal is the 'price'. It is the experience of the author that many a times the business breakthrough was made possible through not competitive pricing but rock bottom pricing. For quoting rock bottom price, an organization should achieve economy of scale in all spheres of business. For example, large international companies such as Starbucks may operate at a loss in some locations but still need a local presence in order to maintain their economies of scale, as well as their reputation as a global player. Therefore, the pricing strategy should be based on your business objective.

Strategic Initiatives based on Knowledge of International Marketing, Culture, Language, Religion, Values and Attitudes, Education & Politics

Culture is the way that we do things around here. Culture could relate to a country (national culture), a distinct section of the community (sub-culture), or an organization (corporate culture). It is widely accepted that you are not born with a culture, and that it is learnt. So, culture includes all that we have learnt in relation to values and norms, customs and traditions. Therefore, international marketing needs to take into account the local culture of the country in which you wish to market.

The Terpstra and Sarathy Cultural Framework helps marketing managers to assess the cultural nature of an international market. It is very straightforward, and uses eight categories in its analysis. These categories are language, religion, values and attitudes, education, social organizations, technology and material culture, law and politics and aesthetics. According to the personal experience of the author, the international buyer greatly values the instant response for his query put forward to the seller. As per Indian standard we take our own sweet time to respond to any sales enquiry which is not at all appreciated by an international buyer as per his culture and practice. Even if you don't quote the price, just thank him for his interest shown in your product and inform him exactly when you will respond to him with details. Again if you don't commit to your words, you are gone.

Language

With language one should consider whether or not the national culture is predominantly a high context culture or a low context culture (Hall and Hall, 1986). The concept relates to the balance between the verbal and the non-verbal communication. In a low context culture spoken language carries the emphasis of the communication, i.e., what is said is what is meant. Examples include Australia and the Netherlands. In a high context culture verbal communications tend not to carry a direct message, i.e., what is said may not be what is meant. So with a high context culture hidden cultural meaning needs to be considered, as does body language. Examples of a high context cultures include Japan and some Arabic nations. Therefore, when you deal with client so of various nations, you need to know the cultural types and communicate suitably.

Religion

The nature and complexity of the different religions an international marketer could encounter is pretty diverse. The organization needs to make sure that their products and services are not offensive, unlawful or distasteful to the local nation. This includes marketing promotion and branding. In 2005 France's Catholic Church won a court injunction to ban a clothing advertisement (by clothing designers Marithe and Francois Girbaud) based upon Leonardo da Vinci's Christ's Last Supper. The author had the experience of product got rejected by the buyer from Saudi Arabia just because of the reason that there was a picture of a women slightly naked on the package of a product. The sketch of women is permitted on the packages in Saudi Arabia but not the real picture.

Values and Attitudes

Values and attitudes vary among nations and even vary within nations. So if you are planning to take a product or service overseas make sure that you have a good grasp on the locality before you enter the market. This could mean altering promotional material or subtle branding messages. There may also be an issue when managing local employees. For example, in France workers tend to take vacations for the whole of August, whilst in the United States employees may only take a couple of week's vacation in an entire year.

Education

The level and nature of education in each international market will vary. This may impact the type of message or even the medium that you employ. For example, in countries with low literacy levels, advertisers would avoid communications which depended upon written copy, and would favour radio advertising with an audio message or visual media such as billboards. The labelling of products may also be an issue. In the People's Republic of China a nationwide system of public education is in place, which includes primary schools, middle schools (lower and upper), and universities. Nine years of education is compulsory for all Chinese students. In Finland school attendance is compulsory between the ages of 7 and 16, the first nine years of education (primary and secondary school) are compulsory, and the children go to their local school. The education after primary school is divided in the vocational and academic systems, according to the old German model. Therefore the knowledge on education level of export marketing country is very essential while designing promotion strategies.

Law and Politics

As with many aspects of Terpstra and Sarathy's Cultural Framework, the underpinning social culture will drive the political and legal landscape. The political ideology on which the society is based will impact upon your decision to market there. For example, the United Kingdom has a largely market-driven, democratic society with laws based upon precedent and legislation, whilst Iran has a political and legal system based upon the teachings and principles Islam and Sharia tradition.

Potential of Indian SMEs to become Export Competitive

SMEs in India are considered to be important members within the supply chain. They are exposed to the competitive pressures either directly from the marketplace or indirectly passed on from their higher ups in the chain. Nevertheless, with their dynamism, flexibility and innovative drive they are increasingly focusing on improved production methods, penetrative marketing strategies and management capabilities to sustain and strengthen their operations.

SWOT Analysis: SMEs in India

Strength	Weakness
Contribution to national economic Growth Generating employment and vitalizing Indian brand to the world Regional development trends Technological innovation Export market expansion	Lack of funds Lack of marketing skills Lack of information Poor adaptability to changing trade Non-availability of technically trained human resources Lack of management skills Lack of access to technological information and consultancy services
Opportunity	**Threats**
WTO regime Bilateral & multilateral trade agreements Enhanced credit support Support for technological upgradation Comprehensive support for cluster development Marketing assistance and export promotion support Growing domestic and international markets	Dumping from developed countries Distrust between SMEs and financial institutions Poor incentive structures for entrepreneurs Virtual absence of enterprise education Non-tariff barriers from developed countries Slow improvement in quality to meet the international standards

The capability of Indian SME products to compete in international markets is reflected in its share of about 34% in national exports. In case of items like readymade garments, leather goods, processed foods, engineering items, the performance has been commendable both in terms of value and their share within the SME sector. In view of this, export promotion from the SME sector has been accorded high priority in India's export promotion strategy which includes simplification of procedures, incentives for higher production of exports, preferential treatments to SMEs in the market development fund and simplification of duty drawback rules. They are thus poised for global partnership to absorb and more importantly to impart latest technologies in diverse fields.

Indian SMEs : Strategic Thrusts for the Future

A flexible combination of state intervention and market freedom, open trade and selective transitional protection, together with a fine-tuned mix of macro- and micro-policies and public-private partnerships are needed for the creation of dynamic exporting SMEs. Drawing from the experience of countries that have successfully promoted the export competitiveness of SMEs, the following section lays down the strategy for Indian SMEs to achieve their export potential and become increasingly export oriented.

Role of Government:. The creation and further development of a business-friendly environment enabling SMEs to start exporting, or to help consolidate the activities of SMEs that are already exporting, is critical. This implies combating of corruption and red tape that hinder the growth and export potential of SMEs.

Measures to improve exporting SMEs' access to finance: This may include providing credits directly from state owned banks to SMEs; liquidity incentives to commercial banks that provide loans to SMEs (lowering of reserve requirements, access to discount lines, etc.); interest rate subsidies; guarantee programmes; and so forth.

Measures to encourage TNCs to create linkages with SMEs: Provided the local suppliers' capacities are sufficient to meet the needs of foreign investors efficiently, these measures include:Prescriptive measures like high tariffs on imports or local content requirements;incentives like benefits such as tax exemptions, the possibility to treat costs related to linkages formation as tax-deductible expenses and granting foreign investors a special status that entitles them to various types of fiscal or financial incentives.

SME trade promotion through public-private partnerships: Governments may approach domestic and foreign large corporations to design specific institutions or tools to provide exporting or promising SMEs with specific services. Such partnerships can take various forms, including training facilities, technology upgrading centres, research and testing labs, scientific hubs, investment funds, start-ups, incubators, etc.

Role of Private Sector

A wide range of measures could also be considered at the B2B level to boost the export capacities of SMEs in India. Key factors and possible measures include:

TNCs: In manufacturing, TNCs and their foreign affiliates can do more to drive or guide the competitiveness upgrading of selected local SME suppliers and subcontractors.

Clusters: Clusters and industrial districts could enhance SMEs' ability to compete in the global economy through a semi-collective organization and specialization among SMEs. National governments, local authorities, TNCs and SME associations should be involved in efforts to identify the optimal division of labour among individual SMEs, large firms and central/local governments in developing countries so as to enable replication of the successes of the best exporting SME clusters and industrial districts (like those in Italy and Taiwan).

Financial and non-financial business development services (BDS): Smooth access to financial and non-financial services can play a role in supporting some SMEs aiming to export or to consolidate regular foreign orders.

Combination of financial and non-financial support services: The rigid separation between financial and technical service providers should be reduced to improve proximity to the real multi-level needs of SME exporters. The combination and teamwork of financial and technical services should be much more systematically explored both by banks and by BDS providers to match SME export needs.

CONCLUSIONS AND IMPLICATIONS

Several factors were identified as barriers that hinder export performance among SMEs, which include lack of finance, lack of export knowledge, lack of qualified personnel, and intense foreign competition. All these factors play a major role in a firm's decision to enter the export market. Various implications derived from the findings of this study concern policy-makers, practitioners, and researchers. With regard to policy-makers, particular emphasis should be given, to the competitiveness of small businesses, the supply of information for the location/analysis of foreign markets and the provision of various tax and other financial incentives.

Apart from all the above-mentioned initiatives there should be measures to educate the business promoters especially in SMEs on how to do international business with its required knowledge related to every aspect of foreign country to which we are planning to export. It is a fact that owners' or managers' export orientation influences a firm's decision to pursue export development strategy. In case the owner is not able to carry out things, they need to have a professional to handle the business. The training and information support services available through the export promotion organizations (EPOs) and organized private sector (OPS) institutions can play a critical role in providing the export knowledge, training, and education needed to SMEs. But how seriously the exporters avail these support is in question. More than everything else an attitudinal change towards the approach of international business will determine the success in this field of business.

REFERENCES

1. Aharoni, Y. (1966). *The Foreign Investment Decision Process.* Boston, MA: Harvard.
2. Barker, A.T. & Kaynak, E. (1992). An empirical investigation of the differences between initiating and continuing exporters. *European Journal of Marketing,* 26 (3), 27-36.
3. Bilkey, W.J. (1978). An attempted integration of the literature on the export behavior of firms. *Journal of International Business Studies,* Spring/Summer, pp. 33-46.
4. Bilkey, W.J. and Tesar, G. (1977). The export behavior of smaller Wisconsin manufacturing firms, Journal *of International Business Studies,* 93-8.
5. Crick, D. Al Obaidi, M. Chaudhry, S. (1998). Perceived obstacles of Saudi- Arabian exporters of non-oil products, *Journal of Marketing Practice: Applied Marketing Science,* 4(7), 187-199.
6. EXIM BANK: Research Brief: "Export Performance of Small and Medium Enterprises in India: - October 2005, International Trade Centre: "Innovations in Export Strategy" Export Strategy"
7. Export Strategies for Small Firms: "New Challenges for Trade Promotion -International Trade Forum" - Issue 1/1999
8. Francis, J, and Collins-Dodd, C. (2000). The Impact of Firms' Export Orientation on the Export Performance of High-Tech Small and Medium-Sized Enterprises, *Journal of International Marketing, 8(3) pp 84-103.*
9. Groke, P.O. and Kreidle, J.R. (1967). Export! Why or why not? Managerial attitude and action for small sized business firms, *Business and Society,* 8, 7 12.
10. Hult G., Snow, C., and Kandemir, D. (2003). The role of Entrepreneurship in Building Cultural Competitiveness in Different Organizational Types. Journal of Management, 29(3), 401-426.
11. Ibeh, K. (2004). Furthering export participation in less performing developing countries, *International Journal of Social Economics,* (311/2), 94-110.
12. Kazem, A., and van der Heijden, B. (2006). Exporting Firms' Strategic Choices: The Case of Egyptian SMEs in the Food Industry", SAM Advanced Management Journal, 71(3), 21-33.
13. Kickul, J., and Gundry, L. (2002). Prospecting for strategic advantage: The proactive entrepreneurial personality and small firms' innovation', *Journal of SmallBusiness Management,* 40(2), 85-97.
14. Kohli, A.K. and Jaworski, B.J. (1990, "Market orientation: the construct, research propositions, and managerial implications", Journal of Marketing, 54, 1-18.
15. Laghu Udyog - Small Industry India - Small Scale Industry (SSI) Information under Government of India www.laghu-udyog.com
16. Leonidou, L.C. (1995), "Export stimulation: a non-exporter's perspective, *European Journal of Marketing,* 29, (8),17-36.

17. Leonidou, L.C. (2004). An analysis of the barriers hindering small business export development, Journal of Small Business Management, 42(3), 279- 302.
18. Marino, L.D., and Weaver, M.K. (2002). Assessing the psychometric properties of the entrepreneurial orientation scale: A multi-country analysis. Entrepreneurship: Theory and Practice. Texas: Baylor University.
19. Rabino, S. (1980). An examination of barriers to exporting encountered by small manufacturing companies, Management International Review, 20 (1), 67-73
20. Small Industries and Development Bank of India www.sidbi.com
21. Suarez-Ortega, S. (2003). Export Barriers: Insights from small and medium-sized firms" International Small Business Journal, 21(4), 403-419.
22. "The Micro, Small And Medium Enterprises Development Act, 2006"
23. Wood, V.R. and Robertson, K.R. (1997). Strategic orientation and export success: An empirical study", *International Marketing Review,* 14(6), 424-444

Websites

www.articlesbase.com/international-business-articles/economy-review-of-india-and-export-business-4336798.html#ixzz1HGFjCieZ
www.tradeforum.org/news/fullstory.php/aid/98/Export Strategies for SmallFirms.html
www.intracen.org/e_discuss/sme/ed3sumday1.htm
www.laghu-udyog.com/sido/export.htm
www.fisme.org.in/views.htm
www.exim.com

14

Challenges of Indian Agriculture Exports

P.A.L.N.S. Kalyani and P.V. Rao

Associate Professor, St. Joseph's PG College, Basheerbagh, Hyderabad
E-mail: satyakalyani.999@gmail.com
Director, Vivekananda School of PG Studies, Srinagar Colony, Hyderabad

ABSTRACT

"Agriculture is the backbone of the Indian economy", said Mahatma Gandhi five decades ago. Even today, the situation is still the same, with almost the entire economy being sustained by agriculture, which is the mainstay of the villages. Not only the economy, but also every one of us looks up to agriculture for our sustenance. Indian agriculture's strengths, weaknesses, opportunities and threats are analyzed in the context of the government's dismantling of the system of quantitative restrictions on imports and its announcement of a strategy to promote agricultural exports as a step towards achieving a 1% share in the global trade. It is concluded that, with the government's proactive role towards the agricultural sector and the cooperation of agricultural research institutes and the private sector, the Indian farmers can get a competitive edge in the future.

Keywords: Agricultural and Processed Food Products Export Development Authority (APFPEDA), National Pulse Development Programme, Contract Farming.

INTRODUCTION

Agriculture sector of Indian economy is one of the most significant parts of India. Agriculture is the only means of living for almost two-thirds of the employed class in India. As stated by the economic data of financial year 2006-07, agriculture has acquired 18 per cent of India's GDP. The agriculture sector of India has occupied almost 43 per cent of India's geographical area. Agriculture is the largest contributor to India's GDP even after a decline in the same in the agriculture share of India. Agriculture also plays a significant role in the growth of socio-economic sector in India. In the earlier times, India was largely dependent upon food imports but the successive stories of the agriculture sector of Indian economy have made it self-sufficing in grain production. The country also has substantial reserves for the same. India depends heavily on the agriculture sector, especially on the food production unit after the 1960 crisis in food sector. Since then, India has put a lot of effort to be self-sufficient in the food production and this endeavour of India has led to the Green Revolution. The Green Revolution came into existence with the aim to improve the agriculture in India. The services enhanced by the Green Revolution in the agriculture sector of Indian economy are as follows:

- Acquiring more area for cultivation purposes
- Expanding irrigation facilities
- Use of improved and advanced high-yielding variety of seeds
- Implementing better techniques that emerged from agriculture research
- Water management
- Plan protection activities through prudent use of fertilizers, pesticides, and cropping applications

All these measures taken by the Green Revolution led to an alarming rise in the wheat and rice production of India's agriculture. Considering the quantum leap witnessed by the wheat and rice production unit of India's agriculture, National Pulse Development Programme that covered almost 13 states, was set up in 1986 with the aim to introduce the improved technologies to the farmers. A Technology Mission was introduced in 1986 right after the success of the National Pulse Development Programme to boost the oilseeds sector in Indian economy. Pulses too came under this programme. A new seed policy was planned to provide entree to superior quality seeds and plant material for fruits, vegetables, oilseeds, pulses and flowers.

The Indian government also set up Ministry of Food Processing Industries to stimulate the agriculture sector of Indian and make it more lucrative. India's agriculture sector highly depends upon the monsoon season as heavy rainfall during the time leads to a rich harvest. But the entire year's agriculture cannot possibly depend upon only one season. Taking into account this fact, a second Green Revolution is likely to be initiated to overcome the such restrictions. An increase in the growth rate and irrigation area, improved water management, improving the soil quality, and diversifying into high value outputs, fruits, vegetables, herbs, flowers, medicinal plants, and bio-diesel are also on the list of the services to be taken by the Green Revolution to improve the agriculture in India.

The Indian Agricultural Scenario

The total geographical area of India is 328.7 million hectares of which 140.3 million hectares is net sown area, while 193.7 million hectares is the gross cropped area, according to the Annual Report 2009-10 of the Ministry of Agriculture.

- **Production**

  India has become the world's largest producer across a range of commodities due to its favourable agro-climatic conditions and rich natural resource base. India is the largest producer of coconuts, mangoes, bananas, milk and dairy products, cashew nuts, pulses, ginger, turmeric and black pepper. It is also the second largest producer of rice, wheat, sugar, cotton, fruits and vegetables.

  As per the Centre for Monitoring Indian Economy (CMIE) farm output was to grow by 10 per cent to 114 million tonnes (MT) in the 2010 Kharif season, while Rabi season was expected to report a 2 per cent increase at 116.6 MT. Oilseeds production was expected to rise by 11.1 per cent during the season to 18.1 per cent, sugarcane to notch up by 15.6 per cent to 321 MT and cotton to grow by 12.4 per cent to 26.9 million bales compared to 23.9 million bales in the last season. The agency pegged the overall food grain output growth up by 5.3 per cent to 229.7 MT. Major agricultural crops, including food grain, oilseeds, cotton, sugarcane, and fruits and vegetables, are projected to grow by 7.2 per cent in 2010-11, while production of non-food crops as a whole is projected to grow by 9.7 per cent in the year.

- **Exports**

  According to the government's agri-trade promotion body, Agricultural and Processed Food Products Export Development Authority (APEDA), India's export of agricultural and floricultural products, fruits and vegetables, animal products, cereals and processed food products was worth US$ 1.14 billion during April-May 2010-11. India's agri-export turnover is expected to rise to nearly US$ 18 billion by 2014, according to APEDA. At present, around 70 per cent of the country's agricultural and processed food exports are to developing countries in the Middle East, Asia, Africa and South America. Indian seed companies are eyeing the export markets in SAARC (South Asian Association for Regional Cooperation) and African countries with a host of hybrid seeds and best farm practices. While some of the companies like JK Seeds, Namdhari Seeds, Nuziveedu Seeds, Nath Seeds, Rasi and Vibha Seeds have already ventured into the export markets in the region.

- **Investments**

  The public and private sector investments in agriculture have been steadily increasing since 2004-05. While public sector investments in agriculture increased from US$ 3.61 billion in 2004-05 to US$ 5.5 billion in 2008-09, private sector investment increased from US$ 14 billion in 2004-05 to US$ 25.5 billion in 2008-09, according to the Annual Report 2009-10 of the Ministry of Agriculture.

Indian Agricultural Sector: 2010

Agriculture is one of the strongholds of the Indian economy and accounts for 14.6 per cent of the country's gross domestic product (GDP) in 2009-10, and 10.23 per cent (provisional) of the total exports. Furthermore, the sector provided employment to 55 per cent of the workforce.

India's agriculture and allied sector grew by 3.8 per cent in the first six months of the current fiscal (2010-11), against one per cent in the year-ago period on the back of better Kharif crop output. According to the GDP data released by the Central Statistical Organisation (CSO) on November 30, 2010, the country's farm sector grew by 2.5 per cent and 4.4 per cent each in the first two quarters of the current fiscal, against 1.9 per cent and 0.9 per cent, respectively, in the same period last year.

The Government is giving highest priority to agriculture and allied sectors. The Eleventh Plan allocation has been considerably higher over the Tenth Plan allocation. An amount of US$ 19 billion has been allocated for the Ministry of Agriculture during the Eleventh Five Year Plan. Capital investment in agriculture increased from US$ 1.2 billion in 2007-08 to US$ 3.26 billion in 2010-11 (inclusive of State Plan Scheme Rashtriya Krishi Vikas Yojana), as per a Ministry of Agriculture press release dated August 3, 2010.

SWOT ANALYSIS OF INDIAN AGRICULTURE SECTOR

STRENGTHS	WEAKNESSES
Water : Numerous rivers, streams, and other water bodies with perennial flow of water in the region, potential for irrigation, hydropower, water transport, fishery etc. ***Tea*** : Climate-topographical situation is most suitable. Fifty-six per cent of India's tea production in the region, most of which is organically grown. ***Oil and petroleum products***: Over half of oil and natural gas production of the country is in the northeast region (NER). ***Forests*** : The region possesses richest bio-diversity, good quality usable wood/timber ***Potential international markets for exports and imports:*** The NER is surrounded in all sides with international borders ***Mineral resources***: Several mineral resources are found in abundance	***Isolation*** : From the main land and shyness of the people ***Socio-cultural closeness:*** (particularly of the tribal), subgroups, multiplicity of ethnic groups, diversity of language and dialects etc. ***Shifting cultivation:*** Though labelled as inefficient, shifting cultivation is a major mode of production in many areas, 16 per cent of the available land area involving 4.5 lakh *Jhumia* families. Due to population pressure, the Jhum cycle is reduced which is a deterrent to local ecosystem ***Lack of capital formation:*** Outside markets for trading the natural resources of the region are in existence from colonial regimes. But the market is unidirectional, inefficient and does not favour capital formation ***Movement of flow of men and material:*** Due to various reasons, the flow of man and material is highly limited ***Lack of data-base:*** Lack of relevant on information on socio-economic and development parameters, is a policy deterrent.
OPPORTUNITIES	**THREATS**
Potential international market: Triangular and quadrangular trade can be promoted ***Close society:*** Better socio-cultural exchange in tribal societies; a model of collective action ***Diversification:*** Agro-based industries using the local raw materials-horticulture, fishery, tea, rubber, jute, oilseed etc.	***Ecological:*** Floods, cyclones and earthquakes occur frequently ***International border:*** Long and difficult terrain in the international border ***Social security:*** Possibilities for border-crossing creating situations of threat to social/national security

Export Competitiveness of India's Agricultural Products

India has a competitive advantage in several commodities for agricultural exports because of near self-sufficiency of inputs, relatively low labour costs and diverse agro-climatic conditions. These factors have enabled export of several agricultural commodities over the years such as marine products, cereals, cashew, tea, coffee, spices, oil meals, fruits and vegetables, castor and tobacco. For certain commodities like Basmati rice. India has a niche market access in spite of competition. The ten most important agricultural products that currently cover more than 80 per cent of the trade in the world market are coarse grain, cotton, rice, soybean, sugar, spices, tea, tobacco, vegetable oil and wheat, commodities in which India has a dominant production. Apart from these, fruits and vegetables (the second largest producer with 150 million tonnes), spices (world's largest producer, with over 3 million tonnes) milk (being the largest producer with 91 million tonnes), poultry (5th largest with 842 million) meat products (with 417 million livestock, the largest in the world), fisheries (8000 km of coastline; 7th largest producer with 6 million tonnes) offer tremendous potential for export. Horticulture occupies about 12 million ha, which accounts for about 7 per cent of the total cropped area. The annual production is about 150 million tonnes. India's share in world production being nearly 10 per cent in fruits and 14 per cent in vegetables. India produces 50 per cent of world's mangoes, 19 per cent of banana, 36 per cent of cashew nut, more than 10 per cent of onion, 38 per cent of cauliflower, 28 per cent of green peas, etc. Despite all this, our share in the world exports of fruits and vegetables is only about 1 per cent. And it is only about 2 per cent of the fruits and vegetables produced in the country is processed and there is considerable potential to increase it to about 10 per cent.

An area with high potential for exports in the years ahead, among the agricultural exports, is the processed food products. The export of fresh fruits and vegetables and processed fruits and vegetables continues to remain a mere 6 per cent of the total value of exports, despite the institutional support to boost their exports, though there are indications of a steady rise in their exports. Processed items include fruit pulps and concentrated pulps, juice concentrates, canned fruits and vegetables, dehydrated vegetables and frozen fruits and vegetables. The level of processing in our country is very low and varies from sector to sector, and is estimated at 2 per cent in case of fruits and vegetables. Even in developing countries such as Malaysia (80 per cent) and Thailand (30 per cent) it is very high. Similarly, value addition in India is estimated at 7 per cent as compared to 45 per cent in the Philippines and 23 per cent in China.

Within the country, there are wide variations in productivity levels. Punjab, Haryana, Andhra Pradesh, Tamil Nadu and Kerala may have attained world standard productivity levels. But other regions are way behind. Thus, the issue of competitiveness is also region specific. A regionally differentiated strategy, taking into account the agronomic, climatic and environmental conditions is, therefore, sought to be pursued to realize the full potential of yield in every region. Comparative advantage, in itself, is a relative concept and it depends upon the relative changes in the international market. A major difficulty faced by India in the international market is the high level of subsidies given by developed countries for their agri-exports. Hence, it is imperative to evolve concrete strategies to make Indian agriculture competitive and enhance its efficiency. For this purpose, on the one hand, we should be seeking substantial reduction in the support given to agriculture by developed countries, on the other hand, Indian agriculture would also require to be supported to maintain and improve its competitiveness.

The annual increase in India's exports on account of WTO and the enlarged market share is estimated to be US$1.25 billion, marginally less than what has been estimated by the Ministry of Commerce at US$ 1.5 billion to 2 billion. A study carried out by National Council for Applied Economic Research (NCAER) which had covered 17 agricultural commodities had rated rice, banana, grapes, sapota and litchi as highly export competitive. Raising the level of productivity and quality standards to internationally competitive levels is one of the major challenges following the dismantling of quantitative restrictions on imports, as per the WTO agreement on agriculture. For several commodities, our national productivity is less than the world average. There is potential for enhancing crop productivity and thereby increasing agri-export.

CREDIT FACILITIES TO AGRI-EXPORTS

Institutional agencies and banks have been playing an important role in extending credit and other support to agriculture and in the promotion of exports. Nationalized commercial banks have been providing credit support by way of pre-shipment and post-shipment. Other support facilities may include foreign exchange transactions including forward cover, provision of cross-currency options, weekly trends in Forex markets, providing country profiles and risk, credit, status report of overseas trading partners, market intelligence, counselling, risk management and optional hedging of foreign exchange exposures in the long term perspective, consulting services on exchange controls, import-export policy and other formalities in foreign trade, inputs supplied to contract farms by exporters as raw materials for export and sanctioning the line of credit to processors, financing bulk purchase of inputs, etc. Given the thrust on agri-exports and the advent of WTO, we need to have a fresh look at the financial assistance being extended to promote agricultural exports with a view to making it more export-friendly. Apart from banks, the other institutions involved in export promotion include the commodity boards like coffee and tea boards, the spices board as also the Agriculture and Processed Food Products Export Development Authority (APEDA).

Major Constraints of Agri-export Sector

(i) Lack of a broad raw material base in terms of the kinds and varieties of fruits and vegetables suitable in all respects for processing and their availability in commercial quantities at prices economical to the processing industry. Invariably, the cost of the raw material is high.

(ii) Low productivity and poor quality of the produce as compared to the very high levels obtained in the advanced countries affect processing and none of the processing units work to full capacity. Much of the produce taken up for processing is devoid of the quality attributes or characteristics required for processing.

(iii) Despite the WTO and the Agreement on Agriculture (which focuses primarily on reduction of tariffs, increased market access, reduction in aggregate measure of support in the form of subsidies) subsidies continue as a result of which the expected gains have eluded developing countries like India.

(iv) Imposition of non-tariff barriers like sanitary and phytosanitary (SPS) conditions on imports from developing countries. Lack of awareness and knowledge about the SPS measures and quality standards required to be adopted by the processing industry and exporters.

(v) Fruits and vegetables are generally constrained by poor price support, credit support and delivery system which affect processing.

(vi) The quality of packaging is poor. Importing countries demand specific packaging for each produce and the use of bio-degradable materials resulting in high cost of packaging.

(vii) The emergence of trading blocs in Asia, Europe and North America has also considerably affected India's agri-export trade.

(viii) Due to poor infrastructure in handling, transport, marketing and processing, horticulture, as an industry, has not grown in our country. Poor infrastructure, particularly transportation, road network, and freight and cargo facilities, cold storage facilities, etc., coupled with inadequate post-harvest management affect the produce and products.

(ix) Inadequate supply of power, water and research and development support add to the constraints.

(x) The freight rates in India are reported to be around 50 to 100 per cent higher than those prevalent in some other countries which does very little to improve our competitiveness.

(xi) It is the residual rather than the fresh produce that is often taken up for processing, which has a bearing on quality.

(xii) Lack of a proper marketing strategy geared to meeting the raw material requirement of processing units and ensuring a sustainable export market for the processed products.

(xiii) Poor and inconsistent quality of processed products and inadequate export promotion are some of the constraints plaguing the processing industry.

SUGGESTIONS FOR PROMOTING EXPORTS

Infrastructure Development: A major impediment to promoting exports is the lack of adequate infrastructure, particularly cold storage facilities and transportation. There is need to encourage public-private partnership in building such facilities and ensuring their proper maintenance. There is no dearth of financial assistance as there are several incentives provided by the Government of India under its capital investment subsidy scheme as well as those available under the schemes envisaged by APEDA. Concerted efforts need to be made in this direction in collaboration with commercial banks.

Marketing Strategy: In the new scenario where all the quantitative restrictions have now been removed and there is increased opportunity for the developing countries to have access to global markets, it is imperative that a marketing strategy is worked out, focusing on major items of import by countries and to concentrate on such products using the comparative advantage. The countries in the European Union, African countries and the CIS countries need to be given greater attention.

Contract Farming: Contract farming needs to be encouraged not only to provide a broad base for raw materials for processing but also for the supply of the right type of inputs and other linkages necessary for the acceptability of the quality standards for competitive exports.

Human Resources Development: There is also a vital need for human resources development and to train the exporters about the quality standards and the sanitary and phytosanitary measures that need to be complied with.

Market access and information: There is a need to provide continuous updating of data on market information, market access, procedures and processed, etc.

Biotechnology: India is recognized as one of the five top biotechnology leaders in the Asia Pacific region. In terms of number of patents filing, India ranks third in Asia. Biotechnology leads to reduction in cost and improvement in productivity. Given the low cost but high calibre workforce, there is a need to optimal utilization of intellectual and biological resources with a view to bringing cost effectiveness in production.

Trade Related Intellectual Property Rights: India should launch genetic and legal literacy movements immediately to sensitize panchayats and rural families on the implications of the protection of plant verities and Farmers Rights Act, 2001 and Biodiversity Act, 2002, since they contain provisions for recognizing and rewarding the contributions of the primary conservers of biodiversity and holders of traditional knowledge.

Credit facilities: The EXIM Bank, in consultation with APEDA and the Ministry of Agriculture, may set up Farm Export Promotion Cells in each AEZ and provide necessary technical support and guidance to the exporters. It can also open offices in each state in order to promote agri-export and also establish overseas branches in countries where Indian exports are favourite destinations.

Economies of Scale: Economies of scale and brand banding can only happen when large and big companies enter the sector. In this respect, contract farming and corporate farming should be extended, credit facilities with liberal terms and making storage, movement, processing, marketing and trade of farm commodities free from regulations and controls. It is necessary to consider streamlining the procedure for export financing of agricultural products which are perishable in nature and making it entrepreneur friendly. Likewise, the procedure for obtaining export credit guarantee cover should be streamlined and made exporter friendly and in this respect a comprehensive insurance cover right from the stage of production to export can also be considered.

THE ROAD AHEAD: STRATEGIES

The strategies are suggested based on constraints and SWOT analysis keeping in view the basic tenets of interdisciplinary, eco-regional perspective, making business with a changing attitude, and with strong O&M motivation. The principles involved include ecology, gender and social equity, economics and employment.

REFERENCES

1. Dr. L Krishnaveni and Sangita Ghosh, (2004). "India's Agricultural Exports: Some Challenges," The IUP Journal of Agricultural Economics, IUP Publications, vol. 0(3), pp. 62-71.
2. Meenakshi, P. (2008). "Rural Financial Institutional in India (A Study on Agriculture Sector)", Banking and Finance.
3. Ramesh Golait, (2008). "Current Issues in Agriculture Credit in India:An assessment", *Indian J. Management.*
4. Sanjiv Chopra, (2009). "The Structure and Organisation of the Agricultural Credit in India: Relationship between Primary Societies, Apex Bodies and CDFAs", Banking Finance.
5. Prof. G. Ram Reddy, (1999). Third Endowment Lecture by Dr. Y.V. Reddy, Deputy Governor, Reserve Bank of India, at Potti Sreeramulu Telugu University Auditorium Public Gardens, Hyderabad.

15

Opportunities and Challenges of Supply Chain Management

Sanjay S. Solanki and Ajay Kumar

Asst. Prof. & HOD, JSPM's Jayawant Institute of Management Studies, Tathwade, Mumbai Bypass Highway, Pune 411033. E-mail: sanjay.solanki123@gmail.com

Director, JSPM's Jayawant Institute of Computer Applications, Tathwade, Mumbai Bypass Highway Pune 411033. E-mail: ajay19_61@rediffmail.com

ABSTRACT

A supply chain is a network of facilities and distribution options that performs the functions of procurement of materials, transformation of these materials into intermediate and finished products, and the distribution of these finished products to customers. Supply chains exist in both service and manufacturing organizations, although the complexity of the chain may vary greatly from industry to industry and firm to firm. The main objective is to understand SCM (supply chain management) and explore the various challenges and opportunities evolving day by day. Firms from established and mature economies are increasingly expanding into emerging markets. Globalization forced companies to change their competitive priorities and redesign the supply chain aggressively with a global focus. For some companies the driving factor is the new markets for its products and for some other it is the access to new suppliers or raw materials from anywhere in the world at low cost, for a third it is about lowering the cost of manufacturing and services through outsourcing. Regardless of a galore of opportunities there are many common supply chain challenges as they enter or expand their business in emerging markets: new risk of disruption of quality, financial uncertainties of the partner, unfamiliar cultures, varied infrastructure, historical reasons and rapid growth and change. Globalization ,vertical disintegration, outsourcing and off-shoring, shorter product life cycles, lesser lead time, JIT inventory are also some factors which led to challenges like information integration, coordination and resource sharing, organizational relationship linkage. Information is the power of modern SCM. A company with modern technology and having and effective supply chain management system with information integration as its foundation will have a definite edge over competitors and various SCM challenges. This paper mostly concentrates on opportunities and challenges of supply chain management in healthcare industry.

Keywords: SCM, Globalization, Resource sharing, Outsourcing, e-supply chain, Real time information challenges.

INTRODUCTION

Supply Chain Management

"Supply chain is defined as the network of organizations that are involved, through upstream and downstream linkages, in the different processes and activities that produce value in the form of products and services delivered to the ultimate consumer." "Supply chain management is defined as management of a network of retailers, distributors, transporters, storage facilities and suppliers that participate in the sale, delivery and production of a particular product."

OPPORTUNITIES IN SCM

Information Technology in SCM

The Internet wave and the emergence of e-business have highly influenced the traditional supply chains by enhancing coordination and communication between the partners. The enabling technologies like EDI, intranet, extranet, electronic market places, ERP, DRP, warehouse management system, CRM, CPFR, etc., have tremendously improved the integration among the buyers and sellers. Information technology has removed the roadblocks of information sharing making the firm smarter every day. E-business has enhanced both supply chain efficiency and responsiveness by sharing real-time information regarding inventory, shipment status and other key information like product design, product availability and demand among partners. The e-supply chain will have customers and suppliers seamlessly linked together, throughout the world, exchanging information almost instantly. As a result of e-speed information sharing the companies are adopting pull strategy instead of push strategy. Fast access to relevant supply chain information can pay-off handsomely in lower product acquisition costs, lower procurement transaction, less inventory, higher quality decision making, shorter lead times, profitable means of disposing unused excess inventory and better customer services. Effective supply chain management can impact and improve upon virtually all business processes, such as data accuracy, operational complexity reduction, supplier selection, purchasing, and warehousing and distribution. Other benefits include:

- Quicker customer response and fulfilment rates
- Shorter lead time
- Greater productivity and lower costs
- Reduced inventory throughout the chain
- Improved forecasting precision
- Fewer suppliers and shorter planning cycles
- More reliable and quality information

Supply Chain Management Software

Supply chain management software (SCMS) is a business term which refers to a range of software tools or modules used in executing supply chain transactions, managing supplier relationships and controlling associated business processes. Some common features of these software are as follows:

- Customer requirement processing
- Purchase order processing
- Inventory management
- Goods receipt and warehouse management
- Supplier management/sourcing

A requirement of many SCMS often includes forecasting. Such tools often attempt to balance the disparity between supply and demand by improving business processes and using algorithms and consumption analysis to better plan future needs. SCMS also often includes integration technology that allows organizations to trade electronically with supply chain patterns.

ERP and SCM

ERP is the battering ram that integrates all that information together in a single application, and SCM application benefits from having a single major source to go to for up-to-date information. New initiative in resource planning, electronic commerce and extended supply chain are fuelling the trend among corporations toward integrating strategic business applications. ERP systems assist enterprises in automating and integrating corporate cross-functions. SCM systems support information flow from various players in the supply side, reducing the transaction cost and facilitating supplier-customer interactions. Normally SCM applications simply automate the logistic aspect of SCM are less dependent upon on gathering information from around the company and are independent of the ERP decision. But current trends in the market are such that you need to have these applications communicate with ERP in some fashion. It's important to pay attention to the software's ability to integrate with the Internet and with ERP applications because the Internet will drive demand for integrated information.

RFID and SCM

It is one of the most notable is Radio Frequency Identification, or RFID. RFID tags are essentially barcodes on steroids. Whereas barcodes only identify the product, RFID tags can tell where the product is, where it has been, when it expires, whatever information someone wishes to programme with it. RFID technology is going to generate mountains of data about the location of pallets, cases, cartons, totes, and individual products in the supply chain. It could produce piles of information about when and where merchandise is manufactured, picked, packed and shipped. It also tells retailers about the expiry dates of their perishable items, numbers that will have to be stored, transmitted in real-time and shared with warehouse management, inventory management, financial and other enterprise systems. Another benefit of RFID is that, unlike barcodes, RFID tags can be read automatically by electronic readers.

SUPPLY CHAIN IN FOOD SECTOR

The food supply chain consists of various players. Logistics is the thread which connects the different components of the supply chain. The supply chain consists of farmers who sell their produce directly to consumers or to traders or manufacturers, cold storage units, food processing entities, packaging units, wholesalers or distributors, retail chains or other form of retailers, hotels, restaurants, caterers and consumers. Supply chain in the case of food sector varies from product to product in terms of number of players and value addition at the level of each player. The efficiency of a supply chain depends upon the way in which the relative activities or processes are conducted such that cost, time and efforts are saved and productivity increases. These cover forecasting supply of and demand for products, sourcing of raw materials and intermediaries, production, inventory, orders, distribution and making the products available to customers. A connecting thread in these cases is the level of technology used, technology-backed information systems and logistics which integrate the various players in the supply chain.

E-FINANCIAL SUPPLY CHAIN SYSTEMS

Cross-border transactions, decreasing cost of technology, speed of transaction and a 24-hour 365 days facility have led to the development of e-financial supply chain. Though e-financial supply chain has been growing, it needs to accelerate at a much faster pace to keep up with global business demands. Comprehensive laws and mitigation of risk of fraud would enhance its use and acceptance. Proper financial supply chain management, using e-payment mechanism, can reduce the cost of working capital and improve supplier relationship management by providing speedy payment.

SCM IN PHARMACEUTICAL INDUSTRY

Outsourcing, the current mantra of pharmaceutical industry, is being used more strategically as an ongoing part of a company's overall business strategy. Outsourced activities can be in various fields right from "drug discovery" till manufacturing of the product. Pharmaceutical companies have a long outsourced function such as manufacturing, packaging, clinical trials and sales force mobilization. Biotechnology companies which have almost doubled in number during the past five years, also contributed to this trend as they seek ways of bringing their products to markets without making capital investment in their own manufacturing facilities, the major benefits of outsourcing are given below:

- Outsourcing reduces the overall cost by 30 to 35 per cent
- Reduces problems faced during the regulatory process
- Improves manufacturing efficiencies
- Reduces excess production capacity by divesting facilities
- Improves net earnings and cash flow
- Is fast and cheaper to have discovery work outsourced as it reduces the drug development cost.

The healthcare industry, in general, lags behind other industries while adopting e-commerce and related technologies. While the financial and telecommunication industries have been in the forefront of usage and deployment of technology, the healthcare industry is still plagued by many stove-pipe systems that do not interoperate. Many times, companies do not have the technological infrastructure to integrate supply-chain applications to each other.

The lack of industry standards for data exchange has promoted the development and implementation of divergent contract administration systems within and between industry segments. As a result, half or all transactions are still paper-driven — requiring manual processing or rekeying. Trading partners experience significant delays, long processing cycles and inefficient use of their resources resulting in increased cost and less profits.

Market surveys have shown that between 85-100 per cent of contract systems in the pharmaceutical industry (manufacturers, wholesalers and group purchasing organizations) are home-grown or specially customized. This has contributed to lack of interoperation and integration of the supply chain. Since business partners are distributed, this creates the need for distributed technologies that can help integrate their systems.

Although technologies exist for distributed computing and integration, agreement between partners is still required on the semantics and syntax for information that is exchanged between them. The supply chain includes many components such as catalogues, contracting, order placement, order tracking, inventory replenishment, and more. Clear and standardized interfaces must be produced between and within each of the business function areas. If an agreement is not established between trading partners, proper purchasing and order fulfilment cannot take place.

There is a need to explore the technical (development and operations), process, organizational and political, as well as security issues that must be overcome to successfully deploy a B2B system across the Internet. Differences between user-to-system and system-to-system integration and security requirements and solutions are to be addressed. Also highlighted is the Pharma Initiative, a prototyping and standardization activity led by several of the supply chain trading partners, vendors, and the Object Management Group need to be developed. Supply chain management is a major issue in many industries as organizations begin to appreciate the criticality of creating an integrated relationship with their suppliers and customers, as well as all other stakeholders. Managing the supply chain has become a way of improving competitiveness by reducing uncertainty and enhancing customer service. The concept of value chain management (VCM) is becoming quite prevalent in industry.

Despite this popularity, there is little evidence of the development of accompanying theory in the literature. Without theory development, it is difficult to identify specific hypotheses and propositions, which can be tested, resulting in research that lacks focus and is perhaps irrelevant. This paper analyses the merits and limitations of SCM in the context of Indian pharmaceutical industry.

The pharmaceutical industry can be defined as a complex of processes, operations and organizations involved in the discovery, development and manufacture of drugs and medications. The pharmaceutical industry is a life line industry, which plays a crucial role in building a strong human capital of a country, and is very essential for economic growth and development. The achievements of the Indian pharmaceutical industry are spectacular in recent times and are praiseworthy.It has evolved as model industry of the country in performance.

The first phase of transitions happened in 1970s, when the regulatory reforms were initiated to encourage the domestic manufacturers to produce and supply quality drugs at an affordable price to the consumers. Pricing of the finished formulations was controlled by the union government through enactment of drug price control order (DPCO). The stage was set for the second phase of growth, when the government began enactment of patent law and up-regulation of policies in an effort to liberalize the economy. Under its commitment to World Trade Organization and patent treaty, the government is taking the following steps:

- Adaptation of product patent by 2005
- Reduction of duties on import of drugs
- Encouraging foreign investments in pharmaceutical sector
- Allowing Indian pharmaceutical companies to invest in foreign countries Encouraging research and development activities

The Indian pharmaceutical sector has come a long way, being almost non-existent before 1970 to a prominent provider of healthcare products, meeting almost 95 per cent of the country's pharmaceuticals needs. The domestic pharmaceutical sales have increased from Rs. 4bn in 1970-71 to Rs. 214bn in 2002, at a CAGR of 13.7 per cent per annum. The total Indian production constitutes about 1.3 per cent of the world market in value terms and, 8 per cent in volume terms. The per capita consumption of drugs in India, stands at US $3, lowest in the world, as compared to Japan-- US $412, Germany-- US $222 and USA-- US $191.

Indian pharmaceutical industry is mounting up the value chain. From being a pure reverse engineering industry focused on the domestic market, the industry is moving towards basic research-driven, export-oriented global presence, providing wide range of value added quality products and services. Government policies will play an important role in defining the future of the pharmaceutical industry. The product patent regime coming into effect from January 2005 will lead to long-term growth for the future.

In the present scenario, the growth of a domestic pharmaceutical company is critically dependent on its therapeutic presence. The old and mature categories like anti-infective, vitamins, analgesics are de-growing while, new lifestyle categories like cardiovascular, central nervous system (CNS), anti-diabetic are expanding at double-digit growth rates. Increased generic penetration, intense competition, fragmentation of the industry has negatively impacted the overall value growth of the domestic pharmaceutical market. In this scenario, to grow in the domestic market, pharmaceutical companies are constantly eyeing for innovation, introduction of new value added products, product life cycle management and enlarging their market reach. Indian companies are putting their act together to tap the generic drugs markets in the regulated high margin markets of the developed countries. The US market will remain the most lucrative market for the Indian companies led by its market size and the intensity of blockbuster drugs going off patent. An estimated US$45bn of drugs expected to go off patent by 2007 in US alone. Outsourcing in the fields of R&D and manufacturing is the next best event in the pharmaceutical industry. Spiraling cost, expiring patents, low R&D cost and market dynamics are driving the MNCs to outsource both manufacturing and research activities. India with its apt chemistry skills and low cost advantages, both in research and manufacturing coupled with skilled manpower will attract a lot of business in the days to come.

Key Activities in Indian Pharmaceutical Industry

Major activities of Indian pharmaceutical industry include manufacture of bulk drugs, formulations, generics, import and export of medicines. The research and development has been more intense focusing on drug discovery new molecular entities. The worldwide competitions and enhanced cost of research in developed countries have made the leading multinational drug companies to tap the resources of talent infrastructure, natural resources to cut down the cost of discovery of new molecular entities.

For example, GE company has opened research centre near Bangalore; Astra Zenaca International Research Center for anti-tubercular drug discovery programme. Another major area of activity of significance is of ethnic medicine and natural drugs, Many ayurvedic drugs and herbal products are in demand in developed countries. There is a belief and faith that ayurvedic medicines and herbal medicines cause less harm and hence, likely to be safer than allopathic medicines. Due to hectic activity in the formulation industry the ancillary industries like machinery, packaging and basic chemical industries are booming with rapid growth rate.

Indigenous research centres of Ranbaxy, Dr. Reddy Research Center, Lupin Pharmaceutical Research Park, Torrent Research Centers, Sun Research Center and Cadila Research Center are few of the research centres which have established research facilities matching the international standards and are focusing on drug discovery processes with an eye on patent regime. The human talent bank is groomed by highly focused educational and research institutions like Niper, Candhigarh, BITS, Pilani, UDCT Mumbai, CDRI Lucknow, IIsc Bangalore, NCL, Pune.

The main drivers of growth have been new products. Market trends in the year 2000 revealed that new products contributed significantly to the overall turnover of most companies. According to the figures of a recent ORG-MARG survey conducted at ten major companies, new products are second only to volumes. For example, 9.1 per cent of Sun Pharma's overall growth rate has come from new products, 5.6 per cent in Cipla's case, 4.8 per cent in Cadila Healthcare's, 2.6 per cent in Nicholas Piramal, 0.7 per cent in Knoll, 0.6 per cent in Pfizer, 3.5 per cent in Ranbaxy, 0.5 per cent in Glaxo Smithkline, 1 per cent in Wockhhardt and 0.1 per cent in Hoechst Marion Roussel.

CONCLUSION

There are several areas where the industry could benefit from standardization. Among others, these include membership and eligibility, contract negotiation, catalogue interfaces, sales history, and more. There are also various related initiatives, related standards and organizations that should be leveraged. The healthcare domain is a complex enterprise consisting of specialized pockets of information as well as a vast number of individuals whose role within the enterprise may be different depending on a certain context or location or both. In order for these individuals to perform their various responsibilities in a productive manner, it is imperative that they have access to the pockets of information that exists within the enterprise. Unfortunately, that information is usually in some ancillary system that is interoperable with any other system in the enterprise and thus making the job of information sharing less than optimal, which, in turn, makes individuals less productive.

Of course, the ideal solution is to have one system for the entire enterprise (not likely to ever be the case) that includes all the necessary ancillary functionality and although many vendors claim such a system and many have tried ultimately, they are expensive, difficult to maintain, extremely difficult to extend and provide general functionality where specialty functionality is needed. Furthermore, the majority of enterprises already have a substantial investment in existing systems. The supply chain management philosophy adaptation is key to the success of Indian pharmaceutical industry in an era of intense global competition.

REFERENCES

1. Arntzen, B.C., Brown, G.G., Harrison, T.P. and Trafton, L. (1995). "Global Supply Chain Management at Digital Equipment Corporation", Prentice Hall.
2. Ballou, R.H. (1992). "*Business Logistics Management*", Prentice Hall, Englewood Cliffs, NJ, Third Edition.
3. Cohen, M.A. and Lee, H.L. (1989). "Resource Deployment Analysis of Global Manufacturing and Distribution Networks", *J. Manufacturing and Operations Management*, Vol. 23, pp. 81-104.
4. Houlihan, J.B. (1985). "International Supply Chain Management. *International Journal of Physical Distribution and Materials Management*", Vol. 15. pp. 22-38.

16

A Study on Performance, Challenges and Opportunities of Indian IT/ITES Industries Export

Mandeep Kaur and Sonal Satish Kakar

Asst Prof., Jayawant Institute of Management Studies, Pune
E-mail: Mandeep.gondara@gmail.com
Lecturer, Jayawant Institute of Management Studies, Pune
E-mail: Kakarsonal2008@gmail.com

ABSTRACT

The growth of IT industry has made a huge impact on economic scene of India; it has now become a significant sector contributing to India's GDP, employment and ancillary industries. Indian IT and ITES companies are extremely profitable and some are stock market pinups. India has emerged as an 'IT super power', especially in the field of software and related services exports. As of now, the export oriented software and service sector has proven as a driving force of Indian IT industry and it is widely held as the engine of growth and earner of foreign exchange. This paper focuses on the study of revenue generated by India through IT sector in terms of exports. The performance of IT exports is elaborated through statistically processed data. This paper also highlights the opportunities and challenges ahead IT exports.

Keywords: Exports, IT/ITES industries, Economy, Foreign exchange.

INTRODUCTION

India is emerging as software hub for many developed as well as developing countries. The IT /ITES industry has contributed to the growth and development of the country in terms of various economic aspects. Scientifically skilled manpower is the one of the biggest advantages of India which is pulling good amount of money through IT firms. BPOs and KPOs as a part of ITES (Information Technology Enabled Services) add more value to IT sector as foreign countries find the good resources (human as well as technical) at the lower costs. India generates good amount of revenue from IT export. IT export includes the export of software, BPO services and KPO services.

SOFTWARE INDUSTRIES

Indian software companies provide the services in the form of developed software as well as maintenance of existing software systems. The current and evolving role of software industry in Indian economy is well established.

BUSINESS PROCESS OUTSOURCING (BPO)

BPO provides customer support services for products and services. The IT BPO sector has become one of the most significant growth catalysts for the Indian economy. This industry is positively influencing the lives of people through an active, direct and indirect contribution to the socio-economic parameters such as employment, standard of living, and women empowerment.

KNOWLEDGE PROCESS OUTSOURCING (KPO)

KPO services include learning solutions, animation design, training, consultancy, legal services, content writing, and business and research solutions, among many subjects. This industry is also fuelling Indian economy through direct and indirect contribution. The Information Technology (IT) and IT enabled services (ITES) industry has become one of the most significant growth catalysts for the Indian economy. Indian economy is the 11th largest economy of the world. The IT/ITES industry has played a significant role in transforming India's image from a slow moving bureaucratic economy to an economy of innovative entrepreneurs in providing world class technology solutions and business services. India has emerged as an 'IT Super power', especially in the field of software and related services export. .Due to export oriented approach, the Indian IT/ITES industry has become the engine of growth in earnings from foreign exchange.

In this paper, we highlight the contribution of IT and ITES industries in the export earnings of the country. We elaborate the opportunities and challenges before IT and ITES industries for export of products and services.

CONTRIBUTION TO INDIAN ECONOMY BY EXPORTS

It is a well known fact that export oriented software and service sector is indeed the driving force of Indian IT industry and it is widely held as the engine of growth and earner of foreign exchange. This segment will continue to show robust growth in future also. Moreover, software export is performing well in terms of its overall contribution to the total export. If export earnings of the industry are considered an indicator of contribution to foreign exchange reserves of the country, the IT/ITES industry has clocked an impressive growth of 31.9% in FY 07.Export earnings for FY 10 stood at approximately USD 46.3 billion as compared to USD 18.3 billion in FY05.

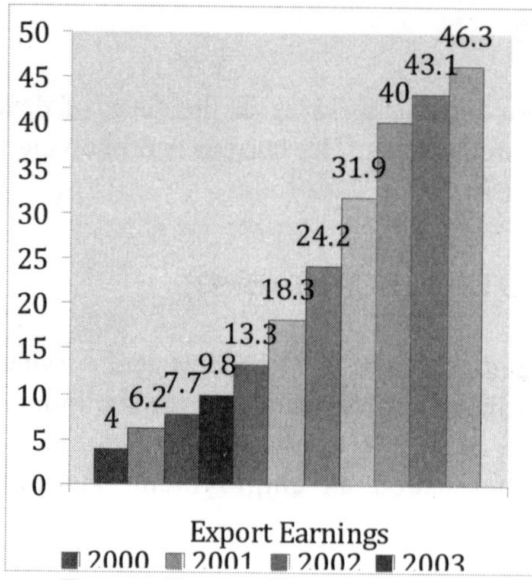

Fig. 1. Export earnings of the IT/ITES industry in USD billions.
Source: NASSCOM

GIANT IT EXPORTERS FROM INDIA

The companies like Tata Consultancy Services Ltd. and Infosys Ltd. have played a vital role for taking India to this height. India has established a definite superiority in software services production. The tremendous growth of Indian IT/ITES export can be attributed to the growing respect for Indian software industry in the international market, continued rise in the offshore services, quality services, timely delivery, entry into new markets, and above all the steps taken by the Indian Government to promote software export such as simplifying procedures, tax concessions, establishments of software technology parks such as STPI and SEZ and more liberal foreign investment policies.

Following are the top 10 IT exporters from India in the year 2010:

Ranking	Company Name
1	Tata Consultancy Services Ltd.
2	Infosys Technologies Ltd.
3	Wipro Ltd.
4	Cognizant Ltd.
5	HCL Ltd.
6	Tech Mahindra Ltd.
7	Mphasis Ltd.
8	Patni Computer Systems Ltd.
9	Aricent Technologies Ltd.
10	L & T Ltd.

SOFTWARE EXPORT CATEGORIZATION

Scientifically skilled manpower is one of the biggest advantages of India which is pulling good amount of money through IT firms. BPOs and KPOs as a part of ITES (Information Technology Enabled Services) add more value to IT sector as foreign countries find the good resources (human as well as technical) at the lower costs. India generates good amount of revenue from IT export.

India exports the software mainly through the sectors like

- Software Product Development
- BPO
- Engineering
- IT & KPO

The share of each of these in the software export for the year 2009-10 is depicted:

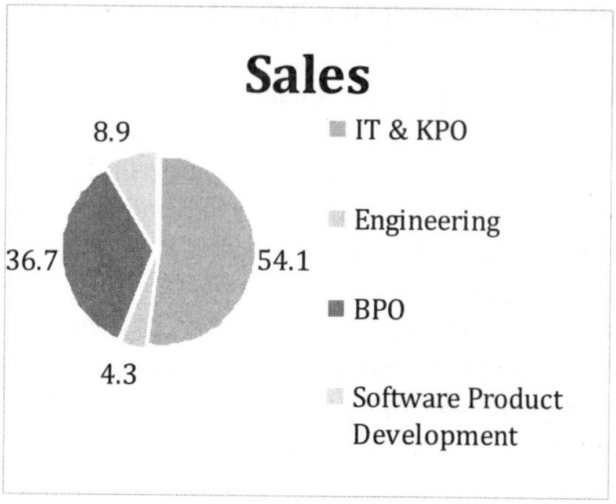

Fig. 2. Sector-wise export by IT/ITES industries.

The above figure shows the total exports from India in the form of IT/ITES services. It includes the contribution from IT & KPO sector which is around 54.1% and next is the contribution by BPO sector (36.7) and the contributions of software product development and Engineering are 8.9% and 4.3% respectively.

CONTINENT-WISE DISTRIBUTION OF SOFTWARE EXPORT

India has become software hub for many Asian as well as European countries. The contribution of Indian software exports to the different continents is shown in the following figure.

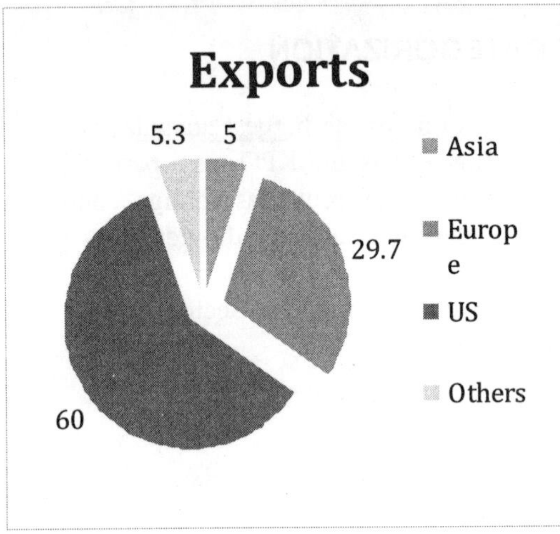

Fig. 3. Continent-wise distribution of IT/ITES exports in 2009-10.

CONTRIBUTION OF IT/ITES INDUSTRY TO GDP

The Indian software and service sector has expanded faster than in any other country of the world of comparable size (Raghavan and Nair, 2001). After independence, Indian IT/ITES industry is the only industry that has shown such a tremendous growth due to its major contribution in Indian exports. In the last two decades, the Indian IT/ITES industry has contributed significantly to Indian economic growth in terms of GDP and foreign exchange earnings by exporting its products and services to the foreign nations.

The contribution of IT/ITES industry in Indian GDP has shown a remarkable increase in the last decade. However, the growth showed slight downfall in financial year 2009 due to global recession but still the economical surveys forecast the upward growth of IT/ITES sector in coming years. This industry will remain a major catalyst in GDP growth of the nation.

EXPORT CHALLENGES AHEAD IT & ITES COMPANIES

Undoubtedly, the building block for the successful endeavour by IT/ITES industry is the widely acclaimed "Global Delivery Model". This business model has helped Indian software companies

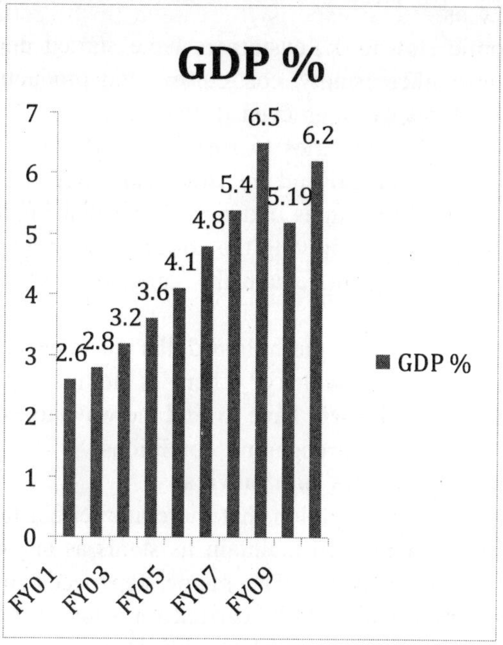

Fig. 4. Contribution of IT/ITES industry to GDP.
Source: NASSCOM

execute software projects, from the simple to complex, for Fortune 500 and other bluechip corporations worldwide from remote and cheaper locations such as India. Offshore outsourcing has gained widespread acceptance in the developed world and the top Indian software companies are riding this wave. Working with this model, the top three companies in the Indian software industry have reached the $1 billion league in revenues. Tata Consultancy Services, the unlisted Tata group company crossed $1 billion (Rs 4,500 crore) in revenues last year, and Infosys and Wipro are on the threshold of entering the one billion dollar club.

In the next phase of growth, say, over the next three to five years, customers are expected to demand a more sophisticated and complex range of services. This is expected to force the top Indian companies to transform themselves into truly global corporations, operating from multiple geographies, employing a multicultural workforce, and across lines of business.

Some of these challenges likely to emerge are:

- **Threat from multinational vendors**

  Since last year, the noise has been growing. The multinational vendors such as IBM Global, Accenture and Computer Sciences Corporation are showing signs of expanding their operations in India, for software services and business process outsourcing.

  As the STPI scheme is going to end up this year. The industries under STPI scheme have to pay huge taxes to the Govt. in terms of customs duty, taxes on earnings from export and corporate taxes. The competition will become hard for domestic companies in the presence of multinational vendors.

- **More IT at Lesser Cost**
  Since the US economic slowdown, customers have started demanding IT products and services at a lesser cost. Increasingly, cost-cutting and productivity benefits have shown upward graph in the export earnings even during recession. But in the coming years, it will become difficult for IT industries to sustain in the same lane as the TAX Holiday given to IT industries is going to end up **this year** under STPI (Software Technology Park India)I. However, the companies under SEZ (Special Economic Zone) can still face these challenges as they will be enjoying the concessions on export earnings till 2020 but the calculation parameters will not remain the same for next ten years.

In the backdrop of these challenges, the billion-dollar question is: Will revenue and margin growth come under pressure for the industry? There is no incompatibility between revenue growth and quality. IT/ITES companies will have to find the ways to export services and products at lower cost along with the survival in changing conditions.

- **Continuous Innovative Practices for Survival**
  The experts are however of the opinion that there are certain things that need to be done in order to make sure that India can maintain its status as one of the leading information technology destination of the world. The major step needs to be taken is to create an environment for innovation that could be carried for a long time. The innovation needs to be done in three areas that are connected to the information technology industry of India such as business models, ecosystems and knowledge. The information technology sector of India also has to spread the range of its activities and also look at the opportunities in other countries. The improvement however, also needs to be qualitative rather than just being quantitative. The skill level of the information technology professionals is one area that needs improvement and presents a considerable amount of challenge before the Indian information technology industry for maintaining its earnings from export.

Opportunities

The World Bank is today rated India as No. 1 by the US people, as far as software outsourcing is concerned. More than 25 per cent of Fortune 1000 companies use India as their software outsourcing centre. UC Berkeley Professor AnnaLee Saxenian, made a study recently and found that somewhere between 27 and 29 per cent of start-ups in Silicon Valley are headed by people of Indian origin. Hotmail, Sycamore, and Exodus are some great examples.

Opportunities for Export of Services by IT/ITES industries

- First, the availability of a large number of professionals who speak English - with a different accent of course, but hopefully reasonably understandable. India has the second largest manpower or talent pool available after the United States. BPOs in India will keep on growing in terms of providing services to countries like USA, U.K. and Germany.
- The attractive wage structure in India is of course a very important point. The average salary for Indian software professional is somewhere around 20 to 25 per cent of the corresponding wages in the US. Therefore, the countries like the USA will continue to outsource the services to India where manpower is required.

- Globalization is also one of the opportunities of exporting services as sourcing the global capital from where it is cheapest, reducing where it is most cost effective, and selling where it is most profitable, without worrying about national boundaries. In keeping with that, the global delivery model reduces the cost to the customer and brings tremendous value. The advantage of globalization are twofold : (1) it is a scalable model because countries like India have a large number of professionals; and (2) it also brings tremendous monetary opportunity for the customer.

Opportunities for Export of Software Products by IT/ITES industries

- The orientation of quality, methodology and technology of Indian companies is yet another important reason why India has been able to grow as a favourite destination in this industry and has got a huge earning by exporting products in foreign nations. In particular, the concept of project management has been extremely well practised in the Indian software industry and created big opportunity for India to handle offshore projects.
- The value proposition of the Indian software industry can be summed up as "faster, better, and cheaper". The Indian companies have taken responsibility on an end-to-end basis for new software development and for re-engineering. Indian software companies have also been very proactive in accepting, embracing, and practising state of the art methodologies and processes; in investing heavily in tools, technology, and infrastructure; in reducing time to market as well as cost; and in improving quality, productivity, and response time. These are the biggest reasons to seek opportunities for growth of exports of software products in India.
- In the new paradigm, the Indian software industries have brought tremendous value in the area of e-commerce. IT companies are getting contracts and exporting products to others nations through e-commerce. All the IT companies can generate huge revenue by doing business in an electronic way.

CONCLUSION

India is emerging as software hub for many developed as well as developing countries. The IT/ITES industry has contributed to the growth and development of the country in terms of various economic aspects. From the statistical analysis, it is evident that IT/ITES sector will work as a catalyst to make India a 'global IT super power'. The share of IT exports in total export and its contribution to GDP has steadily increased over the years. In this paper, along with the export performance of IT sector, we have highlighted the challenges to be faced by IT/ITES industry for exporting products and services. We have also elaborated the opportunities for IT exports in India. By availing opportunities as mentioned in here, the IT industry can earn more from foreign exchange by exporting its products and services.

REFERENCES

1. Arora, A. and Athreya, S. (2002). "The Software Industry and India's Economic Development", Information Economics and Policy, Vol 14, pp. 25-273.

2. Asheref Illiyan, (2005). "Performance, Challanges and Opportunities of Indian Software Export", *J. Theoretical and Applied Information Technology.*
3. Murthy, Narayan, (2000). "The Software Industry in India: Opportunities and Challenges".
4. Thiagarajan, Krishnan, (2004),"Frontline software companies: Challenges in going beyond the billion" in "*The Hindu Business line*".
5. "The Future of Outsourcing – Opportunities and Challenges for India" at http://www.indiun.com
6. "Challenges before Indian IT Industry" at http://www.economywatch.com
7. Debroy, Bilek, Bebl, Ramesh, and Mago, L.D. (1992). "Software Export- World Scenario and Indian Prospects" *Foreign Trade Review*, Vol 27, 2.
8. DIT (Department of Information Technology) (Information Technology Annual Report, 2006-07", Ministry of Information and Communication, Government of India (www.mit.gov.in), 2007.
9. Export Import Bank of India, (1992). "Software-A Sector Study", Occasional paper, Export Import Bank of India, Mumbai.
10. Nasscom, (2008), "Indian IT/ITES Industry: Impacting Economy and Society 2007-08.
11. Nasscom, (2007). "Software Industry in India-A Strategic Review", National Association of Software and Services Companies, New Delhi.

17

Strategic Export Orientation and Internationalization Barriers: Evidence from SMEs in a Developing Economy

M. Dhanabhakyam and V. Anitha

Assistant Professor, Department of Commerce, Bharathiar University, Coimbatore-46
PhD Scholar, Department of Commerce, Bharathiar University, Coimbatore-46,
E-mail: anithavelu_comm@yahoo.in

ABSTRACT

This study examines strategic process and export entry choice of small and medium manufacturing firms in Tamil Nadu. The data were collected from a survey of 72 small and medium-sized manufacturers in Tamil Nadu. Data were analyzed using descriptive statistics, t-test, and Pearson's product moment correlation analysis. Results show that firms' strategic choice to enter the export market was associated with entrepreneurial orientation. Entrepreneurs with high export orientation were exporters and were more involved in the export market than entrepreneurs with low export orientation. Findings also revealed that the most common barriers hampering export development among the firms surveyed include resource constraints, knowledge barriers, corruption, lack of export assistance, and poor infrastructure.

Keywords: Strategic decision, Export orientation, Entry choice, Developing economy.

INTRODUCTION

Internationalization process of many small and medium-sized (SMEs) firms in Tamil Nadu is beset by numerous problems. Many nations have acknowledged the value of small and medium-sized enterprises (SMEs). The benefits of SMEs to any economy are easily noticeable, they include: creation of jobs at relatively low capital cost, a vehicle for reducing income disparities, and development of a pool of skilled and semi-skilled workers. Researchers have argued that promoting SMEs has been described as one of the best strategies for achieving national development goals such as economic and industrial growth. Despite the importance of SMEs and export development in the economic development of sub-Saharan Africa (SSA), scholarly interest in SMEs and export development in the sub-region has not garnered the type of attention it deserves.

Although a great deal of research on SMEs and export development has been conducted, these studies have been primarily conducted in the West. As a result, there has been paucity of research dealing with small enterprises and export development in Africa in general and in Tamil Nadu in particular. Research on this topic has been disappointingly scarce. Since very little research has been done on this topic in Tamil Nadu, there is a knowledge gap in our understanding of this issue with regard to the Tamilian environment. This study attempts to bridge this gap. For SMEs in Tamil Nadu, an awareness of barriers that hamper export involvement and how to deal with those barriers may encourage more SMEs participate in export market. Therefore, this study makes a significant contribution to both practitioners and researchers. This study provides insights to both exporters and non-exporters, as well as to decision makers, that may help to increase performance at the firm level and may be reflected in the nation's macro-economic environment. The purpose of this research, therefore, is to explore export orientation and decision-making processes of SMEs in Tamil Nadu.

LITERATURE REVIEW

An extensive review of the literature reveals that there is substantial interest in the broad issue of business strategy and strategic decision making. Several researchers have asserted that strategic orientation has a powerful influence on both management expectations and organizational performance (Kohli & Jaworski, 1990). Strategic orientation has been described to include many traits including managers'/owners' attitudes towards risk-taking, entrepreneurship, objectivity, assertiveness, and information use (Wood & Robertson, 1997). They argued that an emotional state of a manager's strategic orientation is believed to influence his/her strategy formulation and subsequent decisions. They argued that a manager's strategic orientation affects which specific strategies that he or she would use, value, and bring to fruition. Strategic orientation helps to determine future strategies other organizational strategies such as financial resources, product characteristics, and technological capabilities. In essence, the strategic orientation which managers adopt has a profound effect on what an organization can do and will do, and is associated with the ultimate level of an organization's success.

Knowledge Barriers

Previous studies have shown that export barriers have a major influence on a firm's internationalization process. Aharoni's (1966) study was one of the first studies to explore export barriers. He found, among other things, that lack of knowledge is a major barrier for entry into a foreign market. In another landmark study by Bilkey & Tesar (1977), they found that firms starting export activity face difficulties in identifying opportunities in export markets, also Suarez-Ortega (2003) identified the following as knowledge barriers: lack of awareness of export assistance available to would be exporters, lack of awareness of economic and non-economic benefits of export markets, lack of knowledge of potential markets, lack of qualified staff for export markets, and overall lack of knowledge of how to enter the export market (Suarez-Ortega 2003, p. 409).

Resource Barriers

According to Suarez-Ortega (2003), internal resource constraints refer to the need for a firm to possess resources in order for it to be able to commence export activity. The following factors have been recognized as internal resource barriers: lack of financial resources such as the difficulty in obtaining the necessary funds needed to start export operations. For example, in a study of export barriers in Cyprus, Leonidou (1995) found that one of the barriers facing firms who want to export is how to get the necessary funding to finance export operations. Other researchers have also identified additional barriers as internal constraints that hamper export activity. These include how to obtain and use letters of credit for international transactions, the lack of experienced personnel to devote time to export activities, and banks willing to support firms' international activities.

Hypotheses

H1: Owners/managers of firms with high strategic (proactive) orientation are more likely to be exporters than owners/managers of firms with low strategic (conservative) orientation.

H2: Owners/managers of firms with high export orientation are likely to enter the export market than owner/managers with low export orientation.

H3: Export knowledge barriers within a firm will negatively affect its decision to enter the export market.

H4: Internal resources constraints within a firm will negatively affect its decisions to entry in the export market.

Methodology

This study follows a quantitative research design using a survey method combined with a statistical treatment. A questionnaire was used to elicit responses from (SMEs) in Tamil Nadu. The sample was composed of firms listed in the Manufacturers Association of Tamil Nadu (MAN) export promotion group directory. A random selection of 106 firms from the list was successfully contacted through a letter and fax requesting their participation in the research. The firms identified from the list were personally visited or contacted by telephone for permission to participate in the study. The firms that agreed to take part in the study formed the research sample. To avoid loss and delay due to the weaknesses in the communication and postal system in Tamil Nadu, a drop-off and pick-up method was adopted. This method ensured *Journal of International Business and Cultural Studies* distribution and collection procedures were systematic and controlled by the investigator. A total of 72 usable surveys were received, which provided a response rate of 68%. Of the 72 firms, 38 or (53%) are exporting firms and 34 or (47%) are non-exporting firms.

SURVEY INSTRUMENT

The survey instrument asked questions about the firms' exporting choices, and the firms' attitudes toward exporting. Most questions were asked using the five-point Likert scale. Factor and reliability analyses were used to assure construct validity of the measures for industries selected. All measures were also examined and verified for face validity by six industry executives experienced in exporting and international business, and six university professors who were published authors and have extensive experience teaching and consulting in the areas of international management and marketing.

EXPORT BARRIERS /ORIENTATION QUESTIONNAIRES

Export orientation was measured by the following criteria: (1) I actively look for export market information ;(2) I attend international fairs and export seminars; and (3) management is not interested in exporting, and so forth. The export barrier was measured primarily based on the questionnaire, the respondent was asked to indicate to what extent he/she considered various export barriers to be obstacles to the initiation or expansion of his/her firm's export activity. Five-point Likert scales were used for this purpose, with responses ranging from "not an obstacle" to "major obstacle". Export barriers were measured by the following criteria: (1) Lack of knowledge of best potential markets; (2) Lack of finances for market research; (3) Lack of staff for export planning and (4) Effect of strong foreign competition among others.

FINDINGS

This hypothesis was tested by comparing the mean scores of exporters and non-exporters on export entrepreneurial orientation questionnaire. To conduct the analysis, our sample was split into two exporters and non-exporters for the sole reason of comparison. The results of the t-test of the differences in group mean comparisons are shown in Table 1. The results indicate that the mean scores of owner/managers of firms with high strategic (proactive) orientation were high on strategic orientation of entrepreneurial orientation dimension and were indeed more involved in export than owner/managers of firms who scored low on the export orientation scale. H1 is supported. This result is consistent with previous studies on export literature. Hypothesis 2 speculates that owners/managers of firms with high export orientation are more likely to enter the export market than owners/managers with low export orientation. The results of the mean comparison are shown in Table 1. As shown in Table 2, results indicate that firms with owners/managers who have high entrepreneurial orientation (EO) are more proactive in seeking export markets information and are more likely to attend international trade fairs and export seminars than non-exporters. Results also indicate that proactive entrepreneurs are more likely to initiate export business than firms with owners/managers who have low EO. On the basis of this comparison, hypothesis 2 is confirmed.

To test the third hypothesis, a total of 32 non-exporters were identified from the survey and were asked to rate on a five-point Likert scale (five being very important and one being not important at all) how lack of knowledge about export markets can affect their decision to enter the export market. Results of the data in Tables 2 and 3 indicate that the most important factors are export market knowledge, lack of finance, general lack of knowledge on how to export, lack of export assistance, lack of qualified personnel to plan for export market, and difficulty in handling export documentation requirements. This supports hypothesis two. It is interesting to observe that the least influential factors were corruption and poor infrastructure. One would expect that in a country ridden with corruption and crumbling infrastructure, that these should be ranked in the top five as major obstacles to exporting. However, these findings are consistent with similar results in the export literature.

Appendix

Table 1: T-test of the differences in group means (N = 72)

Variables	N	Mean	SD	DF	t-value
Initiate changes to which our competitors react.					
Exporters	38	4.312	505	70	0.42
Non-exporters	34	2.201	.441		
First to introduce new products/services.					
Exporters	38	3.412	.415	70	0.38
Non-exporters	34	2.101	.331		
We take a very competitive oriented approach					
Exporters	38	4.222	.423	70	0.28
Non-exporters	34	2.301	.311		
We consider new export markets to enter					
Exporters	38	4.412	.305	70	0.32
Non-exporters	34	1.501	.341		
Exporting should not wait for domestic demand					
Exporters	38	1.420	.430	70	0.34
Non-exporters	34	4.641	.417		
Looking for export market information					
Exporters	38	4.616	.301	70	0.42
Non-exporters	34	1.331	.320		
The export market is risky business					
Exporters	38	4.451	.332	70	0.33
Non-exporters	34	4.454	.421		
Opportunities are greater than the risks					
Exporters	38	4.563	.306	70	0.43
Non-exporters	34	1.401	.340		
Accept temporary losses for long-term market share					
Exporters	38	4.631	.362	70	0.30
Non-exporters	34	1.510	.345		
We attend export market seminars and trade fairs					
Exporters	38	4.642	.316	70	0.45
Non-exporters	34	1.749	.124		
We develop new products for export markets					
Exporters	38	4.641	.315	70	0.35
Non-exporters	34	1.506	.203		

To test the third hypothesis, a total of 32 non-exporters were identified from the survey and were asked to rate on a five-point Likert scale (five being very important and one being not important at all) how lack of knowledge about export markets can affect their decision to enter the export market. Results of the data in Tables 2 and 3 indicate that the most important factors are export market knowledge, lack of finance, general lack of knowledge on how to export, lack of export assistance, lack of qualified personnel to plan for export market, and difficulty in handling export documentation requirements. This supports hypothesis two. It is interesting to observe that the least influential factors were corruption and poor infrastructure. One would expect that in a country ridden with corruption and crumbling infrastructure, that these should be ranked in the top five as major obstacles to exporting. However, these findings are consistent with similar results in the export literature.

Appendix

Table 2: Reasons for not exporting (n = 32)

Variables	Mean	Rank
Lack of export market knowledge	4.60	1
Lack of export finance	4.55	2
General lack of knowledge of how to export	4.51	3
Lack of knowledge export assistance	4.49	4
Lack of qualified personnel to plan for export market	4.47	5
Difficulty in handling export documentation requirement	4.45	6
Intense foreign competition	4.36	7
Limited managerial time to deal with exports	4.20	8
Transportation and insurance costs	3.49	9
Language differences (verbal/nonverbal)	3.92	10
Lack of government incentives	3.79	11
Lack of knowledge on how exchange rates work	3.77	12
Corruption	3.76	13
Poor infrastructure	3.74	14

Regarding resource barriers within a firm and how these affect the firm's decisions to enter the export market, Person's correlation method was used to test the fourth hypothesis. The results of the correlations between the four most important variables identified discussed in the literature (lack of support from banks, lack of finance, lack of production capability, and lack suitable staff with export knowledge) and exporters and non-exporters are presented in Table 4. These results indicate that resource constraints, are negatively correlated to non-exporters orientation. This supports hypothesis 4 indicating that resource barriers are obstacles to export development and may influence a firm's decision to not enter the export market.

Appendix

Table 3: Correlation analysis of resource barriers

Resources Barriers	Lack of Support from Banks	Lack of capital to finance export operations	Lack of production capacity	Lack of suitable staff with export knowledge	P
Exporters	.38**	.34**	.32**	.35**	.001
Non-exporters	-.58**	-.54**	-.52**	-.56**	.000

*p < .01 **p < .05 (The correlations are all significantly greater than zero at the .01 and .05 levels).

Discussion

The purpose of this exploratory study is to explore strategic decision processes and export entry choices of SMEs in Tamil Nadu. The results support our hypotheses that entrepreneurs with high export orientation are more likely to enter the export market than entrepreneurs with low export orientation and the decision to enter the export market is negatively associated with the firm's resource constraints and knowledge barriers. The findings suggest that differences exist between low and high involvement exporters.

Although the internal and knowledge resource barriers facing these businesses appear to present common problems regardless of the firm's characteristics, significant differences exist in terms of a firm's decision to enter the export market given its insight of the export barriers. The most common barriers facing all the firms include lack of export knowledge, lack of finance, lack of export assistance, lack of qualified staff, and difficulty in handling export documentation among others. It is surprising to observe that corruption and poor infrastructure were ranked low among thirteen obstacles for not exporting (see Table 2). Tamil Nadu has been identified by Transparency International (2005) as one of the most corrupt **countries** in the world. One would therefore expect that corruption would be ranked among the top barriers to exporting.

Corruption has been identified as a hindrance to small business growth in Tamil Nadu. With regard to poor infrastructure, services such as electricity, telecommunications, roads, and bridges play a critical role in a country's development and are directly and indirectly linked to export success. Poor infrastructure affects export development. Power failures affect production of both export and domestic goods, and slow down services. Condition of roads and bridges, which causes areas to be inaccessible, affects distribution of goods and increases transportation and logistics costs, thus increasing the cost of the products in the international market, making those products relatively expensive and unattractive to the international customers.

CONCLUSION AND IMPLICATIONS

The preceding analysis has demonstrated that Tamil Nadu's small business owners'/managers' decisions to enter the export market is not hitch free, but is plagued by many obstacles of differing severity and significance. This is an issue of paramount importance in the exporting business, since the way these obstacles are perceived by SMEs often determine their future involvement in international business activities.

Results show that owners' or managers' export orientation influences a firm's decision to pursue export development strategy. Several factors were identified as barriers that hinder export development in Tamil Nadu; among them, lack of finance, lack of export knowledge, lack of qualified personnel, and intense foreign competition play a major role in a firm's decision to enter the export market. Various implications derived from the findings of this study concern policy-makers, practitioners, and researchers. With regard to policy- makers, certain policy measures should be taken in order to improve the perceived inhibiting impact of barriers on non-exporters.

Particular emphasis should be given, to the competitiveness of small businesses, the supply of information for the location/analysis of foreign markets and the provision of various tax and other financial incentives. Also, the training and information support services available through the export promotion organizations (EPOs) and organized private sector (OPS) institutions can play a critical role in providing the export knowledge, training, and education needed by SMEs through workshops and seminars.

REFERENCES

1. Barker, A.T. & Kaynak, E. (1992). An empirical investigation of the differences between initiating and continuing exporters. European Journal of Marketing, 26 (3), 27-36.
2. Bilkey, W.J. (1978). An attempted integration of the literature on the export behavior of firms. Journal of International Business Studies, Spring/Summer, pp. 33-46. - Arabian exporters of non-oil products, Journal of Marketing Practice: Applied Marketing Science, 4(7), 187-199.
3. Francis, J, and Collins-Dodd, C. (2000). The Impact of Firms' Export Orientation on the Export Performance of High-Tech Small and Medium-Sized Enterprises, Journal of International Marketing, 8(3) pp 84-103. Journal of International Business and Cultural Studies.
5. Groke, P.O. and Kreidle, J.R. (1967). Export! Why or why not? Managerial attitude and action for small sized business firms, Business and Society, 8, 7-12.
5. Hult G., Snow, C., and Kandemir, D. (2003). The role of Entrepreneurship in Building Cultural Competitiveness in Different Organizational Types. Journal of Management, 29(3), 401-426.

18

Telemedicine's Potential Challenges and Future Diagnosis Renovate of Rural Health in India

M.A. Lalitha Thirupura Sundari and C. Kathiravan

Lecturer in Department of Business Administration, Ph.D. (Part Time Research Scholar), AKD. Dharma Raja Women's College, Rajapalayam

Assistant Professor, Department of Business Administration, Annamalai University, Annamalai Nagar, Tamil Nadu, India

ABSTRACT

It is essential for medical professionals to keep track and organize their patients' medical records. The growing influence of technology, mobile phones and computers, along with the advances in medical devices, is an integral part of healthcare. These technology driven devices are making their way towards becoming essential tools in offices of medical practitioners. With this equipment, record keeping of medical information of patients could be made more efficient, convenient and richer in content, not only including pictures but audio and video records as well. Medical practitioners can take advantage of its technological capacity and geographically extend their practice to be of service to more patients by bringing this to remote areas in India.

INTRODUCTION

India is a vast country of 1.4 billion population occupying an area of 3, 287, 268 sq.km. It consists of 29 states and 6 Union Territories governed by a federal system. There is no national health insurance policy for the country. Government supported healthcare delivery follows Telemedicine, e-health services in India. Telemedicine is the use of information technology and electronic communication to provide clinical services when participants are based at different locations. Telemedicine takes healthcare to remote areas throughout India. It enables health professionals to examine patients by viewing their medical images and records that have been electronically transmitted from one location to another. Telemedicine is a rapidly developing application of clinical medicine where medical information is transferred through interactive audiovisual media for the purpose of consulting, and sometimes remote medical procedures or examinations.

About Telemedicine

Telemedicine is a method, by which patients can be examined, investigated, monitored and treated, with the patient and the doctor located in different places. Telemedicine is an upcoming field in health sector. It may be as simple as two health professionals discussing medical problems of a patient and seeking advice over telephone to as complex as transmission of electronic medical records of clinical information, diagnostic tests such as E.C.G., radiological images, etc., and real time interactive medical video conference with the help of IT based hardware and software video conference using broadband telecommunication media provided by satellite network.

Review of Concepts

According to World Health Organization, telemedicine is defined as "The delivery of healthcare services, where distance is a critical factor, by all healthcare professionals using information and communication technologies for the exchange of valid information for diagnosis, treatment and prevention of disease and injuries, research and evaluation and for continuing education of healthcare providers, all in the interests of advancing the health of individuals and their communities."

Objective of the Study

The main objective is to provide healthcare facilities to rural and remote areas

To find out quality health services.

- To lessen the inconvenience and cost of patient transfers.
- To discover our unnecessary travel time for health professionals.
- To evaluate rural practice by upgrading their knowledge through tele-education.
- To unearth and facilitate patients and rural practitioners to have access to specialist health services and support.

Barriers of Telemedicine

1. Licence problem from state to state.
2. Malpractice from different states and country-wise like licensure.
3. Higher quality resolution and greater capacity for image (bandwidth), result in higher costs.
4. As distinct from face-to-face consultations services payment.
5. Lack of trained manpower.

Applications in Rural Area

70% of Indians live in villages, more than 75% of Indian doctors are based in cities. Rural Indians lack access to basic healthcare facilities. In addition, poor Indian villagers spend most of their ou\t-of-pocket health expenses on travel to the specialty hospitals in the city and for staying in the city along with their escorts. To avoid such difficulties, ISRO has established such network as Telemedicine is a way to bridge the rural urban health divide. This network has enabled thousands of patients in remote places such as Jammu and Kashmir, Andaman and Nicobar Islands, the Lakshadweep Islands, and tribal areas of the all regions of India to gain access to consultations with experts in super specialty medical institutions. Telemedicine may turn to be the cheapest and fastest way to the rural India.

Some other fields using Telemedicine are:

- Teleradiology
- Telecardiology
- Telesurgery
- Telepsychiatry
- Teleneurology
- Telepathology

Current Efforts

Telemedicine programmes are actively supported by

a) Department of IT
b) ISRO
c) Apollo Hospitals
d) Asia Heart foundation.
e) State government

Current Scenario of Telemedicine in India

There are more than 150 telemedicine initiatives today. Most of it are supported by ISRO & IT ministry. On an average close to 6 (range of 2-10) telemedicine encounters take place per day in each of these centres. These figures are very low considering the dearth of healthcare services in India.

Specific activities in E-health in India: HIS (Health Information System) available

Although a large number of products are available in the market, the major players in this field, are WIPRO,TCS and Siemens Information Systems Ltd. in developing HIS Solution in India.

MATURITY OF TECHNOLOGY

Benefits for Healthcare Delivery System to Patients and Healthcare Professionals

Healthcare in rural India

- 70 % of India's population lives in rural areas.
- Lack of investment in healthcare in rural areas.
- 90% of secondary and tertiary care facilities are in cities and towns.
- Low penetration of healthcare services.
- Inadequate medical facilities in rural areas.
- Problem of retaining doctors in rural areas specially the specialist doctors.
- Rural and remote areas continue to suffer from absence of quality healthcare services.

India is ideal setting for IT assisted healthcare

It is feasible to set up a national health grid to be shared by healthcare providers, trainers and beneficiaries taking the advantage of a strong fibre backbone and indigenous satellite communication technology with large trained manpower in this sector. The groundwork on telemedicine has also been established by ISRO, DIT, state governments and specialty institutes/hospitals. National rural telemedicine network will help to provide quality healthcare where there is none and will improve healthcare where there is some.

FINDINGS

- **Better patient management**
  Peripheral devices can also be attached to computers or the video-conferencing equipment which can aid in an interactive examination. With the availability of better and cheaper communication channels, direct two-way audio and video streaming between centres through computers is leading to lower costs.
- **Increased involvement in care**
  The concept of connected health, or telemedicine, extends healthcare beyond the traditional confines of hospitals and doctors' offices to our everyday surroundings. The availability of technology in the home, our aging population, and the dramatic increase of patients with chronic diseases, such as hypertension, diabetes, and obesity, are some of the factors fueling increased interest and growth in connected health.
- **Overall cost stabilization**
  The original initiative started as a telephone link that allowed specialists to consult with attending physicians at two affiliated community hospitals to stabilize patients in the critical care unit prior to transferring them to the main hospital.
- **Connected to patients, who are more educated (provider physician/nurse)**
  Patients are more educated by the doctors how they want to take care by themselves for kind of diseases (by the various state of doctors-remote area).
- **More control of time**
  They are often located in areas where telemedicine is the only way to diagnose and treat

them. The fact is that telemedicine can go anywhere as it is both versatile and effective.

- **Proposition**
  In a few rural-remote areas telemedicine had reached, government have to take more steps to cover all regions.
- **Should reduce video conferencing payment**
  Reimbursement of services by insurers is an area of concern. System related to the payment of consultations by interactive video need to be framed (taking into consideration national policy).
- **Appoint trained consultant**
  Trained employees should be appointed so that they can make less mistakes. If the employees are skilled they will not go off any gaffe while giving patient's details, medical information and video conferencing.
- **Should have Ethical practice**
  Government authorized telemedicine should operate with a will to diminish malpractices. Basic rights of patients to privacy of their medical informationmust be upheld. Patients' privacy should be observed unless waived for a valid reason.
- **Prestige's company should get aware about E-health services**
  IT workers are affected by diseases (like back pain etc.) they can get ideas from e-health. This reduces the patient's expenses and by adopting the telemedicine it saves the patient's time. This awareness should create to the companies,etc., WIPRO Health Services.

CONCLUSION

Telemedicine will soon be just another way to see a healthcare professional just as seeing video conferencing also opens up new possibilities for continuing education for rural health practitioners, who may not be able to leave a rural practice to take part in professional meetings. People can be anywhere, 99% of healthcare problems can be managed by the doctors staying at a remote place-linked by telemedicine.

REFERENCES

1. Ganapathy, K. and Aditi Ravindra, (2007). Healthcare for Rural India: Is Telemedicine the solution?: *J. e-health technology and application,* vol 5, No 3 pp. 203- 207.
2. Kapoor, Lily, Basnet, Rajesh, Chand, Repu Daman, Singh Sandeep, Pradhan Varad, Durgapal, Mishra, S.K. (2007). Analysis of Telemedicine Project deployed in sub Himalayan Region in the Indian State of Uttaranchal: Journal of e-health Technology and Application 5(2): 169-173.
3. Mahapatra, A.K. and Mishra, S.K. (2007). Bridging the knowledge and skill gap in Healthcare: SGPGIMS, Lucknow India initiatives, *J. e-health Technology and Application.* 5(2):67-69.
4. Ganapathy, K. (2004). Telemedicine in the management of Head Trauma: An overview: Indian Journal of Neurotraumatology; 1: 1-74.
5. Kim, M.I. and Johnson, K.B. (2002). Personal health records: evaluation of functionality and utility. *In: J. American Medical Informatics Association* 9: pp. 171-180.
6. Porter, S.C., Kohane, I.S. and Goldmann, D.A. (2005). Parents as Partners in obtaining the medication history. *J. American Medical Informatics Association* 12(3): pp. 299-305.
7. Sharma, D.C. (2000). Remote Indian villages to benefit from telemedicine project, Lancet 355: 1529 Available: www.thelancet.com Accessed 31 Jan 2011. Find this article online.

8. BBC News (2005 February 28) India Unveils antipoverty budget. Available: news.bbc.co.uk. Accessed 31 Jan11
9. ISRO Annual Report 2004-2005: Space Appilcations, Available: www.isro.org. Accessed 31 Jan 2011
10. Chougule, A. (2007). Radiation dose to contralateral breast during treatment of breast malignancy by radiotherapy. *J. Cancer Res. Ther.* 3(1): pp. 8-11.
11. Thulasi, Bai. V. and Srivatsa, S.K. (2007). Design of wearable cardiac telemedicine system, *Int. J. Electron Health.* 3(3): 303-316.
12. George, J.T., Rozario, K.S., Abraham, A. (2007). A Survey in India of doctors' knowledge, attitudes and practice regarding telemedicine and e-health. *J. Telemed Telecare*, 13(6): 322.
13. Introduction to Telemedicine, www.greenstar.org.
14. Telemedicine Station, www.webhealthcentre.com
15. Telemedicineconcepts and requirements, www.medindia.net
16. Telemedicine: Applications, www.telemedconsultant.com
17. Centre for Telemedicine. www.ttuhsc.edu/telemedicine

19

Footwear Cluster Facing the New Competition and Challenges in Agra

Nimeesha Pathak and Ravi Kant Pathak

Assisstant Professor, Department of Management Studies, Anand Engineering College, Agra (U.P).
E-mail: nimeeshapathak@gmail.com
Assisstant Professor, Department of Management Studies, Anand Engineering College, Agra(U.P).
E-mail: pathakravikant@yahoo.co.in

ABSTRACT

Agra has been one of the important centres of shoe production in India since medieval Mughal era, having around 80,000 skilled workers and providing employment to around two lakh persons. This paper examines how producers in a traditional Indian cluster have responded to major recent changes in internal and external markets. It shows that in a heterogeneous cluster such as Agra the answer differs by market channel. The paper investigates how specific groups of producers in particular market channels have prospered while many other producers have closed down or face ever more desperate conditions in the market channel of the last resort.

Keywords: Heterogeneous cluster; Export shoes market; Competitive environment.

INTRODUCTION

Agra is the headquarters of the Divisional Commissioner and SISI with a large area adjacent to it has been one of the premier centres of trade and industry from time immemorial. Agra for a quite long time was also the capital of the country. As back as in 15th century, foundry industry of the region was quite developed.

Leather footwear of Agra is known all over the world for superb craftsmanship. Fully handmade shoes are class apart. No other place in the world does this trade related activity in a day more than Agra. Whooping 90 million per annum production is cost effective too. Apart from catering the best requirement of domestic market, footwear and shoe uppers being exported to Europe and other foreign countries. Garments, purses, valets, belts are other products of leather known for craftsmanship and quality. The range is wide and price/cost is reasonable.

Importance of Clustering

In the present industrial scenario the researchers have highlighted the opportunities created by networking among enterprises located in geographical proximity, i.e., industrial clusters. This process of networking and clustering substantially contributes to the competitiveness, growth, technological dynamism and efficiency of the participating firms. The evidence suggests that horizontal collaboration between small and medium sized enterprises yields collective efficiency in the form of reduced transaction costs, accelerated innovation through rapid problem solving and greater market access. Besides positive externalities are generated by agglomerations through the availability of:

I. Skilled labour and inputs
II. Creation types of infrastructure
III. Innovation generating informal exchanges

Further, political and social institutions along with various policies can play a crucial role in supporting the emergence and development of such a network. In fact, in most of the European success stories of networking in industrial clusters regional and local governments played crucial role. The available evidence of developing countries like China, Korea, etc., also suggests that clustering and networking help small and medium sized firmed (SMEs) to raise their competitiveness.

The Indian Leather Industry

The Indian leather industry occupies a place of prominence in the Indian economy in view of its substantial export earnings, employment generation and growth. There has been increasing emphasis on its planned development, aimed at optimum utilization of available raw material for maximizing the returns particularly from exports. India is the largest livestock holding country with 34% of large animals and 23% of small animals. The export of leather and leather products increased manifold over the past decades. The export increased from Rs. 28 crore in 1956-1957 and from Rs. 3056 crore in 1991-1992 to Rs. 9624 crore in 2003-2004 and 27,465 crore in 2009-2010. Today the industry ranks 6th in the export trade in terms of foreign exchange earnings of the country. The value added finished products presently constitute around 85% of the total exports from the industry, which were 7% in 1956-1957.

The major production centres for leather and leather products are located in Tamil Nadu, West Bengal, Uttar Pradesh, Punjab, New Delhi, Haryana and Mumbai. India produces 3 billion sq ft of leather annually. This industry can be classified in five groups as tanning & finishing, footwear & components, leather garments, leather goods, saddlery and harness articles.

Indian exports of leather and leather products for five year during 2005-2006 to 2009-2010 are given below:-

(value in Million US$)

Category	April-March				
	2005-2006	2006-2007	2007-2008	2008-2009	2009-2010
Finished leather	587.82	623.42	734.20	798.13	825.38
Leather footwear	542.19	555.39	610.30	643.18	743.72
Non-leather Footwear	156.09	159.17	189.94	233.27	245.82
Footwear Components	310.28	460.45	378.75	272.08	295.00
Leather garments	378.72	443.76	421.46	435.36	433.48
Leather goods	54.11	52.66	49.64	43.66	51.94
Saddlery	138.80	124.61	141.15	145.04	155.16
Harness	71.12	76.14	84.02	88.68	92.00
Leather gloves.39	136.23	124.11	139.22	144.34	156.12
Total	2438.4	2673.92	2825.76	2870.76	3081.93

*source survey in 2010

Brief Description of Indian Footwear Industry

The Indian leather footwear industry has undergone remarkable changes during the last three decades, with the large raw material reserves, access to large supply of labour and management. The factory sector of the footwear industry has made rapid strides in the production and export of shoe uppers and full shoes. The government's, trade and industrial policies, institutional support, coupled with progressive entrepreneurship growing demand for export and domestic demand have been the major factors contributing its growth. The clinical changes in the footwear manufacture have brought about traceable and tangible mechanization in the industry. The footwear industry in India is the second largest employer in the country. As per the estimated data available the production capacity of the footwear are as follows:

S.No.	Product	Production (Capacity)
1.	Leather footwear	897 million pairs
2.	Leather shoe uppers	324 million pairs
3.	Non-leather footwear	997 million pairs

Using the market channel approach, this paper provides a dynamic and disaggregated view of how heterogeneous clusters develop. Moreover, this approach enables us to address what is still a key question in the small enterprise development debate: "The issue is not whether small enterprises have growth and employment potential but under what conditions" (Schmitz, 1982, p. 445). The cluster literature has brought us a step forward, as it indicates that clustered small enterprises, as compared to dispersed small enterprises, may indeed stand a better chance to experience evolutionary growth (Schmitz, 1995, 1999).

The market channel approach stresses the need to differentiate within clusters. It shows how growth opportunities fundamentally differ for specific groups of clustered firms within distinct market channels. Therefore, the market channel approach provides us with a more detailed understanding of why some clustered firms may be able to grow, while others merely survive or die.

The paper

- Outlines the market channel approach.
- Introduces some of Agra's cluster characteristics.
- Presents a subsector map of Agra and compares Agra's main market channels.
- Discusses the main changes and how these changes have altered the cluster's composition.
- Presents the cluster level data.
- Shows which firms in Agra have increased interfirm cooperation during and examines whether those firms have also performed better.
- Investigates how different groups of firms in particular market channels have responded to the changes.

The Agra Cluster and its Market Channels in 2011

This section presents the composition of the Agra footwear cluster in 2010-2011, just before the impact of the major changes mentioned above. It introduces the cluster, presents a subsector map, and compares producer-trader relations in the various market channels.

(a) **Cluster characteristics:** Agra, India's most diverse as well as most tightly knit footwear cluster, is a prime example of an artisanally rooted low-tech cluster with predominantly small producers. In 2010-2011 some 70,000 workers, employed in around 5,000 mostly informal small-scale units, produced approximately 3,00,000 pairs of shoes per day. Agra's competitiveness is squarely based on its cheap, abundantly available and skilled artisanal labour. Entrepreneurs can and do draw upon this specialized and flexible labour pool at a moment's notice. Artisans frequently (have to) move from one workshop to another, and also alternate roles as piece-rate factory worker, unpaid family labourer, and running their own home-based unit. Agra's other main local advantage is its central position in the Indian footwear distribution network. With around 250 buyers of shoes, Agra provides producers relatively easy access to substantial markets in all parts of India. Producers also have relative easy access to all sorts of small inputs at short notice. There exists a nourishing industry of input suppliers, like manufacturers of lasts, of all sorts of tools, leather board, carton boxes, etc. Concentrated in one area of the city one could and, in 2010, around 275 shops selling leather, and some 175 shops selling other inputs (PVC soles, laces, counters and stifeners, chemicals, etc.). Moreover, a large variety of agents and dealers for machines, insurance or transport facilities swarm around Agra.

(b) Agra's main market channels notwithstanding its specialization in producing cheap hand-made leather-upper shoes, a wide variety of footwear is produced in Agra for very distinct market segments. Specific producers predominantly manufacture footwear in a narrow price-quality range for just one particular market channel.

We characterize producer-trader relations in the main market channels (see Table 1). This characterization continues to be relevant because the qualitative differences between market channels have remained remarkably stable, in spite of major changes in the overall composition of the cluster in recent years. Any account of producer-trader relations in the Agra footwear industry inevitably starts.

Table 1: Market channel characteristics in Agra footwear industry

Market channel characteristics	Direct Sales	Local traders	Premium domestic	Indirect exports	Direct exports
Type of product unit	Household family labour	Household workshop	Small scale factories	Small scale factories	Small scale factories
Employment per unit	3-5	3-9/9-18	20-50	20-50 & above	200 & above
Sample making, setting of product specification	No samples made	Set by local traders	Initiative by traders, joint development	Set by foreign buyer	Mostly set by foreign buyer
Price setting	Bargaining after production	Bargaining before production	Bargaining in ongoing relation	Set by foreign buyer	Bargaining in ongoing relation
Cooperation between producer and traders	Extremely limited	Limited	High	Very limited	High
Trust between producer and traders	Extremely limited	Limited	Very High	Very limited	Very High
Growth options	Extremely limited	Limited	Very High	High	Very High

With the hereditary occupational structure that follows from the caste system, footwear workers are predominantly Jatavs, a subgroup of the Chamars, and only those born as Chamars "can occupy the status of shoemaker without breaking caste rules" (Lynch, 1969, p. 15). Chamars are found close to the bottom of the caste hierarchy, because they work with leather, a task considered highly polluting in orthodox Hinduism (Khare, 1984; Sharma, 1986). For Agra Jatavs, making shoes is: "..more than a caste occupation; it is a family affair and a way of life" (Lynch, 1969, p. 47). By contrast, traders are predominantly forward caste Hindus born in Punjab or Sindh, Sikhs and some well-to-do Muslims. Most of the influential trading families came from Punjab or Sindh at the time of Partition (1947) and took over positions previously held by Muslim traders. Relations between artisans and traders have since then become more antagonistic (Lynch, 1969; Knorringa, 1999). Therefore, and like many other craft-based industrial cities in South Asia, Agra is characterized by a deep rooted caste-based chasm between an artisanal community that makes, and a trading community that sells local traders are concentrated in the Hingki-Mandi market, the main node in the subsector map, where "... large volumes of product pass through.... restricted geographical space (Boomgard et al., 1992, p. 201). The construction of this central market, at the beginning of the 20th century, solidified the key role of the Agra cluster in the Indian footwear distribution network. Even today, local traders, who deal mainly in basic and cheap footwear, follow two buying strategies: direct sales or transaction on prior order.

(i) Direct sales

In 2011 around 1,800 of the smallest home-based units, run by artisans and using primarily family labour, depended on direct sales. In our 2011 survey, of the artisans who rely on direct sales, 75% transact exclusively with Hing-ki-Mandi traders, and an even larger total of 86% predominantly conduct their transactions on Hing ki Mandi. Traders buy the standardized ready-made shoes from artisans on the spot. As all artisans know which subset of traders may buy particular designs in a specific season and many try their luck. The pierce price haggling is aggravated, first, because artisans need to sell before they can initiate another round of production, and, second, by the caste-based antagonism leading to high levels of ascribed distrust between forward caste traders and "untouchable" Jatav artisans.

(ii) Working on order for local traders

The second main market channel deals with a pool of more than 2,000 owners of small and medium-sized workshops who work on order for local traders. The smaller workshops usually get orders for rather cheap shoes from local wholesalers, while a few of the medium sized workshops are able to get orders for somewhat more fashionable and more expensive shoes. The extent of cooperation with local traders varies by market segment. With small orders for standard cheap shoes, local traders can and do threaten Jatav artisans to "throw" them back into the faceless crowd of direct sales artisans. Producer-trader relations are basically as antagonistic as with direct sales, even though artisans desperately try to build up some earned trust. Our 2011 survey shows that artisan entrepreneurs are almost exclusively involved in direct-sales and cheap and small local orders. In the medium-quality segment owners of somewhat larger workshops usually have a trader's background. Since the early 1970s these trader-entrepreneurs have set up an increasing number of somewhat larger workshops and small-scale factories, in which Jatav artisans are employed on piece rates (Misra, 1980). Step by step, these entrepreneurs have built up trust with local traders, with whom they share a roughly similar socio-economic status. Cooperation may emerge when entrepreneurs feel confident enough, and are skilful enough, to participate in setting product specifications.

(iii) Premium domestic market

By 2011, a few hundred entrepreneurs (18% of all entrepreneurs in the 2011 survey who worked for domestic traders) had outgrown the local traders and directly supplied boutiques for the well-to-do in the metropolitan areas. In this premium, fashion-driven, segment traders and manufacturers frequently need to adjust product specifications overnight. Such an ability to incorporate quickly last minute changes is a prerequisite for success in this volatile segment. Even though traders remain more powerful, producer-trader relations in this premium domestic segment are, relatively speaking, based on close cooperation and a build-up of both ascribed and earned trust. Another group of around 100 producers supplied the premium domestic market segment by working for one of the powerful and well paying large Indian footwear concerns, such as Bata India and Liberty. Supplying entrepreneurs, part of the local footwear elite, often share a similar socio-economic background with purchasing officers, but must first and foremost guard (if not deepen) their laboriously built up earned trust. These large Indian footwear concerns demand continuous high-quality performance. Cooperation remains a rather one-way traffic, since most decisions on product specifications are taken at the headquarters of these large Indian footwear concerns.

(iv) Indirect exports

The indirect export boom to the Soviet Union started in the early 1980s when a small group of Punjabi families, organized in large enterprise groups, secured bulk orders through high government channels in Delhi and Moscow. Apart from the work done in units belonging to these enterprise groups themselves, they also subcontracted especially upper making to around 50 larger workshops on a regular basis. Two out of the five large enterprise groups also served the domestic market with own brand names in the medium-quality segment. In the later part of the 1980s an increasing number of entrepreneurs of independent workshops obtained orders through local representatives of Indian-based export-trading houses. In turn, these Indian traders took orders from an array of foreign buyers who rigidly set product specifications of extremely cheap imitations of previously successful designs for the Soviet Union and also for the lowest-priced market segments in Western Europe. By 2011, at the height of this type of heavily subsidized exports, five purchasing officers in Agra supplied bulk orders to around 275 larger workshops and small-scale factories.

Especially in this market channel, a limited number of large buyers can be seen as nodes in the subsector map where: ... large volumes of product pass through a few hands... (Boomgard et al., 1992, p. 201). Many indirect exporters, without any footwear know-how and thus unable to secure access to other market channels, depended fully on one particular guardian purchasing officer. Without the need for professional cooperation, because product specifications were set and materials supplied, purchasing officers selected entrepreneurs purely on their ascribed characteristics and willingness to provide favours.

(v) Direct exports

Relations with the highest degree of cooperation were found in the fifth and last market channel, where exporters deal directly with foreign buyers from Europe or the United States. In 2011, Agra's top quality shoes were produced by some 25 direct exporters (0.5% of manufacturing units in Agra). They needed to cooperate intensively on fashion oriented sample making, and guard their trust build-up very carefully. To operate successfully so far apart, without opportunities for surprise visits, earned trust is a must. In such relations, interdependency is not a question, but a point of departure, as they build on each other's capabilities. Nevertheless, this leaves unchanged that foreign buyers are more powerful.

(c) Engrained differentiation per market channel

To summarize the market channel description above, my earlier fieldwork confirmed the hypothesis that producer-trader relations in more quality-competitive and fashion-driven market channels are characterized by closer cooperation and higher build-up of earned trust (Knorringa, 1996). Producers with more interdependent relations with traders were also better able to secure regular orders (Knorringa, 1996, pp. 120-123). Moreover, and perhaps most importantly, producers in the more interdependent market channels experienced more regular growth. Obviously, within particular market channels the question of who flourishes and who goes bankrupt is determined by survival of the fittest, and by who is the most knowledgeable and/or the most shrewd. Nevertheless, a tentative calculation of gross and net margins that producers realize in distinct market channels (Knorringa, 1996, pp. 193-195) shows that options for growth are significantly better in market channels with a higher degree of cooperation. Finally, a few firms were able to 'graduate' to more attractive market channels (Knorringa, 1996, pp. 144-145). Put together, in 2011 the Agra cluster consisted of five clearly distinct market channels. The next section examines the impact of the new challenges on the various channels.

The Changing Cluster Compostion: 2006-2011

This section discusses the main challenges put to Agra's footwear industry during 2006-11, and shows how these changes have significantly altered the cluster composition. Looking back, 2006 was a turning point: a break with the past that opened up new opportunities and posed new threats. The most sudden and dramatic change was the collapse of the Soviet Union, which had been Agra's main and easy to satisfy export market for decades. Very rapidly this seemingly solid export market vanished. Moreover, in 2006 economic liberalization in India began to take hold. Step by step, import tariffs were lowered and regulations relaxed, making it easier to import both non-leather components crucial for premium export quality, and to import machines. Simultaneously, export subsidies were lowered. By 2011 it had become clear that Agra's exporters were facing increasingly tough international competition. They had not been able to get out of the especially competitive and price-driven international market segment, and they had lost their previous margin of export subsidies. Moreover, buyers in the price-driven segment have raised quality standards and can choose from an increasing number of potential suppliers. The second process of change is the growing premium domestic market segment. Not only is the size of this market segment increasing but also prices more than doubled over 2006-11.

The common outcome of the turning point is that Agra's producers face higher quality requirements, more exacting markets, and tougher competition. Reacting to a turning point however, is a process that takes time. In 2006-2011 nobody in Agra seemed concerned about quality and speed, in 2007-2008 a few entrepreneurs talked about it but had not yet taken any concrete steps, while in 2011 many had started improving quality and speeding up deliveries. A sample survey among footwear producers in Agra in 2011 indicates that the majority of producers still in operation in 2011 have started to respond to the more exacting demands. But, many firms died in the period 2006-2011. The remainder of this section shows how the size of the cluster (in terms of employment) shrank and how its composition (in terms of employment by market channel) changed.

Changes in Inter-firm Cooperation and Performance

Notwithstanding the importance of distinguishing between market channels, it is also important not to lose sight of the fact that there was a challenge common to all market channels: The need to raise quality and speed up response time. This section shows how the cluster has responded. It presents cluster level data from a stratified random sample of 60 producers in Agra, carried out in February 2011. The survey was conducted to ascertain whether producers in Agra have responded to the common challenge by increasing interim cooperation. Moreover, it was hypothesized that increases in inter-firm cooperation are positively correlated with a strong performance. All questions related to changes over time used the start of economic liberalization in India. Changes in cooperation and performance were assessed by using an ordinal scale with three or five categories: "Decreased (a lot/ a little)," "No Change," "Increased (a little/ a lot)." In interpreting the results from the 2011 survey it is important to mention that home based units relying on the overcrowded direct sales channel were not included and that only firms in operation in February 2011were interviewed, i.e., survivors from 2006 or newly started or restarted firms.

The survey results are presented in three steps. Our first line of enquiry was to establish whether producers in Agra have responded at all. The survey shows that most firms have indeed started to respond to the common challenges. In all, 90% of sample firms have increased average quality of products, while 93% increased the average speed of response time. Most firms increased cooperation with buyers on quality control, though more often in the export sector (94%) than in the domestic sector (55%). Moreover, they have also increased cooperation with suppliers on typical New Competition parameters like quality improvement (in 90% of the cases with leather suppliers; in 86% of the cases with sole suppliers), and speeding up deliveries (92% with leather suppliers; 88% with sole suppliers).

The second line of enquiry investigates whether producers have increased cooperation with buyers, suppliers and other local producers. The first indicator deals with changes in stability of inter-firm relationships. Producers were asked whether they now more frequently changed, for example, their leather suppliers. Table below shows that a clear majority of sample firms have increased stability in vertical relationships with leather and sole suppliers, as well as with buyers. In contrast, most producers did not increase stability in relationships with subcontractors. The second indicator of increased inter-firm cooperation was compiled as follows. In the questionnaire we distinguished four types of inter-firm relationships: "bilateral horizontal" (relationships with other local producers),"backward-supplier" (relationships with suppliers of inputs like leather and soles), "backward-subcontracting" (relationships with local subcontractors) and "forward" (relationships with buyers).

Table 2: Changes in stability in inter-firm cooperation, 2006-2011 (percentage of firms)

Cooperation with	Decreased		No change	Increased		Total
	A lot	A little		A little	A lot	
Leather suppliers	–	2	25	63	10	n = 60
Sole suppliers	–	2	23	58	17	n = 59
Subcontractors	–	–	89	9	2	n = 58
Domestic buyers	3	5	19	68	5	n = 38
Export buyers	–	3	6	91	–	n = 32

Table 2: Composite indicators of changes in inter-firm cooperation, 2006-2011 (percentage of firms)

Cooperation with	Decreased		No change	Increased		Total
	A lot	A little		A little	A lot	
Bilateral-horizontal	3	5	47	31	14	N = 59
Backward-supplier	–	–	5	12	83	N = 58
Backward-subcontracting	–	2	48	17	33	N = 58
Forward	–	–	10	32	58	N = 60

Responses by Market Channel

The previous sections showed changes in the composition of the cluster and in the extent of cooperation in inter-firm relationships. This section focuses on changes within particular market channels to identify more precisely the profile of strong and weak performers. Apart from the already introduced 2011 survey, this section also draws upon in-depth interviews with key informants from each market channel.

The strong performers are found in particular among direct exporters (73%) and premium domestic suppliers (72%). In contrast, only 19% of producers for local traders display strong performance. Indirect exporters are partly strong performers (62%) and partly weak performers (38%). Five out of the nine weak performers in the sample are indirect exporters, together with two workshops in the domestic market and one direct exporter. Moreover, Table 4 shows a statistically significant relationship between the main market channel of a producer and its performance, based on a qualitative ordering of market channels in line. The remainder of this section focuses first on producers for the domestic market and then on exporters.

(a) **Producers for domestic markets:** The informal home-based units relying on direct sales were not represented in the 2011 survey. Field impressions indicate an increasingly overcrowded direct-sales segment, but also increased differentiation.

Previous employees of larger workshops, pushed back into this segment of last resort, run home-based units that produce a significantly higher quality and appear to do good business, especially in selling directly to consumers. Also in other segments of the domestic market the crowding out effect has led to increased differentiation. For example, producers selling to local traders that have not been able to upgrade, now face direct and tough competition from previous suppliers to premium domestic demand or former indirect exporters. Even in the growing premium domestic market segment, with 72% of strong performers in our 20011 sample, two particular groups of firms present in this segment in 2006 have at least partly been squeezed out. First, large Indian concerns lost their strong market position because they were not able to adequately respond to the increasingly volatile and exacting demand. This has led to declining orders for producers in Agra.

Second, mainly because the premium domestic market has become increasingly similar to international demand, direct exporters have invaded its upper segment. Therefore, the premium-domestic suppliers from 2006 now have to compete with, and have at least partly been squeezed out by, former suppliers of the large Indian concerns and direct exporters.

(b) **Producers for export markets:** The export market for Agra's producers is clearly differentiated between indirect and direct exports, as was shown in earlier sections. Therefore, these two market channels are discussed separately.

I. INDIRECT EXPORTS

Indirect exporters were most suddenly and severely hit. After the collapse of the Soviet Union, very few indirect exporters have been able to respond adequately and find alternative market channels at short notice. The first generation Punjabi entrepreneurs, running four out of the five large enterprise groups, had for decades successfully relied on their contacts with high placed government offcials in Delhi and Moscow and were considered unassailable powerhouses in early 2006.

Performance per market channel in Agra's footwear industry, 2006-2011 (percentage of firms)

Performance	Local traders	Indirect exports	Premium domestic	Direct exports	Total
Poor	12	38	7	7	16
Average	69	-	21	20	29
Strong	19	62	72	73	55
	100%	100%	100%	100%	100%
	N=16	N=13	N=14	N=15	N=58

By 2009, one large enterprise group had successfully penetrated other markets, one had gone out of business, and the third just kept its head above water, but had gone under by 2011. Moreover, all five large enterprise groups stopped giving out labor-intensive subcontracting work to larger workshops, forcing them to move back into the domestic market. The usually young owners of larger workshops supplying shoes to the local purchasing offices of international trading houses were even harder hit. They were not able, and often not interested in gaining access to other market channels. Most of them, seeing this market channel as an easy way to earn rents, left the footwear industry altogether. Only entrepreneurs with at least some footwear know-how and with larger financial reserves to outlive the initial shock, who were usually already supplying local traders, were able to survive. Moreover, a new type of indirect export has come up: small workshops and even home-based units that supply to relatively small traders, often Muslims with contacts in, for example, the Gulf countries or the Muslim countries of the former Soviet Union.

II. DIRECT EXPORTS

While most of the currently successful firms are direct exporters, at least five aspects can be distinguished to elucidate the paradoxical situation in this market channel. First, as shown in Table 5, 73% of direct exporters in our 2011 sample performed well. Moreover, many successful direct exporters have doubled their employment and started a second factory during 2009-2011. Second, and a reason for concern, direct exporters face an extremely competitive price-driven international market segment. For example, even though all but one of the direct exporters in our 2011 sample claims to have increased product quality and speed in delivery, 10 out of 15 direct exporters have not been able to enforce an increase in the price of their product. Third, among direct exporters a shift has taken place from one dominant type of entrepreneur professionals without roots in Agra to another. These professionals usually came to Agra to start a footwear firm because of the abundant availability of cheap skilled artisanal labour. They all possess substantial know-how, and usually also formal training, in the actual manufacturing process. During 2009-2011 second-generation Punjabi trader-entrepreneurs have pushed out many of the outside professionals. This shift has wider implications. Outside professionals consciously aimed to utilize Agra's comparative advantage of abundantly available cheap skilled artisanal labour, in combination with a selective upgrading of technology. By contrast, the second generation Punjabi entrepreneurs increasingly set up more mechanized units in which the labour force consists predominantly of women workers and persons with some formal technical training.

This shift strongly influences the international market segment within which direct exporters compete. In short, this new strategy solidifies a focus on the international price-driven market segment, turning Agra into "just" another cheap production location.

Fourth, in their vertical relations, the two main groups of entrepreneurs rely on different mixes of trust. While outside professionals have always predominantly relied on earned trust, second generation Punjabis often rely on a subtle combination of ascribed and earned trust. Even though community ties and extended family relations remain important, nowadays all direct exporters agree that also community and even family members need to perform up to the mark. In direct exports, the market channel where the volatile and exacting demands of the new competition are felt most directly, ascribed trust cannot shelter nonperformers. Indeed, as Schmitz (1995, p. 559) suggested, it appears that partners need not necessarily change, but the foundation of trust (from ascribed to earned) does. Agra's new elite predominantly chose a cautious way forward, not by changing partners, but by continuing with those partners who are now also "earning" their trust. Fifth, direct exporters have realized they are too small to operate on their own in the world market and have started to experiment with selective horizontal joint action to sustain their success. While I did not come across any horizontal cooperation among direct exporters or any other type of producers in 2006 and 2009, by 2011 87% of direct exporters in the 2011 sample had increased making use of local associations. The two most remarkable new initiatives for joint action by direct exporters are discussed below.

III. NEW JOINT ACTION BY DIRECT EXPORTERS

The first initiative was the establishment of the Agra chapter of the Council for Leather Exports (CLE), in 2011. It took a very active government official, acting as a cooperation catalyst (Humphrey and Schmitz),more than one year to convince entrepreneurs of the potential gains of such an initiative. The list of invitees reads like a who's who of the Agra footwear industry. The first meeting focused on the need to upgrade skills of workers. Moreover, they also decided to focus on trying to solve common institutional problems, such as the absence of a state tax office in Agra. Another common problem which puts Agra at a competitive disadvantage, is that on average it takes about one week to get a shipment of shoes from Agra to Bombay, another week to get them cleared in the harbour, and four weeks to ship the shoes to Europe. To make up for this slow response time, Agra's manufacturers have to be 15-20% cheaper in comparison to suppliers from countries such as Turkey and Brazil[13] Moreover, this slowness inhibits access to more fashion-oriented market segments where speed is crucial. Establishing a "dry port" near Agra could solve some of those problems.

Perhaps Agra's main institutional problem is its well-earned bad reputation with foreign buyers. Before leaving the footwear business altogether, many of the more unscrupulous indirect exporters further damaged Agra's reputation by taking on orders at extremely low prices and then compromising on the quality of all inputs. Even CLE officials would disseminate Agra's bad reputation, and up till recently would not take foreign buyers to Agra. Fortunately, the same cooperation catalyst mentioned above is trying to put Agra back on the map. In all, the establishment of the Agra chapter of the CLE is a significant step in developing collective action to solve common institutional problems. A second joint action initiative involves the establishment of a much more informal agreement among some of the more outward-oriented entrepreneurs to pass on orders to each other. These entrepreneurs, with complementary specializations and recognition of the need to specialize in a smaller range of products, predominantly pass on orders to each other that they may book at fairs. After having learnt the hard way that it is better to refuse an order than to deliver substandard products, they now channel such orders to a colleague in Agra. This practice also makes it easier for foreign buyers to deal with one reliable person for all their orders in Agra. Most direct exporters have successfully shifted gears during 2006-2011 by increasing horizontal cooperation in associations while also further strengthening vertical interim relationships with suppliers and buyers. It remains to be seen however, whether strengthening interim relationships will succeed. In the conclusion I will brief address this issue.

SWOT Analysis of the leather industry in Agra

Strengths

- High growth
- Ready availability of highly skilled and cheap manpower
- Large raw material base
- Policy initiatives taken by the Government
- Capability to assimilate new technologies and handle large projects
- Continuous emphasis on product development and design upgradation

Opportunities

- Rising potential in the domestic market
- Growing fashion consciousness globally
- Use of information technology and decision support software to help eliminate the length of the production cycle for different products
- Use of e-commerce in direct marketing

Threats

- Major part of the industry is unorganised
- Limited scope for mobilising funds through private placements and public issues (many businesses are family-owned)
- Difficulty in obtaining bank loans resulting in high cost of private borrowing
- Stricter international standards
- High competition from East European countries and other Asian countries
- Lack of communication facilities and skills

Weaknesses

- Lack of warehousing support from the government
- International price fluctuation
- Huge labour force resulting in high labour charges
- Lack of strong presence in the global fashion market
- Unawareness of international standards by many players

CONCLUSION

Industrial clusters in developing countries have recently become a focus of attention because clustering seems to help firms to overcome growth constraints, upgrade and compete in distant markets. This paper addressed the question of how firms in the Agra footwear cluster have responded to the main challenges of the 2011 a collapse of Agra's main and easy to satisfy export market, economic liberalization, tougher international competition and a growing premium domestic market segment. I have argued that to answer such a question in a heterogeneous cluster such as Agra one needs to distinguish between market channels. Nevertheless, it is also important not to lose sight of the fact that there was a common challenge to all market channels: the need to improve quality and increase speed.

Our 2011 survey shows that a clear majority of producers have indeed responded by improving quality and increasing speed. A large majority of producers has increased cooperation in vertical inter-firm relationships, except for relationships with subcontractors. In contrast, relationships with other local producers more often remained unchanged and were only weakly correlated with performance. Even a negative relationship was found between increased cooperation with other local producers and increased cooperation with buyers. Moreover, without inferring causality, a statistically significant relationship was found between the main market channel of a producer and its performance. These cluster-level findings support the market channel approach that stresses vertical relationships over horizontal relationships.

Notwithstanding the common challenge to all market channels, to a large extents the recent changes affected distinct market channels differently. Due to the collapse of the Soviet Union and dismantling of export subsidies, employment in indirect exports nose-dived. Many entrepreneurs in this market channel had relied predominantly on ascribed trust relations with local purchasing officers or high government officials in Delhi and Moscow. They were unable, or not interested, in gaining access to other market channels, and left the industry altogether. Some of the remaining entrepreneurs and almost all affected artisans flooded the already overcrowded domestic market. Moreover, the large Indian concerns were unable to maintain their market share in the increasingly volatile premium domestic market. They substantially decreased their number of Agra suppliers, and offered less attractive conditions to the remaining suppliers. The others, together with the former indirect exporters, seized the more attractive orders in the domestic market. This led to a cumulative crowding out process. Therefore, most producers in the domestic market, irrespective of the fact that many of them have increased cooperation with buyers and suppliers, have not performed well. Notwithstanding this severe overall crisis, two market channels direct exports and the premium domestic segment have seen remarkable evolutionary growth and have shown at least some signs of shifting gears to adjust to the New Competition. In both these market channels, however, the existing producers in 2006 have to a large extent been squeezed out by a group of second-generation Punjabi trader-entrepreneurs.

This group of very successful direct exporters, who have also invaded the top of the premium domestic market, increasingly rely on earned trust in their close cooperation with buyers and suppliers. Moreover, they have engaged in selective joint action with similar local producers. The 2011survey finding which shows a positive and statistically significant relationship between an increased involvement with the business association and a strong performance refers primarily to this group of producers. This small but very successful group of producers is becoming increasingly disconnected from the main part of the cluster. A picture emerges of a large stagnant and low quality segment where an increasing number of Jatav artisans face ever more desperate conditions, and a small dynamic and relatively higher quality segment that is in the process of shifting gears and has performed very well in recent years.

An area for further research would be to investigate the sustainability of this success in the dynamic segment. To keep up with the New Competition shifting gears in inter-firm relationships needs to be complemented with a parallel upgrading in intra-firm relationships. The cluster literature, with its focus on inter-firm relationships, has so far neglected intra-firm issues. It is increasingly recognized however that to remain competitive, actors in particular market channels will need to simultaneously upgrade inter- and intra-firm relationships. Those market channels in which the various activities and skills are more effectively geared to each other would be in a better position to keep up with the New Competition. Moreover, such market channels may well offer relatively better growth opportunities for small producers. A key question in the Agra context would be the extent to which entrepreneur-worker relationships pose a major constraint on quality improvements because of the caste-based chasm inhibiting professional cooperation between Jatav artisans as workers and Punjabi traders as entrepreneurs. At present they fight with each other instead of competiting. Therefore, the gap between the increasingly close cooperation in inter-firm relationships and the antagonistic deadlock in entrepreneur-worker relationships becomes more harrowing day by day.

NOTES

1. In their conclusion Boomgard et al. (1992, p. 209) also mention the need to develop our understanding of these less tangible aspects.
2. This typology is based on Zucker (1986). She uses the terms "characteristic-based" and "process-based" trust. I agree with Schmitz (1995) that "ascribed" and "earned'" trust more vividly illustrate the distinction.
3. According to surveys held in 1960 and 1974 around 85% of footwear workers were Jatavs (Lynch, 1969; Misra, 1980).
4. In India, hierarchical large enterprise groups were often split up into many formally independent small scale manufacturing units, because of the existence of a wide range of subsidies to stimulate small-scale manufacturing, but these units were directly controlled by centralized management (Sandesara, 1988).
5. Even though tariffs on imports of shoes were lowered, the import of finished shoes is still negligible.
6. The government provided an important stimulus for the export boom previous to the liberalization program by paying a 20% subsidy on each exported pair (up to 30% in some periods).
7. While, for example, 85% of strong performers increased subcontracting of upper cutting, only one or two of the average and weak performers (thus in most cases less than 10%) did so. This finding is statistically significant for all stages of production that are subcontracted: upper cutting, upper making, sole cutting, lasting and finishing.
8. By contrast, only 15% of indirect exporters, and none of the suppliers to local traders have increased making use of business associations.

9. The CLE, strong in other parts of India, had never been important to Agra, due to the indifference of the leading families of Agra's large enterprise groups.
10. Entrepreneurs feel that courses by existing training institutes are too theoretical. Moreover, training institutes appear to focus more on training supervisors than operators.

REFERENCES

1. Axelrod, R. (1984) The Evolution of Cooperation. Basic Books, New York.
2. Best, M. H. (1990) The New Competition. Institutions of Industrial Restructuring. Polity Press, Cambridge.
3. Boomgard, J. J., Davies, S. P., Haggblade S. J. and Mead, D. C. A subsector approach to small enterprise promotion and research. World Development.
4. Gambetta, D. (ed.) (1988) Trust. Making and Breaking Cooperative Relations. Basil Blackwell, New York.
5. Gere, G. (1994) Capitalism, development and global commodity chains. In Capitalism and Development. ed. L. Sklair. Routledge, London.
6. Hays, W. L. (1968) Statistics. 4th edn., Hott, Rinerhartand Winston, New York.
7. Misra, S. (1980) Living and Working Conditions of Labourers in Leather Industry in Agra. Ph.D.
8. Naidu, B. Krishnama (1993) Study on Employment, Production and Marketing of Footwear in the Informal Sector. Ph.D. Thesis, Department of Economics, Sri Venkateswara University, Tirupati, India.

Journals

Journal of Development Studies 34(4), 32-61.
Journal ; www.iupindia.in/.../IJMR_Buying_Behavior_of_Shoes_in_Kolkata_39.html
Journal ; www.ihd**india**.org/.../Paper-4-A-Case-Study-of-Footwear-**Industry**-in-**India**
Journal; footwearsinfolinethree.tripod.com/**india**_footwear
*Journal ; www.gfe.de/Publication/**India**n%20**Leather**%20**Industry***

Websites

www.indianshoebazaar.com/publications
leather.indiabizclub.com/.../indian_leather_industry
www.indianleatherportal.com
www.leatherindia.org
www.scribd.com

20

Export of Hair: A Golden Opportunity to India

K. Jagannathan and N. Panchanatham

Associate. Professor, Dept. of Management Studies, A.V.C. College of Engineering, Mannampandal, Mayiladuthurai- 609 305, E-Mail: jaganavcce@yahoo.co.in, blackjagan@gmail.com
Prof. & Head, Department of Business Administration, Annamalai University

ABSTRACT

India is one of the heritage countries in the world. India is crammed by Hindus. They have customs of sacrificing their belongings as a gift to God. After the recovery through bad times of all sorts they have a practice of thanks giving by sacrificing, donating, gifting and so on to the temples. Likewise in some parts of of the country they also donate their hair to the God as thanksgiving. All age groups and gender donate their hair to the temples. Donating or sacrifice hair is called "tonsure" hair. Temple authorities collect the tonsure hair and sell the hair to exporters and processors through auctions.

INTRODUCTION

Human hair is a big business industry in Chennai. This is a busy and multicrore industry. In today's business world everything should be made profitable. In any manufacturing concern, there is waste and scrap from its main products. This scrap, after being processed, can be converted into utilizable products through effective techniques. Likewise human hairs have also some uses. In India the business peoples are involved in exporting the raw human hair and its products to various countries after processing them. Raw Indian human hair and its products are very much in demand all over the world because of its quality. It increases our economic value in the export market and also creates a lot of employment opportunities both directly and indirectly.

Chennai is one of the hubs for exporting human hair. The business people engaged in export of human hair is quite less in number compared to other businesses like exporting of leather, cosmetics, textile, chemicals, etc. Business people collect the tonsure hair from various temples through auctions and process it and market the hair and its products to all over the world.

Background of the Study

India is one of the largest exporters of human hair and its products to various countries.

About Hair

The main component of hair fibre is keratin. The hair can be divided into three parts lengthwise, (1) the bulb, a swelling at the base which originates from the dermis, (2) the root, which is the hair lying beneath the skin surface, has also three parts, (i) the medulla, an area in the core which contains loose cells and airspaces (ii) the cortex, which contains densely packed keratin and (iii) the shaft, which is the hair above the skin surface; and (3) the cuticle, which is a single layer of cells arranged like roof shingles.

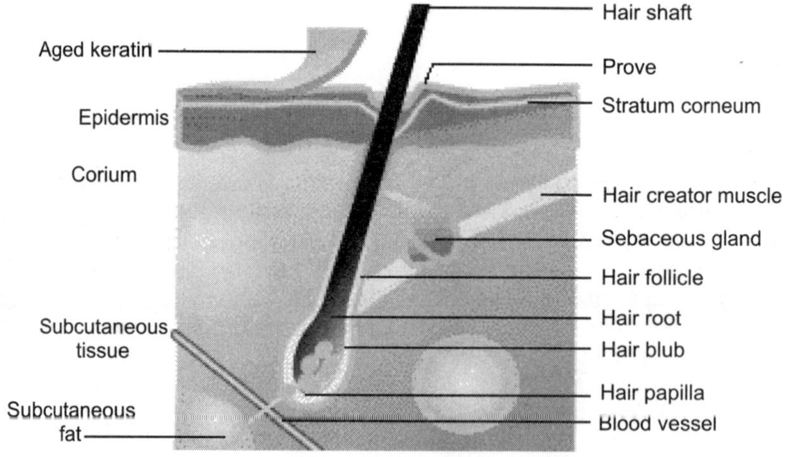

Source: -www.geocities.com/HotSprings/4266/chem.html

Major uses of Human Hair

- Hair extension
- Wig making
- Amino acid
- Fertilizer
- Crafting a rope (to twist hair fibres together to make strong ropes)
- Suturing material

Types of Hair Harvested in India

- Temple hair
- Village hair
- Barber hair

Temple Hair

Temple hair is the most abundant source available. Each year, thousands of worshipers make pilgrimages to temples where their hair is cut off as an act of religious sacrifice, devotion and thanksgiving. This custom is lucrative that temples designate certain women to ensure all the pilgrims' hair are properly braided before being cut. By having the hair cuticles face the same direction; temples are able to sell the locks to wig makers for big bucks. The Balaji Temple in Tirumala—the second busiest in the world—collects tonnes of hair each week, thereby generating an estimated annual income of ten thousand dollars for the temples.

Village Hair

Village hair is regarded as of lower quality than temple hair because it's derived from women's hair combs and brushes. The hair is collected monthly by what is known as hackers. The hair is exchanged for sweets, plastic, toys, etc.

Barber Hair (Thukku)

Finally, barber hair, or "Thuku" as it is known, comes from the sweepings off the floor from barber shops.

Of all the above the temple hair is very much in demand all over the world, because of its length and quality.

Export of Human Hair

Data like demand of importing countries, values of human hair and their quantity are analyzed. The analyzed report helps to identify the opportunity to enter into the hair business. India is one of the biggest sources for the human hair importing countries. Human hair trade has become a large export orientedmarket. The demand of human hair is still increasing day by day. India is one of the biggest sources of hair market through regularized regulations and procedures that enhance the potential of hair market.

Table 1: Export trend of human hair overall (Export value crores in 2010)

Year	Value	Value	Value	Value
	Sum	Mean	Minimum	Maximum
2005	1614164881	981852	41	43685890
2006	2098414345	1418947	0	48526528
2007	3544973025	1956387	0	66177504
2008	3013227071	2705197	0	71349542
2009	3766533839	1224315	0	43035712
2010	4519840607	1514240	1	53265250

Source: TANSTIA FNF Service – Chennai

The data above indicates that export value has increased from Rs,161.41 crores in 2005 to 451.98.

Chart 1: Export trend of human hair overall

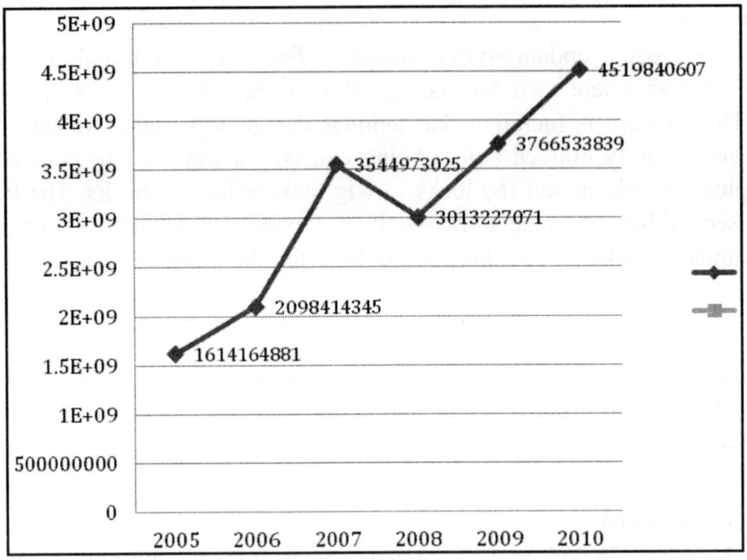

Table 2: Top ten countries importing human hair from India

S.No.	Country Code	Export values (in Rs)
01	ES	496553849
02	KR	73234909
03	HK	1266819202
04	CN	9194559644
05	BR	1498090604
06	US	553741034
07	ID	318390076
08	LB	177505795
09	IT	1309648235
10	DE	80515429

Source – TANSTIA - FNF SERVICE – Chennai

Apart from these more than seventy countries also import human hair from India. In this manner we identify the opportunities to attract and improve the hair business through effective marketing strategies.

Chart 2: Top ten countries importing human hair from India

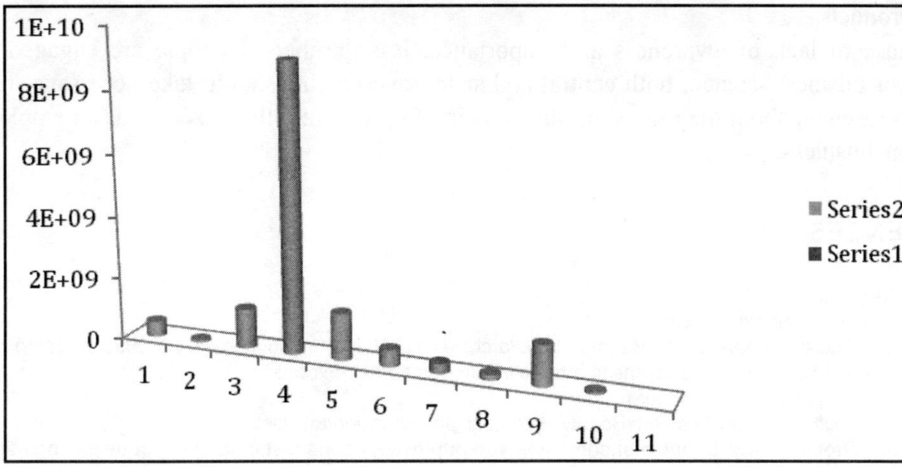

Country Codes and Names

CN – China
BR – Brazil
IT – Italy
HK – Hong Kong
US – United States
ES – Spain
ID – Indonesia
LB – Lebanon
DE – Germany
KR – Korea

Challenges Faced by the Exporter

- Human hair exporting companies are less in number and hence, tough competition exists among the top most companies.
- The major source of hair availability is Hindu temples.
- The procurement of human hair from temples is through auctions only, so only economically sound companies can only participate.

CONCLUSION

India exports the human hair and its products to various countries after collecting and processing them. Indian human hair and its products are very much demanded all over world because of its quality and its length. It increases our economic value in the export market and also creates lot of employment opportunities both directly and indirectly.

Human hair trade is largely export oriented. The demand of human hair is increasing day by day. Chennai has become one of the largest processing and manufacturing hubs for human hair and its products.

Because of lack of awareness and importance, less number of people are engaged in the human hair business. Hence, both central and state governments should take necessary steps for creating awareness about the usages of human hair and promoting this business as an employment generation business.

REFERENCES

1. www.hair.co.in
2. www.hair.co.in/hair-extensions
3. Hair and There - Amaranth K. Menon, –http://archives.digitaltoday.in/indiatoday/20060821/coversco
4. www.articlesbase.com/online-business-articles/indian-human-hair-exports.
5. www.perfectlocks.com/indian-hair-history
6. www. timesofindia.indiatimes.com/Beauty/Hair_gets_an_extension/articleshow
7. A Hairy Problem by Economist.com/ Newyorkhttp:/www.economist.com/blogs/freeexchange/2007/01/hair_market.cfm.
8. Hair – raising business ideas! – opportunities – Manufacturing, Written By–Mohita Nagpal, Friday 31 October 2008–; http:/www.dare.co.in/opportunities/manufacturing/hair-raising-business—ideas/

21

An Empirical Study on Competitive Positioning in International Logistics using Neural Networks: Chennai Port

M. Dhanabhakyam and K. Vimaladevi

Assistant Professors, Department of Commerce, Bharathiar University, Coimbatore-46.
Ph.D(F.T), Department of Commerce, Bharathiar University, Coimbatore-46
E-mail: vimala.sri@gmail.com

ABSTRACT

Firms involved in international logistics must develop a system of service attributes that gives them a way to be profitable and to satisfy customers at the same time. How customers trade-off these various attributes in forming satisfaction with competing international logistics providers has not been explored well in the literature. This study explores the ocean freight shipping sector to identify the system of attributes that maximizes customers' satisfaction. Data were collected from shipping managers in Chennai using personal interviews to identify the major concerns in choosing and evaluating ocean freight services. The data were then examined using neural networks and decision trees, among other approaches to identify the system of attributes that is connected with customer satisfaction. The results illustrate the power of these methods in understanding how industrial customers with global operations process attributes to derive satisfaction. Implications are discussed.

INTRODUCTION

In the 1990's, the so called "Logistics Renaissance" (Council of Logistics Management, 1995) reflected the new era of supply chain management. This "renaissance" compelled firms to examine their supply chain efficiencies to cut costs while simultaneously enhancing customer satisfaction. International logistics operations have become critical in recent years given that about one-fifth of the output of U.S. firms is produced overseas and one-fourth of U.S. imports are between foreign affiliates and U.S. parent companies (Dornier et al., 1998). Moreover, costs associated with logistics operations now make up the most significant portion of international trade expenses (Rodrigues, Bowersox, & Calentone, 2005). Amidst this dramatic change, international logistics providers need to identify the most important attributes that determine the value of the services they offer to logistics users looking to improve their supply chain effectiveness. The business environment for logistics service providers is notably competitive especially as more firms outsource their logistics solutions to third party logistics providers. Yet, how industrial customers (or supply chain participants) choose logistics service providers is not well understood. Which service attributes have the strongest impact on satisfaction? What combination of service attributes maximizes satisfaction? The purpose of this paper is to explore this choice process by investigating firms which ship their goods using one type of logistics provider, the ocean freight shipping service. We use the techniques of neural networks and decision trees as our approach to understand this process. The literature reports no application of these techniques to probe the mindset of industrial customers. The paper first begins with a discussion of Porter's (1996) ideas on how to construct a profitable system of attributes and its strategic importance. Subsequently, we examine service satisfaction, its antecedents, and its consequences. Next, we offer a brief discussion of the features of neural networks and decision trees and their usefulness in our research. We then present our research method, including a description of the sample and survey measures consisting of structured and unstructured questions. After providing the results, we discuss the efficacy of such analytical techniques in understanding the formation of customer satisfaction in the logistics industry. The paper concludes with implications for firms that provide international logistics services and insight into developing their system of offerings. Our paper contributes to a better understanding of international logistics by investigating an important area that has received little attention.

Strategic Importance of Constructing a Profitable System of Service Attributes

Porter (1996) argues that firms must understand the trade-offs that exist in establishing a competitive position in the marketplace. The essence of strategic positioning is to choose activities that are different from rivals; strategy rests on these unique activities to deliver a unique mix of value. It is, therefore, essential that international logistics companies identify what type of service attributes or offerings (e.g., price, reputation, delivery speed, claim handling) to focus on so that service satisfaction remains high–even if the company does not provide maximum service levels in every aspect of the service delivery. The question "What are the key drivers of customer loyalty?" is essentially about finding the right combination of activities at various levels that provide superior value and high levels of customer satisfaction as Porter (1996) advocates. Unfortunately, there is no easy answer to this question, perhaps due to the diversity of customers and industry situations. Because a service is intangible, it has properties regarding quality that make it much more difficult to identify and, therefore, to quantify drivers of loyalty. Becoming the best service provider may seem initially like the surest route to success if the costs are not considered. For international logistics firms with limited resources, key decisions must be faced in terms of the trade-offs involving giving maximum service versus focusing on optimal profitability. These trade-offs in logistics costs are crucial in determining customer service levels in supply chain decisions. Given the need to develop a combination of logistics attributes, we now examine the role of customer satisfaction in building this combination.

Techniques to Understand Satisfaction : Neural Networks and Decision Trees

One way to quantify the importance of various service attributes or features and reasons in driving satisfaction is via ordinary regression analysis or path analysis. These analytic techniques are constrained by assumptions regarding linearity of relationship between satisfaction and its determinants and the possibility of multi-collinearity among the determinants of service satisfaction. However, the relationship between service satisfaction and its determinants may not always be linear. Moreover, multi-collinearity causes instability among parameter estimates, thereby limiting the applicability of traditional analytic methods. In this scenario, other techniques such as neural networks or decision trees offer a better promise. Neural networks can be used when there is a non-linearity in the relationship between customer satisfaction and its determinants. These networks, which mimic how the brain may work, are helpful in sorting the most important service features that drive customer satisfaction. Decision trees, on the other hand, are particularly useful in mapping out the combination of service satisfaction attributes that maximize satisfaction. Knowing this combination would allow a firm to develop a more profitable "system" of service features or attributes that would lead to higher levels of satisfaction among its customers. Neural networks and decision trees, therefore, offer an analytic power that regression analysis cannot provide. The discussion below gives greater details concerning the features and application areas of neural networks and decision trees.

Neural Networks

The concept of a neural network is based on a mathematical abstraction of the way the human brain works (McMillen & Henley, 2001). In the human brain, information is processed by cells which are also called neurons. Each neuron collects information from other neurons that are attached to it, and it aggregates that information and passes it along to other neurons. In an artificial neural network, elements called nodes function similarly to the neurons in our brain. Each node sums information that it receives from nodes connected to it, and it passes the processed information to the nodes that it connects to. When several nodes are connected together, they process information in parallel, allowing the system to find complex relationships quickly. In this network, the "neurons" or "nodes" are organized into "layers." There are typically three layers in a network: the input layer, the hidden layer, and the output layer. Each layer consists of several nodes or neurons. Further, each node is linked to every neuron in the preceding layer by connections that have strengths or **weights** attached to them. The first layer is called the **input layer** since it consists of nodes that uniquely represent each input or predictor variable. Input values for the predictor variables are presented to these input nodes. The information then flows through the network and is processed by nodes in the second layer, also known as the **hidden layer**. The hidden layer represents a sort of black box in that the nodes of this layer are hidden from the input and output. This layer is essential for mapping nonlinear relationships between the target output and the predictor inputs. It is important to point out that the hidden layer is an intervening layer and it facilitates the propagation of information from the input layer to the output layer. The third layer (called the **output layer**) consists of one or more output nodes. These output nodes combine information from the hidden nodes to generate predictions for the target variables. Once a neural network is set up by defining a set of nodes and how they are connected, the network has to be trained. The network trains itself by looking at one record at a time. For each record, it makes a guess against the actual value for that case. It then adjusts the weights so that its next guess will be better. This implies that the network learns from its mistakes. Initially all weights are randomly set to small values and the predictions that come out of the network are likely to be nonsensical. However, as the network processes more and more data, it gets better and better at making predictions. Another important feature of the neural network is that the input for each hidden neuron is the weighted sum of data values from the input nodes that are transformed using a **nonlinear** function. Typically, such a function is the logistic function, though other transformation functions can also be applied.

In our study, we use this approach to assess the relative importance of various service features of ocean freight shippers in predicting satisfaction of their clients. The model developed (using customer service variables) was able to predict customer churn rates better than the more traditional logit regression models. Most recently, the neural network modeling approach to evaluate service quality. Given the wide range of applications of neural network analysis, it can also be used to examine how customer satisfaction is formed. The neural network in our paper represents mental processes of the industrial customers of logistics service providers. We employ this technique to understand the relative importance of various drivers of customer satisfaction.

Decision Trees

In simple terms, a decision tree is a tree in which each branch node represents a choice between a number of alternatives, and each leaf node represents a classification or decision. The tree shows how the value of a target variable can be predicted by using the values of a set of predictor variables. The graphical representation of the tree shows a number of inter-connected "nodes." Each node represents a set of records (rows) from the original dataset. Nodes that have child nodes are called "interior" or "branch" nodes. Nodes that do not have child nodes are called "terminal" or "leaf" nodes. The topmost node is called the "root" node. While a real tree has its root at the bottom, decision trees are represented in such a way that the root node is always at the top. The root node in a decision tree represents all of the rows in the dataset. A decision tree is constructed by a binary or non-binary split that divides the rows of the root node into two or more groups (child nodes) based on categories of the "best" predictor. The same procedure is then used to split the child groups based on other predictor variables. This process is called "recursive partitioning." The splitting process continues until no more statistically significant predictors can be found. Decision trees can be applied to solve both regression type problems and classification type problems. Among the decision tree based techniques, CHAID (chi-squared automatic interaction detector) (Biggs, de Ville, & Suen, 1991; Kass, 1980) and

C&RT (classification and regression trees) (Brieman et al., 1980) have been widely applied in segmentation, stratification, and interaction identification studies in the areas of direct mail, credit scoring, human resources, market analysis, and health care (Sargeant & McKenzie, 1999, Sargeant & Msweli, 1999, Wyner, 1995).

In our study, Decision tree analysis is used for predicting the response to a target variable or for classifying consumers into mutually exclusive groups based on responses to several predictor variables. It does not attempt to model the brain, but instead, tries to identify how various attributes are linked to one another in combinations. This technique is particularly suitable over traditional regression analysis when the relationship between the target variable and its predictors is nonlinear or when there are interactions among the predictor variables.

Methodology

Study location and sample

Our study focuses on the ocean freight shipping sector of the logistics industry. Data were collected from Chennai based companies that used services of ocean freight shipping lines. We chose the Port of Chennai since it is the India's busiest port in terms of shipping and cargo tonnage and the second busiest for container throughput. In 2005, Chennai terminals handled 22.28 million twenty-foot equivalent units (TEUS) of containers through 4 container terminals and 2 multi-purpose terminals. The Port links shippers to an excellent network of 200 shipping lines with connections to 600 ports in 123 countries. The Chennai Strait is one of the world's busiest waterways used by international shipping. Additional details on the importance of this port can be found at the Port of Chennai Authority website. Two phases (as outlined below) were used to collect data from shipping managers and shipping line executives of various organizations in Chennai who regularly use the services of ocean freight shipping companies for their exporting requirements.

Phase I

Names of 985 key accounts were obtained from a large shipping company in Chennai. Some of the shippers on the list were customers of that shipping company, while others were customers of competing shipping lines. From this list, 234 accounts were randomly selected; 222 of these agreed to participate in the study resulting in a 95% response rate. Personal interviews were conducted with these shipping managers. They were asked to provide five reasons why they selected a certain shipping line to take care of their logistics requirements and to list five reasons why they would avoid such a shipping line. Next, they were asked to list three major problems they encountered with shipping lines in general. The shipping managers in the sample also described the companies that they represented on several criteria.

Included among those criteria were company size in terms of annual sales, annual freight expenses of these companies, and how often these companies reviewed the shipping lines' performance on a comprehensive basis.

Results of phase I

Responses to the first phase survey measures were analyzed using SPSS. Results are described in Tables 1 and 2. As shown in Table 1, the sample of shipping companies that use ocean freight shipping services varies in size, with annual sales turnover ranging from under 10 million (45.3% of the sample) to over $100 million (9.4%). The annual freight expenses of these companies ranged from less than $10000 (7.6%) to over $100000 (31.8%). Responses to the question "How frequently do these companies conduct a comprehensive review of their shipping lines' performance" varied from rarely or never (12.4%) to continuously (56%). Table 2 lists the reasons for choosing or avoiding certain shipping lines. It is clear one of the primary reasons behind the choice of a shipping line is competitive freight rates indicated by sixty nine percent of the sample. 46.2% of the customers would not select a shipping line if it does not offer competitive freight rates. Other important reasons for choosing are good service, having a regular service (or frequency of operation), maintaining good relationship, how short the transit time is, punctuality, reliability, and trustworthiness of the shipping line. At least 20% of the customers cited each of these reasons for their choice of a shipping line. Absence of these qualities in a shipping line would prevent the customer companies from patronizing that firm. Somewhat less significant reasons for selection, but noteworthy reasons nevertheless, are speedy documentation, good reputation, and prompt shipment. The significance of these key service features can also be gauged from the major problems that customer companies experienced with shipping lines. The results presented in Table 2 identify the features that shipping lines should focus on to enhance customer satisfaction. To find out whether the reasons for choosing shipping lines varied on the basis of customer company characteristics, we performed a series of cross tabulations using the "multiple response set" feature of SPSS. Results indicate that the same set of key service features as identified above are cited by all customer companies, irrespective of their size, annual freight expenses, or how frequently they review shipping lines' performance. In sum, the first phase of the survey identified competitive freight rates, good service, regular (or frequent) service, good relationship, short transit time, punctuality and reliability, and trustworthiness as key service features that customers of ocean freight shipping lines care about and that are likely to have an impact on customer satisfaction.

Phase II

In the second phase of the survey, we measured customer evaluations of key service features as identified in the first phase along with overall customer satisfaction. Unlike most studies that adapt generic rating scales to measure the determinants of satisfaction (e.g., service quality), we developed specific scales based on customer input. Such customized measures are likely to be more powerful when evaluating logistics service providers since they capture the perceptions of shipping line customers. The list below outlines the themes of those service features, the number of scale items to measure them, and examples of scale items. Insights obtained during preliminary interviews with shipping line executives and a small sample of customer companies facilitated the development of these measures. We verified the face validity of these scales by discussions with managers and experts in logistics. For all scale items, 7-point rating scales anchored by "poor" and "excellent," were used. We summed the item responses for each dimension to derive a composite score. Parenthetically, factor analysis also supported uni-dimensionality of the following seven services features.

1. Competitive freight rates (3 items) (e.g., Competitive rates, Has lowest rates; scale reliability as measured by coefficient alpha is .73)
2. Good Service (3 items) (e.g., emphasize customer satisfaction, good after sales service; scale reliability is .80)
3. Regular Service (1 item) (good frequency of sailings)
4. Good relationship/cooperation (4 items) (e.g., listens to customers, values customers' input, responsive to customers' requests; scale reliability is .76)
5. Short transit time (2 items) (e.g., short transition time; scale reliability is .71)
6. Punctual (3 items) (e.g., punctuality of sailings, good on-time performance; scale reliability is .70)
7. Reliable and Trustworthy (4 items) (e.g., trustworthy, delivers on promises, gives correct/proper information; scale reliability is .76)

The questionnaire also measured subjects' overall satisfaction with their most preferred shipping line's service on a scale from 1 (Extremely Poor) to 7 (Excellent). In phase 2, the same managers again provided responses to the 20 scale items measuring the 7 service features and overall service satisfaction as identified above. A total of 117 useful responses were available for analysis. To keep the survey length manageable, customers were asked to evaluate the service features of only their most preferred shipping lines. We used this data to perform neural network analysis and decision tree analysis.

Results of Neural Network Anaysis

Responses to the second phase of the survey enabled us to examine the relationship between the key service features and overall service satisfaction. The seven service features that we measured in the second phase serve as the predictors of satisfaction. Correlations among the predictors varied from .53 to .82. In view of the potential for multi-collinearity among the predictors, possibility of interaction effects among predictors, and the likelihood of a non-linear relationship between those variables and satisfaction, traditional regression analysis or path analysis is not appropriate. For this reason, we analyzed the data using neural network analysis and decision trees. Clementine 6.5, a data mining package marketed by SPSS, was used for this purpose. We first performed a neural network analysis using the simple multi-layer Perception model. This model consists of one hidden layer besides one input layer and one output layer. There are seven input nodes (or neurons), one for each predictor variable, with customer responses serving as inputs. Customer satisfaction is the target variable that served as the output node. The number of hidden layer nodes is determined by the software program. In our case, the model used four hidden layer nodes to fit the data. The neural network detects the best relationship between the seven service features and satisfaction based on supervised learning. Considering our sample size (n = 117), we used 85% of the sample for training the network and the other 15% for validation purposes. Results of the analysis, presented in Table 3, are very encouraging; the prediction accuracy of the model is 83.5. Table 3 also indicates the relative importance of the service features. Clearly, the key drivers of satisfaction are reliability and trustworthiness of the shipping line, quality of relationship the shipping line maintains with its customers, good service, and regular (or frequent) service. Relatively less important features are punctuality, competitive freight rates, and short transit time. These results offer important insights for shipping lines as to how to maximize satisfaction. It is likely that there were no differences in customer responses with respect to features such as punctuality because all shipping lines are adequate in these areas; hence, these attributes are not differentiating drivers of satisfaction in the minds of customers.

Results of Decision Tree Analysis

When unlimited resources are available, a shipping line would be able to significantly enhance its service offering in every aspect, whether it involves competing more aggressively on freight rates, offering superior quality service, or reducing the transit time. When faced with resource constraints, however, the shipping line would have to make trade-offs in terms of what service features to devote most of its resources. In this scenario, the question is what combination of service features either enhances or undermines customer satisfaction? To address this issue, we performed a decision tree analysis. As with neural network analysis, the target variable for decision tree analysis is satisfaction, and the predictor variables are the seven service features. Prior to performing decision tree analysis, we dichotomized responses to the predictor variables using the "mean split" criterion whereby those customers who rated the shipping lines above the mean on freight rates were recoded as 1 (i.e., "stronger" rating) and those below the mean were recoded as 0 (i.e., "weaker" rating). Next, we used the C&R (classification and regression) tree technique for generating the decision tree (cf. Breiman et al., 1980), as this technique is considered to be robust in the presence of problems of missing data and large numbers of predictor variables. Also, the tree that is developed using this technique is considered to be easier to understand. It is a binary tree growing algorithm. As with any tree growing algorithm, C&RT technique splits the root node (or parent node) consisting of all data records into a number of branches and sub-branches (or child nodes) consisting of more homogeneous data records. Clearly, results of the decision tree show what steps a shipping line must take in order to enhance customer satisfaction.

Discussion

For all types of ocean freight shipping line customers, irrespective of their size, annual freight expenses, or how frequently they perform a comprehensive review of various shipping lines, "competitive freight rate" is the number one listed reason for choosing a certain shipping line, followed by "good service." Other notable reasons are "regular service," "good relationship," "short transit time" and "reliability and trustworthiness." These results suggest that ocean freight shipping firms cannot trade off price/wider network for service. Exclusively focusing on some service attributes may not be attractive to customers if the freight line operates a small fleet with fewer destination choices. Highly competitive rates coupled with poor service will also turn away customers. So, it is clear that logistics companies should either offer everything (e.g., best price & service) or offer a small network with great service, but integrate operations with partner lines so that customers see a seamless connection (as in Star Alliance for airlines). These results confirm the logic suggested by Porter (1996) in how to develop effective strategy. When comparing the neural network and decision tree results, we find some similarities as well as some differences. For example, both techniques identify good relationship/cooperation and reliability/trustworthiness as important for customer satisfaction. In the case of neural networks, good relationship and reliability/trustworthiness are the most important predictors of satisfaction followed by quality of service and "regular service" (or service frequency). In decision tree analysis, customers' perception of good relationship is the basis for segmenting them into two groups–those who rated service providers as low on good relationship and those who rated service providers as high on good relationship. For the first group, the overall satisfaction decreased, while it increased for the later group. The primary objectives of the two techniques are different, however. For this reason, we find some differences in the results for these two techniques. The purpose of neural network analysis is to identify the relative importance of factors when the objective is to predict customer satisfaction. For logistics providers in the shipping industry, the factors that are the most important for predicting satisfaction are reliability/ trustworthiness of the service provider and good relationship with the service provider. The purpose of decision tree analysis is to segment customers into several sub groups based on their perceptions of various service features and their overall satisfaction. Nonetheless, it is important to note that relationship quality surfaced as important in both types of analysis. Relationship quality is highly intangible and subject to marketing control. Ocean freight shippers firms could potentially use this quality as a way of differentiating themselves to enhance customer loyalty. Analysis of customer complaints (or problems) with ocean freight shipping companies provides clues concerning the attributes that may enhance customer satisfaction. For example, customers frequently cited shipping delays, document delays, and communication breakdown as the major problems; suggested possible solutions that logistics firms could use were more knowledgeable staff and advance notification of shipping delays.

IMPLICATION AND CONCLUSION

Our study provides ideas that contribute to understanding the dynamics of the service attributes in logistics that have not been explored well in the literature. We can offer several implications for logistics service providers in general and ocean freight shipping lines in particular based on our analysis. Neural networks and decision trees provide a powerful lens into the workings of these attributes. First, research on satisfaction can be deceptive depending on the method used. In particular, responses to open ended questions would suggest that freight rates as the most important factor. Yet, such a conclusion may hide what is happening under the surface (in the minds of users). Using neural network we can see that trust, cooperation, etc. are relatively more important. Why the difference? On a basic level, freight rates are clearly a key driver. Yet, a firm cannot easily differentiate it as the low cost provider if others can offer similar low prices as Porter (1996) would argue. Providing low cost rates is not likely to be a sustainable competitive advantage. If all customers provided the same ratings to shipping lines on freight rates then there is very small variation in freight rates vis a vis customer satisfaction. This understanding does not mean that freight rates can be ignored. Freight rates, in general, are not the differentiating factor in enhancing satisfaction when you look at the entire data. Trying to understand how satisfaction develops through the conventional methods of surveys and descriptive statistical analysis does not penetrate the complexity involved in the way the human brain may function. Using simple frequencies for reasons for preferring or rejecting shipping lines only scratches the surface. Neural networks facilitate our understanding of how humans process information to derive an emotional response, namely satisfaction. There is a clear implication of these findings in terms of Porter's (1996) framework of strategy. Firms that are highly successful learn how to develop attributes that other firms cannot imitate easily. Sustainable competitive advantage comes from developing a unique position in the market place. For example, Southwest Airlines in the USA has developed a unique position in the marketplace that emphasizes less service, frequent departures, and low fares (Porter 1996). In the case of ocean freight shipping services, the results indicate that it is not enough to provide a good price, i.e., freight rates. Instead, firms must realize that there is a sequence or combination of service factors that maximizes service satisfaction. Discovering the best sequence depends in part on the segment that the firm is pursuing or the extent to which firms all seem alike. In sum, our exploratory study finds important results related to developing a system of attributes that are of value to customers of logistics services. By using cross tabulations, decision trees and neural network analyses, we show how ocean freight shipping firms in the logistics sector should go about in identifying the sequence or combination of service factors that maximizes service satisfaction and, in turn, loyalty–this is exactly what Porter (1996) suggests firms should do to find a sustainable competitive advantage in the marketplace.

Table 1: Profile of shipping lines' customers annual turnover in US dollars

	Frequency	%
Up to 10 million	101	45.3
10 to 25 million	54	24.2
26 to 50 million	25	11.2
51 to 100 million	16	7.2
Over 100 million	21	9.4
Annual freight expenses in US Dollars		
	Frequency	%
Less than 10000	17	7.6
Between 10000 and 24999	33	14.8
Between 25000 and 49999	55	24.7
Between 50000 and 99999	43	19.3
Above 100000	71	31.8
Frequency of Comprehensive Review of Shipping Line's Performance		
	Frequency	%
Never/Rarely	26	12.4
About once in 2 to 3 yrs	8	3.8
About once a year	25	12.0
Every 6 months	33	15.8
Continuously	117	56

Table 2: List five reasons why you chose a particular shipping line? Responses across the five reasons are summarized as shown below

		Percent of cases
Competitive freight rate	➢	69.0
Good service	➢	50.0
Regular service	➢	44.3
Short transit time	➢	24.8
Good relationship/ooperation	➢	24.3
Customer's choice	➢	13.3
Punctual	➢	12.4
Reliable / trustworthy	➢	10.0
Speedy document	➢	7.6
Good reputation	➢	7.1
Prompt shipment	➢	6.7
Wide network	➢	4.3
Efficient	➢	3.3
Gives me priority	➢	3.3
Ample vessel space	➢	2.4
Special equipment	➢	1.4
Others	➢	1.4

Note: Service features identified are used as input to Neural Network and Decision Tree Analysis

Table 3: Importance weights of predictor variables based on neural network analysis (Dependent variable: Service satisfaction)

Service Variable	Important Weight
Reliability / Trustworthiness	0.31
Good Relationship	0.16
Regular Service	0.06
Good Service	0.06
Short transit time	0.01
Competitive freight rate	0.00
Punctual	0.00
Prediction Accuracy of Model	83.5%
Mean Service Satisfaction	
Original Data	5.97
Estimated by Model	5.86

REFERENCES

1. Anderson, E.W. and Sullivan, M. (1993). The Antecedents and Consequences of Customer Satisfaction for Firms. Marketing Science, 12(2), 125-43.
2. Bearden, W.O. and Teel, J.E. (1983), "Selected Determinants of Consumer Satisfaction and Complaint Report," Journal of Marketing Research, 20(February), pp. 21-8.
3. Collins, E., Ghosh, S. and Scofield, C. (1988). An Application of a Multiple Neural Network Learning System to the Emulation of Mortgage Underwriting Judgments. IEEE Second International Conference on Neural Networks, 8, 459-466.
4. Council of Logistics Management (1995). World Class Logistics: The Challenge of Managing Continuous Change. Oak Brook, IL: Council of Logistics Management.
5. Dadzie, K.Q., Chelariu, C. and Winston, E. (2005). Customer Service in the Internet-Enabled Logistics Supply Chain: Website Design Antecedents and Loyalty Effects. Journal of Business Logistics, 26 (1), 53-78.
6. Fung, P. and Wong, A. (1998). Case Study: Managing for Total Quality of Logistics Services in The Supply Chain. Logistics Information Management, 11(5), 324-329.

7. Hair, J., Anderson, R., Tatham, R. and Black, W. (1998). Multivariate Data Analysis with Readings (5th ed.). Englewood Cliffs, NJ: Prentice Hall.
8. Johnson, M.D. and Fornell, C. (1991). A Framework for Comparing Customer Satisfaction Across Individuals and Product Categories. Journal of Economic Psychology, 12(2), 267-86.
9. Sargeant, A. and McKenzie, J. (1999). The Lifetime Value of Donors: Gaining Insight through CHAID. Fund Raising Management, 30(1), 22-27.
10. Stank, T.P., Goldsby, T.J., Vickery, S.K. and Savitskie, K. (2003). Logistics Service Performance: Estimating Its Influence on Market Share. Journal of Business Logistics, 24(1), 27-55.
11. Tam, K. and Kiang, M. (1992). Managerial Applications of Neural Networks: The Case of Bank Failure Predictions. Management Science, 38(7), 926-948.
12. Vanecko, J.J. and Russo, A.W. (1999). Data Mining and Modeling as a Marketing Activity. Direct Marketing, 62(5), 52-55.
13. Witten, I.H. and Frank, E. (2000). Data Mining: Practical Machine Learning Tools and Techniques with Java Implementation. Morgan Kaufman: San Francisco, CA.
14. Wyner, G.A. (1995). Segmentation Analysis, Then and Now. Marketing Research, 7(1), 40-43.

22

The Current Scenario in Export of Indian Agriculture

Jimmy Mathew and G.S. Jayeesh

Postgraduate Student, Department of Business Administration, Annamalai University.
E-mail: jimmym28@gmail.com
Assistant Professor, Department of Business Administration, Annamalai University

ABSTRACT

Agricultural products provide a better alternative for diversification of Indian exports in view of higher returns available from them. Agricultural sector helps in improving productivity of land, generating employment, improving economic conditions of the farmers and entrepreneurs, enhancing exports and foreign exchange earnings. To make exporting of perishable goods conductive and favourable, the exporter should have the knowledge of production, cold storage, packing, transportation, warehousing, documentation and mainly the quality requirement of the importing country. This paper traces this process, analyses its effects on fruits and vegetables productivity and growth and discusses the problems and prospects for globalization to draw policy implications for the future of fruits and vegetable industry.

Keywords : Globalization, Agricultural products, Exports, Cold storage, Transportation, Vegetables, Fruits, Storage, Packing, Air waybill, Consignee, Consignor, Cargo, IATA, ICAO.

Abbreviations : AEZ - Agri Export Zone, APEDA - Agricultural Product Export Development Authority, BSE - Bovine Spongiform Encephalopathy, GBR - Geographical BSE-Risk, EU-European Union, WTO - World Trade Organization, MRL - Maximum Residual limit.

INTRODUCTION

The process of globalization and WTO agreement by Europe and its allies has touched every aspect of Indian life including agriculture sector. Conditions for increasing production of agricultural crops are very favourable in the country. This is partly because production is labour-intensive. India endowed with abundant labour in relation to capital has competitive advantage in production and exports. Agricultural products not only have good potential for generating employment in cultivation but also in processing, marketing, and distribution. India with its wide diversity in climate and soil has given rise to the formation of a variety of ecosystems. It produces a large range of fruits commercially in various agro-climatic zones.

Horticultural products have a high income elasticity of demand. As income goes up, demand rises rapidly, especially in the middle and high-income groups in developing and developed countries. In developed countries, the growing concern for health and nutrition has caused consumer preferences to shift from high-fat, high-cholesterol foods, such as meat and livestock products, to low-fat, low-cholesterol foods, such as fish, fruits and vegetables. Also, there is an increasing tendency in developed countries to diversify the diet by consuming a wide variety of fruits and vegetables, This, in turn, has led to and is facilitated by increasing imports of new and non-traditional horticultural products, especially from the tropical developing countries.

Currently the challenges faced by the agricultural industries from globalization are the result of lack of increased production and productivity, absence of economies of scale of production, lack of scientific methods, slow pace of crop diversification, few value added products developed, inadequate research and development support, Logistics development, cold storage and marketing of products. Short term strategies aim at addressing the above concerns at the earliest possible time.

Objectives

The objectives of the paper are

- To analyze the factors or problems which are affecting the export performances of fruits and vegetables industry
- To analyze the strategies that are used to overcome the factors affecting export performances.

GLOBAL SCENARIO

Fruit Crops - Global

The global fruit production during 2010 was 715 million tons. During the past 15 years, production of fruits in China has gone up by 246 per cent, which helped China to become the largest producer of fruits (114.24 million tons) in the world from its third largest producer position. It contributes 16 per cent share in production. India is the second largest producer of fruits by producing 78 million tons and contributes 12 per cent share in global fruit

Table 1: Fruit production in major countries of the world countries production in million tons.

Countries	1991	2001	2004	2010
World	353.32	472.24	511.04	715.00
China	24.08	68.92	83.24	114.20
India	28.04	43.00	49.29	78.28
Brazil	31.59	33.31	36.01	46.15
USA	24.70	30.06	30.19	36.00
Italy	17.52	18.29	17.92	29.00
Spain	12.79	15.14	16.69	23.80
Mexico	9.63	14.30	14.76	21.40
Indonesia	6.61	11.66	14.75	20.22
Iran	7.58	12.67	13.14	14.80
Philippines	8.21	11.12	12.37	14.76

Table 2: Production of major fruits arranged in descending order

Fruits	Year				
	2002	2003	2004	2005	2006
Bananas	10,820,000.00	11,954,300 1	1,388,000 1	1,710,300.00	11,710,300.00
Guavas, mangoes, mangosteens	10,640,000.00	10,780,000.00	1,830,700.00	11,140,115.00	11,140,115.00
Coconuts	8,942,000.00	9,313,505.00	9,048,403.00	9,534,845.00	11,000,000.00
Fruit, nec	9,250,000.00	9,530,000.00	9,530,000.00	9,530,000.00	9,530,000.00
Oranges	3,120,000.00	3,070,000.00	3,312,388.00	3,469,354.00	3,469,354.00
Apples	1,160,000.00	1,470,000.00	1,521,600.00	1,739,000.00	1,739,000.00
Lemons and limes	1,440,000.00	1,420,000.00	1,539,791.00	1,617,783.00	1,617,783.00
Grapes	1,210,000.00	1,150,000.00	1,474,800.00	1,546,300.00	1,546,300.00
Pineapples	1,180,000.00	1,310,000.00	1,234,200.00	1,229,400.00	1,229,400.00
Papayas	700,000.00	700,000.00	750,627.00	783,383.00	783,383.00

Table 3: Production of major vegetables arranged in descending order

Vegetables	Year				
	2002	2003	2004	2005	2006
Veg,nec	27,180,000	34,740,000	35,000,000	35,000,000	35,000,000
Potatoes	23,920,000	23,268,700	23,060,100	23,631,300	23,910,000
Eggplants	8,350,000	7,830,000	8,477,300	8,703,800	8,703,800
Tomatoes	7,460,000	7,600,000	8,125,600	8,637,700	8,637,700
Cassava	6,834,000	5,426,200	5,945,300	5,854,800	7,620,200
Onions, dry	5,450,000	4,506,100	5,922,500	6,434,600	6,434,600
Cabbages	5,680,000	5,800,000	5,594,600	6,147,700	6,147,700
Chick peas	5,473,000	4,236,800	5,717,500	5,469,400	5,600,000
Cauliflowers	4,890,000	4,800,000	4,940,200	4,507,900	4,507,90

Table 4: The details of arrivals of important perishables in the Trivandrum market is given below

Sl. No.	Name of commodity	Average Kerala arrivals	Average out of state arrivals
1.	Carrot	00	431
2.	Banana	738	1474
3.	Beet root	00	412
4.	Tomato	00	1209
5.	Brinjal	00	721
6.	potato	00	830
7.	cabbage	00	1135

Table 5: The value wise export targets for the five years of the XI Plan period are given in the table

		Value: Rs in Crores				
Sl. No.	Commodities	2008	2009	2010	2011	2012
1.	Floriculture Products	381	437	502	580	665
2.	Fruits/Veg. Seeds	163	188	216	245	285
3.	Fresh Fruits & Veg.	2775	3190	3665	4115	4845
4.	Processed product	2655	2837	3264	3758	4320

production. Brazil occupies the third position, with 46 million tons and contributes 7 per cent in global production. The other countries among top ten producers are USA (5%), Italy (4%), Spain (3%), Mexico (3%), Indonesia (3%), Iran (2%) and Philippines (2 per cent). India occupies first place in production of mango, banana, litchi, papaya, pomegranate, and sapota, second place in limes and lemons and fifth place in pineapple production in the world. The productivity of grape is highest in the world. India has higher national average productivity in banana and sapota compared to world average productivity, while in citrus, mango, apple, guava, pineapple, papaya; India has substantial low productivity in comparison to the world average.

Vegetables - Global

China is the leading producer of vegetables in the world. India is the second largest vegetable producer with 11% production share in the world and Brazil is the third. India is also the second largest producer of most of the important vegetable crops at the global level, namely brinjal, cabbage, cauliflower, pea, onion and tomato except for potato and okra, where its ranking is number 3 and 1 respectively. However, it falls behind in productivity in most of the crops except for tomato where India ranks at number 1. In okra, it is at par with world productivity and in cauliflower it is quite close to the world productivity.

INDIAN SCENARIO

Fruits - Indian Scenario

India, with its wide diversity in climate and soil, has given rise to the formation of a variety of ecosystems. It produces a large range of fruits commercially in various agro climatic zones. India accounts for 12 per cent of global total production of fruit crops. Increase in the production and productivity is largely due to the adoption of improved technologies, which include quality planting material, balanced nutrients and timely protection against major insect-pests and diseases.

Vegetables - Indian Scenario

Total vegetable production in India before independence was 15 million tons and since independence for decades the growth rate was stabilized around 0.5%. The impetus on vegetable research and policy intervention to promote vegetable crops witnessed a sudden spurt in growth rate of 2.5%, a hike of five times during the last decade. The potential technological interventions with improved gene pool and precise management have taken growth rate to nearby 6% per annum. This may lead to increase production of vegetable crops close to 140 million tons by 2012.

Major Importing Countries

The major markets for Indian horticulture products are the West Asian countries and UK, Germany, the Netherlands in Europe. The top five destinations for various product groups are listed below.

Product Group	Major importing countries
Floriculture	USA, The Netherlands, UK, Germany, Japan
Fruits and vegetable seeds	USA, Pakistan, Japan, Bangladesh, The Netherlands
Fresh onions	Bangladesh, Malaysia, UAE, Sri Lanka, Bahrain
Other fresh vegetables	UAE, Nepal, UK, Saudi Arabia, USA
Walnuts	Spain, Germany, UK, Egypt, The Netherlands
Fresh mangoes	Bangladesh, UAE, Saudi Arabia, UK, Nepal
Fresh grapes	The Netherlands, UK, UAE, Bangladesh, Germany
Other fresh fruits	Bangladesh, UAE, Nepal, Saudi Arabia, The Netherlands
Dried and preserved veg.	Bangladesh, Sri Lanka, USA, UK, UAE
Mango pulp	Saudi Arabia, The Netherlands, Yemen, UAE, zz
Other processed fruits/veg.	USA, Israel, Saudi Arabia, UK, the Netherlands

Production: The cultivation of fruits and vegetables is done as per the international standards, i.e., the amount of pesticides and manure to be used to yield maximum results. The harvesting of fruits and vegetables has to be matched with shipment date as time is very important. It has been found that only some of the farmers do cultivation with the intention of exporting and some of the exporters procure the product from open market which leads to quality degradation and rejections by importers.

Storage and Packing: Proper packing to be made as per international standard so that aging and decaying of perishable goods may be controlled before it reaches its destination. Some of the exporters are very careful in their packing and use standard packing methods. Perishable goods have to be stored in a temperature controlled warehouse for preservation. Since lack of such facilities will have adverse effects on price fluctuations as well as quality of the product.

Transportation: Aging of fruits and vegetables starts from the time of harvest. So time is an important factor for exporting of perishable goods. Most of the time is taken in transportation of goods. So it is very important that logistics of transportation has to be planned with precision and preferably cold storage transportation is required. Since there is very small number of cold storage vehicles available most of the time exporters uses only ordinary goods vehicle to transport it to the airport.

Air Cargo: Air cargo is becoming an increasingly important dimension of India's growing trade in perishable goods, as it reduces the time of travel by 80% compared to sea cargo. Even though there is an increase in exports, numerous problems and bottleneck to trade persist like complicities of customs procedure and documentation. As a result the dwell time of cargo at Indian airports is significantly longer than that of other major airports in Asia. This compromises the competitiveness of Indian industry reducing trade potential.

POST HARVEST LOSSES

Storage and Packing

Horticultural produces are of perishable nature. Losses in quantity and quality affect horticultural crops between harvesting and their consumption. The magnitude of post-harvest losses in fresh fruits and vegetables is estimated at 5-25% in developed countries and 25-50% in developing countries. In India, the estimated losses range up to 40% depending upon the commodity.

Fruits and vegetables are the fastest growing sectors within agriculture. In the Tnth Plan it is proposed to double horticulture production by 2011-12 through National Horticulture Mission. The subgroup of Eleventh Five Year plan revealed that there is 97% marketable surplus in fruits, which means that, then there is need to have strong post-harvest infrastructure for post-harvest management of these perishables. This is not only loss of produce of crores of rupees but also wastage of labour, energy and inputs involved in production.

Thus, creation of post-harvest infrastructure and awareness need utmost attention to increase the availability of quality foods. To reduce these losses, producers and handlers like wholesalers, agents, sub-wholesalers and retailers must understand biological and environmental factors involved in deterioration and use of post-harvest technology to minimize these losses so that best possible quality could be maintained. With the technological advancements in horticulture, it is a proven fact that per unit reduction of post-harvest losses is cheaper than equivalent increase in production of high value horticultural crops.

Cold Storage

Cold storage plays an important role in the preservation of perishables especially fruits and vegetables. It helps in scientific preservation of perishables, stabilizes prices by regulating marketing period and supplies. It also helps the primary producer from distress sale and encourages farmers to produce more. In view of the fall in prices of fruits and vegetables immediately after the harvest and to avoid spoilage of fruits and vegetables, it has become necessary to create cold storage facilities in the producing as well as consuming centres to take care of the existing and projected production of fruits and vegetables. The most obvious losses after harvest are caused by mechanical injury, decay and aging. Losses in moisture, vitamins, sugars and starches are less obvious, but they adversely affect quality and nutrition. Rough handling and holding at undesirably high temperature or too low temperature increase losses. Such losses can be substantially reduced by adopting the recommended cold storage practices.

Product Quality and Suitability

Maximum storage life can be obtained only by storage of high quality commodities soon after harvest. Different lots of fruits and vegetables may vary greatly in their storage behaviour. Storage potential may be influenced by variety, climate, soil and cultural conditions, maturity and handling practices. When products are transported from a distance, grown under unfavourable conditions, or are deteriorated, appropriate storage allowance should be made.

Fresh fruits and vegetables intended for storage should be as free as possible from skin breaks, bruises and decay. Bruises and other mechanical damages not only detract from the appearance of the product and allow entrance of decay organisms. Much more decay will develop on bruised areas of apples than on non-bruised areas. Mechanical damage may also increase moisture loss by as much as 400%. The amount of incipient decay infection, which influences storage potential of grapes and apples, can be predicted by forcasting of decay early in storage period. Only lots with good storage potential should be held for late season marketing.

Pre-cooling Methods

Produce may be cooled by means of cold air (room cooling and forced air cooling), cold water (hydro-cooling), direct contact with ice, and evaporation of water from the produce (evaporative cooling and vacuum cooling).

Transit Cooling

Temperature at night is lower than that during the day. Therefore, if the produce is to be shifted on the day of harvesting to a place at considerably long distance, it may be transported at night. Cooling of the produce during transportation offers the same effect by stimulating the forced air-cooling method, especially in winter. Once the produce is placed in the cold store, it radiates heat to the room by virtue of field heat and heat of respiration. The sooner the produce is brought to its optimum storage temperature then the sooner respiration is brought under control, which results in maximum storage life of the produce.

Cold Storages

After pre-cooling, the produce is brought to cold storage to extend its shelf-life. Commercial refrigerated preservation of perishable commodities is a short-term process. Costly produces like dry fruits, potato, orange, chemicals, processed foods like fruit juices, pulp, concentrate, dairy products, frozen meals; fish, poultry, etc., are stored in cold storages. These cold storages should be multi-chambered, having facilities for storage of various kinds of fruits, vegetables, spices, etc., at different temperatures and humidity. This helps in better utilization of cold storages, throughout the year and is more economical.

Storage Facilities in Kerala

Kerala is considered a consumer state and it imports most of the fruits and vegetables from the neighboring states. The agricultural production in Kerala is reducing day by day, due to rapid urbanization and also due to high labour cost.

Exporters in the state procure the product from neighboring states. As regards cold storages in the state, almost 95% of them are for storage of marine products. These cold storages are not available for rent and used for the captive use of exporters. Kerala exported Rs.120 crore worth of fruits and vegetable products in 2009. Banana and pineapple are the main fruits exported from the state. As regards vegetables bitter gourd, long beans, snake gourd, etc., are exported from Kerala. New cold storages are constructed by the exporters depending upon the export demand. There are very few cold storages for horticultural commodities and the development of such cold storages in the state is slow. There is no concession for cold storage industry in the state. Considering the fact that almost 60% of the operating expense for a cold storage is electricity bill, some sort of concession to the electricity tariff for horticultural based cold storages may be provided by the state govt. as done in the neighbouring states.

It may be seen from the table that the arrival of fruits and vegetables in the market is very good. There is however no cold storage in the district for fruits and vegetables. Being the capital city there is good potential for such cold storage here. Considering the fact that there is an international airport in the city, there is good potential for export and import of perishables. Vegetables and fruits can be also be brought from Madurai, Trichy, etc., and stored here. There is a cold storage at the international airport for the benefit of exporters but the capacity is only 10% compared to requirement, and the facilities are not as per exporter's requirements.

Packaging and Grading

Packing can be viewed as a convenience in achieving orderly marketing. The package is a convenient unit for transporting the produce from the place of production to point of sale or consumption. Packing may be in wooden boxes, bamboo baskets, jute bags, plastic crates, and corrugated fibre board boxes. These could be used depending upon the availability of raw material for packaging and type of market where the produce is to be marketed.

Grading of horticultural commodities is an important aspect particularly from marketing point of view. It is, however, not being followed generally at producer's level in our country. Maturity, shape, colour, quality and other physical parameters have to be kept in view while going for grading of products. It is well known that graded products get better price in market even that farmers do not follow it because of slackness only while on the other hand some size grading is done by sub-wholesaler or retailers.

Creation of grading/packing infrastructure is an important aspect. However, it is not up to the desired level. Some states governments have taken steps while others have not. For example, Andhra Pradesh is one of the largest producers of fruits and vegetables in the country, yet there is no match between production and post-harvest infrastructure. The state government is developing cool chain facilities, especially in mango growing areas and has also identified Agri Export Zones for three important horticultural regions in the state. The state government is also providing financial support for establishment of packing houses and packing materials.

TRANSPORTATION

Transportation is a big and often the most important factor in the marketing and exporting of fresh produce. Fresh produce is transported by many means from head-load to air-freighting.

Road Transport

Most of the fresh produce is transported through road, particularly by trucks, open pickup or bigger trucks to sorting and packing location or to the airport. Specialized transport vehicles should be used for transporting the horticultural produce, which may have separate cabins and partial shade so that losses during transportation are minimized.

Air Transport

Air transport is mainly used for export of fresh produce. Even though it is costly, exporters prefer it because of time — an important factor for exporting perishable goods.

Containerization

The use of containers for the transportation of goods was recently introduced in India. Relatively little attention has however been given to the use of containers for the transport of fresh horticultural produce. Containerization provides an excellent system for the shipment of goods from one place to another.

Refrigerated Containers

Refrigerated containers are used in the transportation of fruits, vegetables and flowers in many developing countries.

Ventilated Containers

The design and fabrication of ventilated containers which incorporate evaporative cooling systems should be considered for the Indian context. One of the greatest advantages of the container is that it can be placed on truck or rail, without interfering with the movement of the vehicle. Palletization and containerization will go a long way in developing local and international trade.

Non-refrigerated Vehicles

Non-refrigerated vehicles are generally open-sided trucks, with wire mesh frames. This type of transportation is inexpensive, convenient and easy. Truck can be used for the delivery of fresh produce, other goods and passengers when required. Layers of produce are not however separated in order to prevent heat generation. Often the produce is stacked too high. Non-refrigerated vehicles are used for transporting produce over distances of up to 850 km. On arrival the produce must be unloaded or sold as quickly as possible to overcome overheating. Fresh produce must not be watered prior to loading, as this will lead to decay.

Transportation of Exports Goods in Kerala

Roads in Kerala are narrow and congested, containerization and specialized vehicles for transporting perishable goods are not available, mainly due to bad roads and high cost of transportation. So the exporters use ordinary vehicles and goods movement is done mostly in the nights. Another peculiar issue is the labour cost for loading and unloading of goods from the vehicle. Here the workers union are strong and charge exorbitantly.

Air Cargo Complex at Trivandrum Airport

Due to time factor, exporting of perishable goods is mainly done via Air cargo, even though the cost is much more than the sea transport. Trivandrum cargo complex facility is maintained by KSIE (Kerala State Industrial Enterprises). KSIE had carried out two major expansion projects at TACT (Trivandrum Air Cargo Terminal). It has also obtained quality certification from the Bureau of Indian Standards as per IS:ISO 9001-2000 standards. TACT is the major centre for export of perishables from South India. Nearly 75 MT per day of vegetables, fruits and other perishables like meat, fish, flowers etc. are exported from TACT.

Processing of Fruits and Vegetables

In India, less than 2% of fruits and vegetables produced are processed as against 65% in the US, 70% in Brazil, 78% in the Philippines, 80% in South Africa and 83% in Malaysia. The annual wastage of fruits and vegetables is estimated to be Rs 25 thousand crore. The value addition is only 7% in India as against 23% in China and 88% in UK.

Due to rapid expansion of internal and external market of processing industries, it is essential to develop such techniques, which reduce post-harvest losses, do value addition and improve quality of the product. Changing dietary pattern, demand of fruits and vegetables in domestic market has increased. To meet the challenge fruit and vegetable production has increased manifolds in the last few decades. There has been unprecedented increase in the export of some fruits like mango, walnut and grapes in the last few years. If more fruits are processed then there will be less wastage of perishable goods. India is one of the largest fruit and vegetable exporters in the world. This strong footing in agriculture provides a large and varied raw material base for food processing. There should be technology upgradation, quality management, firm adherence to export commitments and acquisition of appropriate negotiation skills. India's exports of processed fruits and vegetables has increased from Rs. 2454.61 crore (USD million 554.46) in 2007-08 to Rs. 2502.28 crore (USD million 555.07) in 2008-09.

The Indian food processing industry is primarily export oriented. India is the largest mango producer in the world, and has the range of varieties in mango and processing mangoes. Export of mango pulp is significant. Two main clusters of mango pulp are there in the country which has only around 45 processing units with a good backward linkage of Alphanso and Totapuri variety of mangoes. These clusters are Chittoor in the state of Andhra Pradesh and Krishnagiri in the state of Tamil Nadu. Most of these processing units are HACCP certified and conform to required standard. India's geographical situation gives it the unique advantage of connectivity to Europe, the Middle East, Japan, Singapore, Thailand, Malaysia and Korea. One such example indicating India's location advantage is the value of trade in agriculture and processed food between India and the Gulf region.

FINDINGS - GLOBAL FACTORS AFFECTING EXPORTS FROM INDIA

Artificially Low Prices in Global Trade due to Export Subsidies and Domestic Support by the Developed Countries

The biggest challenge which Indian exporters of agro and food products face in the international markets pertains to low prices as an influence of the excessive export subsidies and domestic support extended by the developed countries to their farmers. We can hardly survive the price war unleashed by the subsidy rich farmers of the USA and the EU. Negotiations under WTO, so far have not made much headway in persuading the rich nations to stop giving subsidy to their farmers in different forms. There has to be a balance between the three pillars of the negotiations. If tariffs were to go down it is essential that developed countries reduce export subsidies and domestic support implying reduction in production and increase in possibilities of import of foodstuffs by them from developing countries most of which are low cost producers.

Testing Standards Issues

The Agreement on Application of SPS Measures contains detailed provisions on transparency, harmonization and standardization. However, the very high level of standards set by some developed countries makes it amply clear that developing countries with their current level of industrial expertise would find it difficult to achieve these levels. Many of these standards are set not on the basis of adequate scientific justification but are driven by commercial considerations. Hence, they tend to operate as non-tariff barriers affecting trade performance of developing countries. Standards set by private bodies have been started in many Western European countries which include parameters relating to social and environmental factors also.

The matter regarding upgradation of India's status to GBR level-I (signifying no risk of BSE) by European Commission has been pending for several years. APEDA has taken these issues relating to specific products with respective member countries during bilateral discussions. However, the experience on pace of such deliberations leaves much to be desired.

Local Factors Affecting Exports from India

1. Lack of post-harvest infrastructure facilities and methods.
2. Lack of knowledge on quality of products to be maintained.
3. Delay in air lifting of cargo due to procedural delays in central excise and customs clearance department.
4. Charges for using facilities in air cargo terminal are very high.
5. Lack of cold storage units near to production centre.
6. No proper road connectivity from the place of production.
7. Less cargo space availability in aircraft than required, as there is only few aircraft flying to European and gulf countries.
8. There is only one cargo aircraft flying to Dubai from Trivandrum airport.

AGRICULTURAL EXPORTS PROJECTIONS AND PLANS

Promotional Activities by Government

Agriculture export zones

With a view to promoting agricultural exports from the country and remunerative returns to the farming community in a sustained manner, the concept of the agriculture export zones (AEZ) was floated. These zones have been set up for end to end development for export of specific products from a geographically contiguous area.

AEZ are to be identified by the state government, who would evolve a comprehensive package of services provided by all state government agencies, state agriculture universities and all institutions and agencies of the Union Government for intensive delivery in these zones. Corporate sector with proven credentials would be encouraged to sponsor new agri export zone or take over already notified agri export zone or part of such zones for boosting agri exports from the zones.

Services which would be managed and coordinated by state government/corporate sector and would include provision of pre- post-harvest treatment and operations, plant protection, processing, packaging, storage and related research and development etc. APEDA will supplement, within its schemes and provisions, efforts of state governments for facilitating such exports.

Government assistance in bio-fertilizer production and quality assurance

To attain production targets, the Government of India implemented a central sector scheme entitled "National Project on Development and use of Bio-fertilizers (NPDB)" during the Ninth Plan for the production, distribution and promotion of bio-fertilizers. A National Bio-fertilizer Development Centre was established at Ghaziabad as a subordinate office of the Department of Agriculture and Cooperation with six regional centres. The purpose of the scheme covered organization of training courses for extension workers and field demonstrations and providing quality control services, R&D and HRD related activities. Capacity creation and production was, however, encouraged through one time grant for new units. The financial assistance, given as grant-in-aid to the tune of Rs. 13 lakh and now increased to Rs. 20 lakh per unit and thrown open for all, was routed through NABARD/NCDC.

Suggestions - thrust areas of Improvement

- India needs to standardize pre- and post-harvest management system and harmonize them with the international standards. Technical experts should participate in all Codex and SPS/TBT related meetings and conferences.
- India needs to invest in post-harvest and laboratory infrastructure, technology upgradation, quality/food safety and training. We also need to re-orient our own extension machinery with an element of motivation.
- India need to implement "India GAP" (the draft national program for good agricultural practices, currently under consideration of the Govt.) in the country on a project mode as soon as possible. Here again, training at all levels will be a critical factor.
- It will be extremely important to introduce a new scheme to encourage value addition in agricultural products with the aim of converting India from being an exporter of bulk agri products into an exporter of agri products in consumer packs.
- Market intelligence activities and competence should be strengthened in India to meet the increasing global competition. If necessary, we should position experts in our mission at key locations.

- Invest vigorously in market promotion activities on a project basis, both on a generic basis and for brand building to enable exporters export ready-to-eat products in consumer packs for direct retail by retailers / supermarkets.
- Government should provide support to NABARD in an appropriate manner to enable NABARD to work out an arrangement with commercial banks so that finance to agri processing units is available at a concessional rate of interest. This will encourage viable investments in the AEZs.
- Make available concession on premium on crop insurance in the AEZs, where contract farming arrangements are prevalent. This concession could be up to 50% of the premium amount.
- India needs to clearly define our own food safety objectives and invest in scientific risk analysis activities to monitor imports.

CONCLUSION

India's growth in exports of perishable goods has grown exponentially in the last few years. It is mainly attributed to the opening up of global market, improved quality conscious, information on export opportunities and major trust and push given by the government of India.

To maintain the growth momentum, India has to improve its productivity and storage techniques as we know that 30 to 40% of our produce is wasted or perished due to lack of scientific handling of product and storage. Movement of goods in India is 20 miles per hour compared to 60 miles per hour in developed counties. So it is very important to improve supply chain infrastructure such as cold storage, packaging, transportation and cargo shipment of both air and sea has to compete with international companies. Promoting R&D facilities and human resource development will also improve the productivity.

REFERENCES

1. Acharya, S.S. (1998). "Agricultural price policy and development: some facts and emerging issues", *Indian Journal of Agricultural Economics*, vol. 52, No.1: 1-47.
2. Desai, M. (1999). "What should be India's economic priorities in a globalized world?", Indian Council for Research on International Economic Relations, New Delhi.
3. Gulati, A. and Sharma, A.N. (1995). "Subsidy syndrome in Indian agriculture", *Economic and Political Weekly.*
4. Kalirajan, K.P., Mythili, G. and Sankar, U. (eds.). (2001). *Accelerating Growth Through Globalization of Indian Agriculture*, Macmilan, India.
5. Schumacher, Jr., A. (2000). "International agricultural trade at a crossroads", *Economic Perspectives*, An Electronic Journal of the US Department of State.
6. Sivakumar, S.D., Balasubramaniam, R. and Srinivasan, N. (1999). "Growth linkage effects of agro-industrialization", *Indian Journal of Agricultural Economics*, vol. 54, No. 3, pp. 412-419.

Websites

- www.apeda.com
- www.eximguru.com
- www.nabard.org
- www.infrastructure.gov.in

23

The Distressing Issues in Performances of Clearing and Forwarding Agents in Chennai

R. PRABUDOSS AND I. JOSEPH RAJ

B.E., Final MBA Student, Department of Business Administration, Annamalai University
B.E., MBA., M.Phill. Asst.Professor, Department of Business Administration, Annamalai University

ABSTRACT

This paper deals with the growth of export industry with the leverage given by the government of India by way of incentives and other factors favouring the exponential growth of export. This in turn created a huge market requirement for clearing and forwarding agents. Whether the clearing and forwarding agents have geared for handling the increase in export activities is a case in point. This study aims to analyze the factors and problems which affect the performance in clearing and forwarding agents and also to analyze why the performances are varied year to year. In this study, the clearing and forwarding agents face problems in documentation side, exporter side, and importer side and also in custom house while paying duties. The study also made some findings on how the problems and disputes are settled.

Keywords: C&F agents, Consignment agent, Export house, Warehouse, Cargo.

Abbreviations: C&F Agents – Clearing & Forwarding Agents, **BL** - Bill of Lading, **BE** - Bill of Entry, **FOB** – Free On Board.

INTRODUCTION

With today's cut-throat economy every company needs to act quickly and professionally in order to succeed. Being able to ship goods from one country to another in an efficient manner is essential to stay above the competition. Freight forwarding services are dedicated to making the shipping process a lot easier and quicker. A professional freight forwarder will act as an intermediary between your company and the transport companies, handling everything that is related to the shipping process. C&Fs (customs clearing and forwarding agents) grew out of the need to provide businesses with smart shipping resources and provide up-to-date imformation to get through customs quickly and easily. One of the primary jobs of a C&F is to keep your shipping costs low, by providing a range of available transportation modes with services related to shipping, like packaging, and acting as experts in clearing customs. The best service they can provide for you is tailoring shipping needs particularly suited for your business according to the goods that you ship and where they are sourced. For importing clients, they work to get the best mode of transportation from the manufacturer or wholesaler to the local customs office upon arrival. For exporting, they choose the best method to take goods from your doorstep to the destination's customs office. A C&F can greatly reduce shipping expenses and the time you spend on customs forms, etc.

Objectives

The objective of the paper is

- To study the distressing issues which are affecting the performances in C&F Agents
- To suggest strategies that are used to overcome the problems and to develop the performance of C& Fs.

International Role of C&F Agent

International freight forwarders are companies specialized in moving cargo to foreign destinations at the client's request. The main advantage of collaborating with a professional freight forwarder is the agent's extensive knowledge of all the overseas transport elements. Freight forwarding services are very familiar with import and export regulations, specific rules of foreign countries, shipping methods and all the documentation needed for foreign trade. These days, shipping freight overseas is virtually impossible without the expertise and advice of an experienced freight forwarder. Freight forwarders practically assist exporters with everything related to the freight shipping process. Furthermore, freight forwarding services must keep you informed of all the potential costs involved in the shipping process. Therefore, a freight forwarding company must offer advisements on foreign costs, port charges, consular fees, special documentation costs, insurance costs and all of their handling fees. The forwarder may also recommend special packing methods that will protect your cargo during transit and make all the arrangements for the packing process. The key elements such as price, date, packaging and shipping method, the freight forwarder will review all of the documents to make sure everything is in perfect order. This step is particularly important in order to avoid any unpleasant surprises in customs. The freight forwarding company is also required to prepare any required special documentation such as the bill of landing or non-vessel operating common carrier (NVOCC) documents. A forwarder can also make arrangements with foreign customs brokers to make sure the cargo fulfills the customs export documentation regulations. Warehousing, international payment methods and risk assessment are also provided by the freight forwarder as part of the service package.

C&F Agents

C&F agent means any person who is engaged in providing any service, either directly or indirectly, concerned with the clearing and forwarding operation in any manner to any other person and including a consignment agent.

Therefore, a service will fall under the C&F agents service, if it includes:

- ✓ A person
- ✓ Engaged in providing any service connected with the clearing & forwarding operations; and
- ✓ Includes a consignment agent

Meaning of Person

The term 'person' has not been defined in the content of service tax. But the term 'person' has been defined as "Person shall include any Company or Association or Body of Individual, whether Incorporate or not" according to clause (42) of section 3 of General Clauses Act, 1897. Therefore, C&F agents may be artificial or juristic person or may be a natural person.

Consignment Agent

The term 'consignment' means 'the act of consigning: the things consigned together'. A 'consignment agent' is also included in the definition of 'C&F agents', but it has not been defined in the context of service tax. Therefore, it should be understood in its commonly understood meaning and scope. In common commercial practice, the principal sends the goods to the consignment agent known as consignee for the purpose of sale and distribution. The consignee is entitled to agreed commission/remuneration for his services. The government in Para 2.1.2 of the circular No. 59/8/2003, dated 20-6-2003 has clarified that nature of service provided by a consignment agent is different from that provided by a commission agent. It is clarified that exemption to commission agent from the whole of service tax under Notification No. 13/2003, dated 20-6-2003 is not available to consignment agent, which remains taxable under the category of 'clearing and forwarding services'

Clearing & Forwarding Operations

A C&F agent normally undertakes the following activities:

- Receiving the goods from the factories or premises of the principal or his agents.
- Warehousing these goods
- Receiving dispatch orders from the principal
- Arranging dispatch of goods as per the directions of the principal by engaging transport on his own or through the authorized transporters of the principal.
- Maintaining records of the receipt and dispatch of goods and the stock available at the warehouses.
- Preparing invoices on behalf of the principal.

Function of C&F Agent and Consignment Agent

The C&F agent's functions are to perform all the functions of clearing and forwarding operations, but a consignment agent does not necessarily undertake all the above activities. A consignment agent receives the goods from the principal and stores them on behalf of the principal and in case sale is made by the principal directly then dispatches the goods to the customs on the direction to principal. But normally the consignment agent undertakes to sell the goods on behalf of the principal and even realizes the payments from the customers and acts as declared agent and also takes his separate registration under sales tax and central exercise in his own name. Therefore only those consignment agents are covered under C&F agents service who perform the function in relation to 'clearing & forwarding operations', in other words receive the goods from the principal and dispatch them on the direction of the principal. If consignment agent undertakes at his own and dispatches the goods stored by him on behalf of principal at his own discretion, raises bills/challans, keeps records for stock and sale made by him, realizes the payment from the customers and remits to the principal and acts as declared agent. There is no doubt to say that where consignment agents functions is to sell the goods on behalf of principal, such function cannot be regarded as service in relation to 'clearing forwarding operation', hence no service tax is applicable on sale of goods by consignment agent under the category of 'clearing and forwarding service'.

Service of C&F Agents

The C&F agents are engaged/appointed by manufacturer of goods (excisable and non-excisable goods), producer and distributors of goods and shall also be included such agents appointed for agriculture and mineral goods. Normally in there is a contract between the principal of C&F agents, indicating the commission or remuneration to which the clearing and forwarding agent is entitled. Generally, a C&F agent receives goods from the factories or premises of the principal or his agent and stores these goods, dispatches these goods as per orders received from the principal or owner, arranges transport, etc. For this service, the C&F agents receive the commissions on the basis of agreed terms. Therefore, an essential characteristic of any service, to fall in the category of C&F agents, is that the relationship between the service provider and receiver should be in the nature of principal (owner) and agent. The C&F agent carries out all activities in respect of goods right from stage of their clearance from the premises of the principal to its storage and delivery to the customers.

The Distressing Issues faced by C&F Agents

The C & fFagent face problems in:

- ✓ Documents
- ✓ Transportation
- ✓ Exporter side
- ✓ Importer side
- ✓ Customs house

Documentation

- Documentations are generated as per import documents, i.e., invoice, BL.
- If any mismatch occurs due to wrong entry of product or quantity, then EPR code is generated because only EPR code can indicate where mismatch has occurred.
- If BE will be generated with any error, then the C & F agents have to amend that problem in 48 hours.
- Once the problem identified the earlier EPR code is cancelled and the process of documentation is repeated to generate the fresh EPR.

Transportation

- Trucks not available in time.
- Cost for transportation varies for each consignment, so that every time hard negotiation takes place.
- Insufficient cranes to upload the cargo.
- In case of local transporters strike.
- Any uncertainty during travel.

Exporter Side

- Any mismatching of goods with respect to invoice.
- Customs do not accept the documents or release of goods for various reasons.
- C&F agents inform the buyer and seller. The seller issues the certificate of documents for clearing the issues, for releasing the goods.

Importer Side

- In case of cheating by importers and they close the company. At that time the C&F agents will settle the dispute to customs house.

Custom House

- Since C&F agents act on behalf of the exporter or importer any issues with the customs house, agents will have to bear all the consequences.

Process of C&F Agents in Import

- Agent clears the goods to the importers from the ship.
- The following documents are submitted to the customer house for clearing the goods.
  - ✓ Bill of lading
  - ✓ Invoice and packing list
  - ✓ Certificate of origin
  - ✓ Letter of credit (During conflict)
  - ✓ Analysis certificate, catalog (if necessary)
- After providing these documents to customs and paid the duty.
- Then approach steamer agent and submit original bill of lading.
- Then the steamer agent issues the delivery order after paying the charges

The local charges are:
- ✓ From port to customs notified area (CFS)
- ✓ Local transportation charges
- ✓ Harbour dews

- ➢ Along with delivery order, customs duty payable challan, BE, BL, invoice, packing list, certificate of origin are submitted to Inspection Officer in CFS.
- ➢ After checking the document he visits the cargo as per the document.
- ➢ If all things are clear then only he releases the goods, otherwise they go for negotiations.
- ➢ Then BE is issued by customs.

Process of C&F Agents in Export

- ➢ First determine either buyer choose CIF, FOB or C&F in terms of contract.
- ➢ Prepare the invoice and packing list according to rule and as per the client's requirement.
- ➢ Submitting the document to customs for generating the shipping bill.
- ➢ Bring the cargo to customs notified area in case of central excise is not covered in factory. They check the exports goods with respect to packing list, invoiceand shipping bill. If all formalities are in order, they allow to stuff the cargo in container and permit for shipment.
- ➢ If central excise is covered in factory means, container is brought to the factory and stuffs the goods, which is verified by central excise people and they attest invoice & packing list and also seal the container.
- ➢ The attested invoice and packing list is submitted to the customs office. They check if the previous copy and then only they generate shipping bill.
- ➢ After completion of all document formalities the cargo is allowed to be shipped.
- ➢ The shipping bill is submitted in duplicate to steamer agent after completing the customs formalities.
- ➢ Streamer agent lifts the container to appropriate vessel.
- ➢ After loading the container into the vessel, the steamer agent issuing the bill of lading (for evidence of completing shipment).
- ➢ Then send one set of documents such as
  - ✓ Bill of lading
  - ✓ Certificate of origin (optional)
  - ✓ Invoice
  - ✓ Packing list
  - ✓ Shipping bill is used for remittance of payment or receiving of payment.

To the C&F agent who in turn give it to the exporter.

CONCLUSION

A first-class C&F agent will have knowledge and access to several modes of goods transportation. To keep track of what document you require and who need them, C&F agents work on clients behalf to gather all the necessary documents to clear your goods through customs. They also keep up with changes in customs and staying abreast of updated regulations is essential, especially if you ship internationally from multiple countries. A good C&F agent should also have connections to link via the web to various customs and port authorities to access current information about your shipments. An excellent C&F agent will also have access to warehouses that can store your goods as they move along the shipping process from the point of origin to delivery. In some countries, having access to a secure warehouse facility is vital to avoid loss of goods or damaged goods.

The C&F agent is invaluable, because they help with:

1. Customs and duty forms
2. Legal documents
3. Certificate of origin
4. Estimating costs for entering the country
5. Choosing the most efficient mode of transport and packaging for clearing customs

REFERENCES

1. C. Rama Gopal, Export Import Procedures- Documentation and Logistics: New Age International Publishers.
2. EXIM Policy Manual- 2009 to 2014.
3. N. Kumar, R. Mittal, Export Management: Anmol publisher.

24

Evaluation of Electronics and IT Exports in India

A. Senthilkumaran and M.G. Loganathan

B.E., Final MBA Student, Department of Business Administration, Annamalai University
MBA, LLB, M.Phil, Asst. Professor, Department of Business Administration, Annamalai University

ABSTRACT

This paper examines the growth of dynamic capabilities of the Indian software industry by looking in some detail at the changing constraints, opportunities and competition facing incumbent firms. It emphasizes the important role played by government in adapting to the requirement of the industry by changing the rules and formalities. Tight labour market conditions in inducing investment in process capability and the role of entrepreneurial experimentation in evolving a business model (outsourced software) are best suited to limited resource advantages of Indian software firms.

INTRODUCTION

Electronics and information technology is proving to be the growth engine in the current day economies of the world. The liberalized policy initiatives of the Government of India in the last decade have propelled the Indian IT industry on to a path of development and prosperity. Over the years, the electronics hardware industry has evolved to offer several innovative products for the convenience of mankind. Electronic devices have become an integral part of human life and are playing a major role in their everyday routine activities. The electronics hardware industry is identified as one of the fastest growing segments in terms of international trade. The electronics hardware and computer software/services industry, a comparatively new entrant in India's export horizon, has emerged as a forerunner among all industries and has been consistently treading on a high growth path in recent years.

India has embarked on a policy agenda, which aims to restructure its economy with enhanced global participation. Foreign Direct Investment (FDI) to supplement domestic investment for achieving a quantum jump in growth rate is now an integral part of government of India policy initiative. Imparting greater transparency to business procedures and integration with global marketplace are seen as the hallmark of the new industrial, trade and fiscal policies. Salient features of the industrial policy for the electronics and IT sector are:

Licensing virtually abolished except for manufacturing aerospace and defence equipment. Private sector entry into defence manufacturing is permitted. There is no reservation for public sector enterprises in the electronics industry and private sector investment is welcome in every area except aerospace and a few strategic defence industries. Electronics and IT units can be set up anywhere in the country subject to clearance from the authorities responsible for control of environmental pollution and local zoning and land use regulations. Industries exempted from licensing are only required to file information in the prescribed industrial entrepreneurs memorandum (IEM) with the Secretariat for Industrial Assistance (SIA), Ministry of Industry, Government of India.

The IT industry has shaped up as a major success story in Indian economy. Exports of computer software and IT enabled services have become a large component of the exports of the country. This is also an area where the government's role has been very different from that in some other industries. The important contribution of the government in the growth of this industry consists of telecom policies, which enabled low cost computer networking in the country and investments in human capital such as through the IITs. Today, India's competency in information technology, more significantly in computer software and IT enabled services, is recognized globally. Over the last decade, the Indian IT industry has been growing by leaps and bounds.

Research Methodology

Collect data/information about cargo through

Secondary data collection:

- Internet
- e-journal

Research Design

Research design is the based framework, which provides guidelines for the research process. It is a map or blueprint according to which the research is to be conducted. The research design specifies the methods for data collection and data analysis determines the source of data. Most specifically it was a kind of "descriptive conclusive research" which takes care of who, when, where, what, how and why aspects of the investigation further the researcher used the statistical method to serve the purpose of the project, it permitted the research to derive more accurate generalization whose reliability could be measured.

India's Electronics and Computer Software/services Industry (2008-09)

India's electronics and computer software/services industry was estimated to be Rs. 3,79,754 crore (US$ 82.57 billion) during the year 2008-09.

The Share of Electronics Hardware

The industry is estimated to be Rs. 94,690 crore (US$ 20.58 billion) and that of computer/services sector is Rs. 2,85,064 crore (US$ 61.98 billion). In percentage share terms, production of electronics hardware accounts for a share of 24.93 per cent and software/services accounts for 75.07 per cent. Production of electronics and computer software/services sector during the year 2008-09 registered a growth of 23.93 per cent (8.49 per cent in US$ terms) over the year 2007-08 when the total production of electronics, computer software/services was estimated to be Rs. 3,06,420 crore (US$ 76.11 billion).

Share of Electronics and Computer Software/services Industry in India's GDP During 2008-2009

The production of Electronics and Computer Software/Services estimated at Rs. 3,79,754 crore (US$ 82573 million) accounts for a share of 7.70 per cent in India's GDP at current prices during 2008-09. This is slightly higher than the share of this sector in India's GDP in 2007-08 estimated at 7.64 per cent. The share of electronics and computer software/services industry in India's GDP is continuously increasing as it can be seen from the graph above.

World Electronics and Computer Software/service Market and India's Share

The world production of electronics and computer swoftware/services during the year 2008-09 was estimated to be US$ 2640 billion. The world electronics hardware production was estimated to be US$ 1700 billion and IT services market is estimated to be US$ 940 billion. India's total production of electronics and computer software/services estimated at US$ 82.57 billion accounts for a share of 3.13 pe cent in the world production.

Electronics and Computer Software/services Exports (2008-09)

India's electronics and computer software/services export registered a growth of 38 per cent (21 per cent in US$ terms) during 2008-09 over the year 2007-08. In value terms, export of electronics and computer software/services during the year 2008-09 was estimated to be Rs. 2,59,060 crore (US$ 56.33 billion) up from Rs. 1,88,200 crore (US$ 46.74 billion) estimated in the year 2007-08. Export of electronics, computer software/services sector has been maintaining an outstanding annual average growth rate of 31.57 per cent (31.57 per cent in US$ terms) during the period 2003-04 to 2008-09.

Share of Electronics and Computer Software/service Export in India's Total Export

India's overall export during the year 2008-09 is estimated to be Rs. 13,55,049 crore (US$ 294.6 4 billion). India's electronics and computer software/services export valued at Rs. 2,59,060 crore (US$ 56.33 billion) accounts for a share of 19.12 per cent in India's over all export during the year 2008-09.

Major Items of Export under Electronics and Computer Software/services Sector During the Year 2008-09

Computer software/services valued at Rs. 1,64,828 crore (US$ 35.84 billion) is the top item of export in this sector during the year 2008-09. ITeS/BPO valued at Rs. 63,006 crore (US$ 13.70 billion) is the second top item of export. Followed by are the items under the electronics hardware category. Telephone sets which includes mobile phones were the major items of export under the electronic goods during the year 2008-09. In value terms, export of telephone sets during 2008-09 was estimated to be Rs. 11,142 crore (US$ 2.42 billion). Solar cells which were at the sixth position in the year 2007-08 registered a high growth of 149 per cent (118 per cent in US$ terms) and became the second major item of export under electronics hardware during the year 2008-09. The other major items of export during 2008-09 were parts of switches, rectifiers, recorded video tapes of educational nature and news/views, television sets, etc.

Region-wise Export Destinations for India's Electronics and Computer Software/services Sector

North America maintains the top position for India's export of electronics and computer software/services during the year 2008-09. This region accounts for 53.09 per cent of the total exports of electronics and computer software/services from India. Export to North America during 2008-09 was estimated to be Rs. 1,37,547 crore (US$ 29,908 million) up from Rs. 1,10,496 crore (US$ 27,446 million) estimated in 2007-08 registering a growth of 24.48 per cent (8.97 per cent in US$ terms). Export to EU countries remains second major destination for export of electronics and computer software services. Export to this region registered a growth of 52.39 per cent (33.40 per cent in US$ terms) during the year 2008-09 over the year 2007-08. In value terms, export of electronics and computer software/services to EU countries increased from Rs. 50,493 crore (US$ 12,542 million) estimated in 2007-08 to Rs. 76947 crore (US$ 16731 million) during the year 2008-09.

Singapore, Hong Kong and other South Asian countries, were at the third position for India's export of electronics and computer software/services during the year 2008-09. There was a growth of 53 per cent (34 per cent in US$ terms) to this region during 2008-09. Export to Middle East countries registered a high growth of 190 per cent (154 per cent in US$ terms) during the year 2008-09 over the year 2007-08. In value terms export to this region increased from Rs. 3947 crore (US$ 980 million) estimated in 2007-08 to Rs. 11460 crore (US$ 2492 million) during the year 2008-09 resulting in shifting of Middle East Region to fourth major destination for India's electronics and software exports. Export to African countries also registered a high growth of 256 per cent (212 percent in US$ terms). Export to Japan, Korea and other Far East countries and Latin American countries registered decline during the year 2008-09 over the year 2007-08.

Export Segments under Electronic and Computer Software/services Sector

Electronics and computer software/services sector can be broadly segmented as below:

1. Computer software and related services
2. ITeS / BPO
3. Computer hardware
4. Electronics components
5. Electronic instruments which includes
    - Industrial equipment
    - Medical equipment
    - Office equipment
    - Strategic, electronics equipment
6. Consumer electronics
7. Telecommunication hardware and related services.

The sectoral contribution of the above segments in the electronics and computer software / services export during the year 2008-09 is as shown.

Findings of the Study

- India's lack of success in exporting electronics hardware to the global market is deeply rooted to a variety of reasons which range from market dynamics to inadequacy of support policy initiatives;
- Low level of technology;
- Poor basic infrastructure;
- Long business cycles;
- Inadequacy of domestic investment, inability to attract foreign investment, mega investments from multinational companies;
- Lack of large scale manufacturing, and competitive product pricing;
- Lack of strong domestic market growth trends;
- Lack of decent profit margins;
- Lack of international branding;
- Inadequate promotional activities;
- Absence of strategic market plan;
- Lack of initiatives for new product development;
- Inadequate investment in research and development;
- Lack of global strategic partnerships;
- Lack of Indian grey market and lack of Indian brand recognition.

Recommendations

Government of India and the Indian electronics hardware manufacturers have to work in tandem, and take some proactive initiatives.

The initiatives to be taken by the Government include:
- Identification of a vision and strategic growth plan;
- Reducing operational costs of manufacturing and improving business attractiveness;
- Promoting single manufacturing clusters (for example, Motors Port Valley, Southern England);
- Promoting R&D activities and human resource development;
- Promoting India as an ideal destination for electronics hardware manufacturing;
- Promoting anchor investment in Indian electronics hardware industry;
- Relaxation of labour laws;
- Identification of thrust areas and development of incubators;
- Skill development;
- Proactive policies for development of entrepreneurship in hardware sector like software.

The industry level initiatives to be taken include:
- Developing mass production capacities;
- Global Partnerships for rapid technology acquisitions;
- Strategic exploitation of niche markets such as optoelectronics, Laser Diodes, LCD Monitors, nanotechnology, automotive electronics, passive components, OLEDs, DVD technology and Contract Manufacturing;
- MADE IN INDIA product branding and new products;
- Initiation of a Marketing Campaign through participation in International Fairs, India Contact Programmes, Release of print ads in International Publications and participation in the program for video documentaries about Indian advantages and profile in the form of CD for large distribution to leading companies in the world;
- Initiative to build the image of India as a manufacturing hub.
- Efforts need be made to model ESC after JETRO, Japan; EDB, Singapore, and HKTDC, Hong Kong and strengthen it with additional technical and secretarial manpower backup support so that it can open a separate wing within itself to promote horizontal and vertical growth of electronics and IT industry in India and exports

Major Obstacles and Suggestions for growth in FDI Flow in Electronics Hardware Sector

- Lack of awareness of investment opportunities in India.
- Wrong perception about setting up of operations in India.
- Poor infrastructure facility.
- Lack of publicity of India advantage.

Suggestions

- FDI flow necessitates a pro-business and pro-growth policy regime, projection and publicity of image of India emerging as the logistically and economically viable manufacturing hub for supply to the SAARC, Central Asian markets.
- India is to be promoted as an emerging potential market with low barriers and hassle-free to operate; and foreign investors are welcome in any special economic zones.

CONCLUSION

The Indian software exports have grown in spectacular fashion. Its success has, for the most part, been a combination of resource endowments, a mixture of neglect and active encouragement from the government, and good timing. The bulk of the Indian software exports consists of fairly mundane services such as low level programming and maintenance. The marked reliance on the access to low cost human capital has prompted considerable skepticism about the ability of the Indian software industry to sustain its performance, given the rapid growth in the demand for engineers and the relatively inelastic supply of engineers. The technological structure of export matters for their growth and learning and path dependence mean that structures are difficult to change as technologies evolve. Trade liberalization is insufficient. Indian manufactured exports suggest that their structure and positioning are not suited to sustained growth. The base for rapid structural change through FDI or domestic capabilities is weak. The current export slowdown in India reflects external conditions and may end soon; however, this does not assure rapid future growth.

Websites

- www.escindia.com
- www.moneycontrol.com
- www.nasscom.in
- www.teck.in
- www.financeexpress.com

Appendix

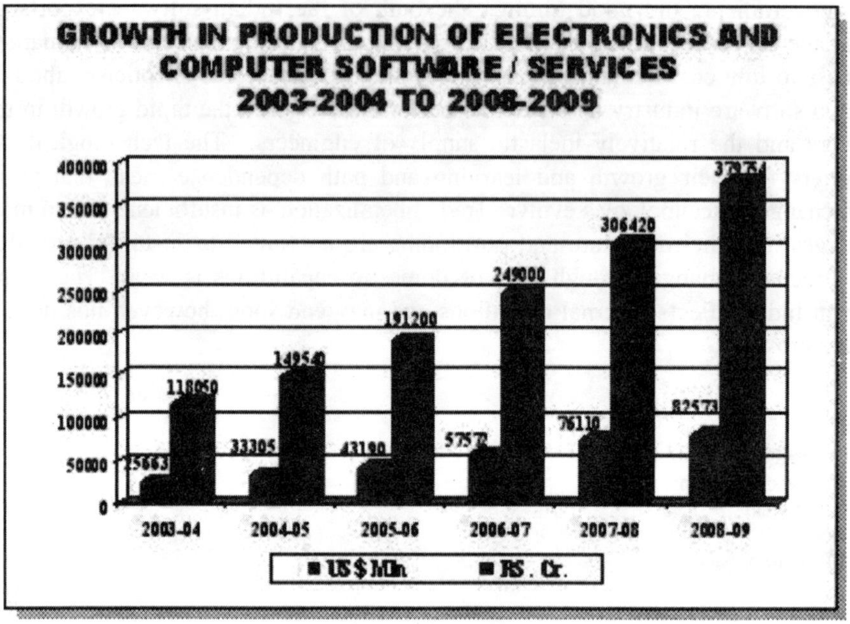
GROWTH IN PRODUCTION OF ELECTRONICS AND COMPUTER SOFTWARE / SERVICES
2003-2004 TO 2008-2009
400000
350000
300000
250000
200000
150000
100000
50000
0
25663
118050
33305
149540
43190
191200
57572
249000
76110
306420
82573
2003-04
2004-05
2005-06
2006-07
2007-08
2008-09
US $ Mln.
RS. Cr.

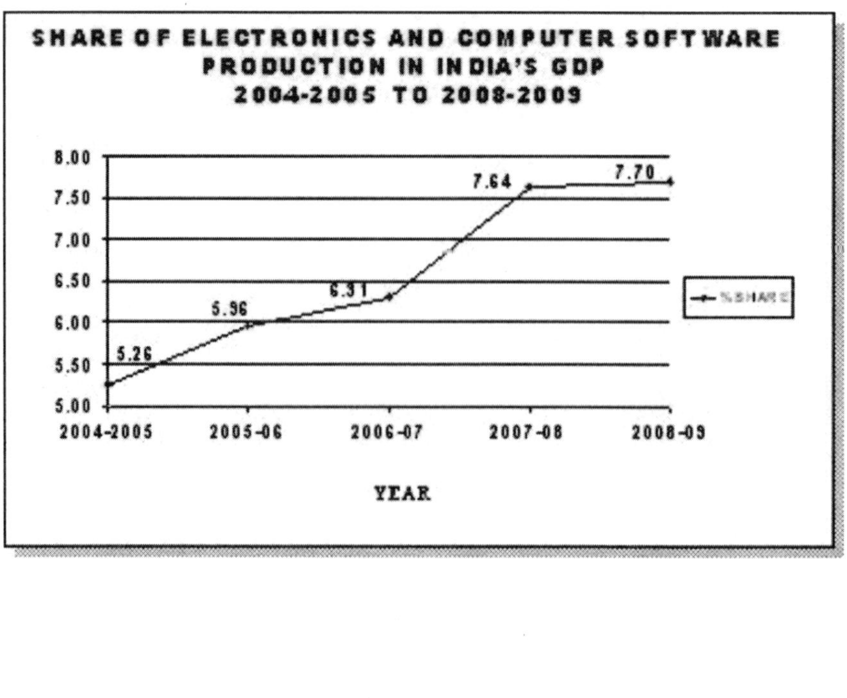
SHARE OF ELECTRONICS AND COMPUTER SOFTWARE PRODUCTION IN INDIA'S GDP
2004-2005 TO 2008-2009
8.00
7.50
7.00
6.50
6.00
5.50
5.00
5.26
5.96
6.31
7.64
7.70
2004-2005
2005-06
2006-07
2007-08
2008-09
YEAR
%SHARE

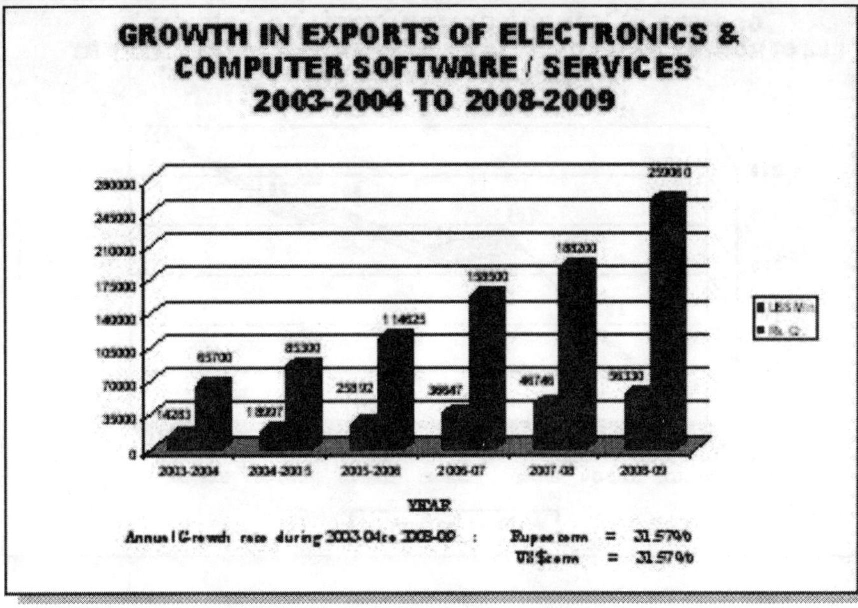
GROWTH IN EXPORTS OF ELECTRONICS &
COMPUTER SOFTWARE / SERVICES
2003-2004 TO 2008-2009
280000
245000
210000
175000
140000
105000
70000
35000
0
65700
85300
114825
14283
25932
2003-2004
2004-2005
2005-2006
2006-07
2007-08
2008-09
YEAR

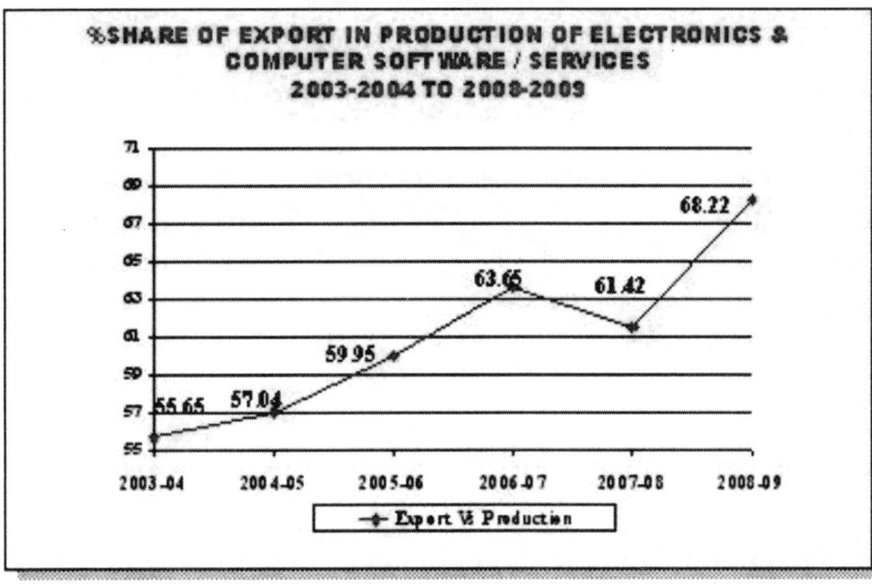
%SHARE OF EXPORT IN PRODUCTION OF ELECTRONICS &
COMPUTER SOFTWARE / SERVICES
2003-2004 TO 2008-2009
71
69
67
65
63
61
59
57
55
55.65
57.04
59.95
63.65
61.42
68.22
2003-04
2004-05
2005-06
2006-07
2007-08
2008-09
Export Vs Production

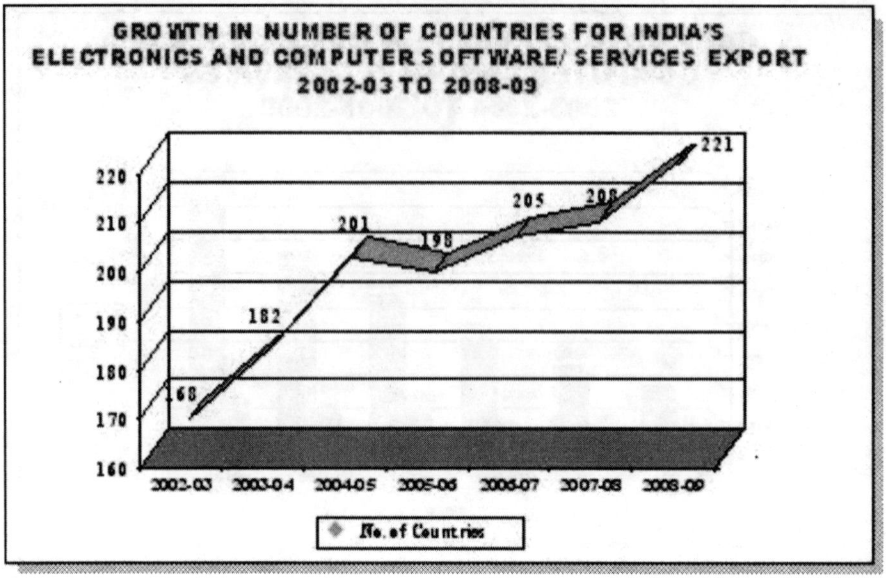

Major Destinations for electronics & computer software / services 2008-2009

Destination	2008-2009	
	Value	Total %
NORTH AMERICA	137547.12 (29908.05)	53.09
EUROPE (EU COUNTRIES)	76947.17 (16731.28)	29.70
SINGAPORE HONGKONG & OTHER SOUTH ASIAN COUNTRIES	14269.17 (3102.67)	5.51
MIDDLE EAST COUNTRIES	11459.92 (2491.83)	4.42
AFRICAN COUNTRIES	6253.74 (1359.80)	2.41
AUSTRALIA &OTHER OCEANIC COUNTRIES	4028.18 (875.88)	1.55
JAPAN, KOREA & OTHER FAR EAST COUNTRIES	3835.01 (833.88)	1.48
EUROPE (NON EU COUNTRIES)	3568.67 (775.97)	1.38
LATIN AMERICA	805.25 (175.09)	0.31
RUSSIA & C.I.S. COUNTRIES	345.27 (75.08)	0.13
TOTAL	259059.50 (56329.53)	100.00

Average Exchange Rate 1US$ = 45.99

Electronics and computer software production and Exports 2008-2009

SECTOR	2008-09	
	US$ MLN.	RS. CR.
CONSUMER ELECTRONICS		
PRODUCTION	5651.23	25990.00
EXPORT	565.34	2600.00
COMM. & BROADCASTING EQUIP.		
PRODUCTION	5355.51	24630.00
EXPORT	2669.28	12276.00
INSTRUMENTATION & STRATEGIC EC.		
PRODUCTION	4257.45	19580.00
EXPORT	913.24	4200.00
ELECTRONIC COMPONENTS		
PRODUCTION	2391.82	11000.00
EXPORT	2283.11	10500.00
COMPUTER HARDWARE		
PRODUCTION	2933.25	13490.00
EXPORT	358.77	1650.00
TOTAL (A)		
PRODUCTION	20589.26	94690.00
EXPORT	6789.74	31226.00
EXPORT Vs PRODUCTION	32.98	
B . COMPUTER SOFTWARE		
PRODUCTION	61983.91	285064.00
EXPORT	49539.90	227834.00
EXPORT Vs PRODUCTION	79.92	
TOTAL (A+B)		
PRODUCTION	82573.17	379754.00
EXPORT	56329.64	259060.00
EXPORT Vs PRODUCTION	**68.22**	

Average Exchange Rate 1 US$ = 45.99

NOTE : Production figures of Electronic Hardware Panels Source : Published figures of MIT in their annual report.

25

The Evaluation of Import and Export Performance in Cargo with Reference to Chennai Port Trust

A. JUSTINEDIRAVIAM AND S. SHANMUGASUNDARAM

Final MBA Student, Department of Business Administration, Annamalai University
Asst. Professor, Department of Business Administration, Annamalai University

ABSTRACT

This paper examines the factors affecting performance of Chennai Port Trust from the clearing and forwarding agents' point of view. The data were collected from a survey of 50 clearing and forwarding agents in Chennai, Tamil Nadu. The data were analysed with different types of tools: ANOVA, Chi-square and Correlation. The study also made some findings on how to solve the problems.

Keywords: Documentation, Berthing, Tariff, Dock, Quay, Transit shed.

Abbreviation: AD – Ambedkar Dock, BD – Bharathi Dock, C & F- Cost & Freight, CCTL – Chennai Container Terminal Pvt. Ltd, CHAs – Custom House Agents, ChPT – Chennai Port Trust, CONCOR – Container Corporation of India Ltd, CPCL – Chennai Petroleum Corporation Ltd.

INTRODUCTION

For any business transaction, some documentation and procedures are required. In case of export trade, it is called export documentation. In case of import trade, it is called import documentation. Export – import documentation is commonly considered to be the most cumbersome part of export- import.

History about Chennai Port Trust

Chennai, formerly known as Madras, is the capital of the state of Tamil Nadu and is India's fourth largest city. It is located on the Coromandel Coast of the Bay of Bengal. The 400-year-old city is the 36th largest metropolitan area in the world. Chennai port is the 2nd largest port in India in terms of cargo handled, achieving a key milestone of 50 million tons in march 2007. The port service of the geographical regions of Tamil Nadu, pondichery, south Andra Pradesh and parts of Karnataka has now emerged as hub on the east coast of India. In 1983 the first modern container terminal of India was established here. It is ranked third among 12 major ports of the country. Today Chennai port boasts of world facilities in 23 alongside berths spanning three docks Dr. Ambedkar dock, Jawahar dock and Bharathi dock. The Chennai port handles iron ore, coal petroleum products, fertilizers, cars, containers and general cargo items with an upgrading of infrastructure as well as operations on the anvil, the port of Chennai is all geared up to face the challenges of the rapidly growing global shipping industry.

Location of Chennai Port Trust

Chennai port is situated at a latitude of 13006 north and longitude of 80018 east. Chennai port is an artificial harbour on the Coromandel Coast in south-east India.

Port Facilities

The total quay length available at Chennai port trust is around 5.5 km. It has in all 23 berths spread over 3 docks i.e Ambedkar Dock, Jawahar Dpck, Bharathi Dock. The maximum draft available at Chennai Port trust is 17.4 m at some of these berths. There is 7 km of entrance Chennai with the depth of outer Chennai being 19.2 m and that of inner channel being 18.6 m. The port has a total land area of 240 ha (approx). Chennai port was the first port to start container handling operation in 1983 which were handled over to CCTL in 2001 for operating under BOT basis. A second container terminal has recently been awarded to PSA SICAL at Ambedkar Dock recently to augment the container operations.

Import Performance of Chennai Port in the year of 2005 to 2010 (In Tonnes)

Commodity	2005-2006	2006-2007	2007-2008	2008-2009	2009-2010
Minerals, Oil & others	1,06,92,250	1,09,65,978	1,10,90,540	1,12,84,498	1,19,17,619
Chemical manures including phosphate	9,82,532	9,38,106	7,78,751	7,10,383	5,50,205
Coal	58,95,343	79,26,752	78,59,986	81,91,857	79,67,976
Coke	11,82,796	11,68,209	18,38,047	16,56,115	17,89,954
Sulphur	89,753	79,113	72,220	72,527	61,002
Edible oil	4,09,925	4,71,185	5,17,882	8,20,643	10,79,982
Iron ore	6830139	8124581	7656899	6846463	7130652
Barites	551202	578650	508556	694042	746911
Other ore	142951	121431	3211108	1571405	991309
Mineral oil	2420889	2021333	1623104	1848479	1402847

Meaning of Wharf

The place in front of the berths used for shipping operations of the vessel.

Meaning of C.T.B. (Container Terminal Berth)

Where container vessels are berthed.

Meaning of I.C.D. (Inland Container Depot)

A place approved by the customs for storing and stuffing of container in place away from parts.

MEANING OF MANIFEST

A document field by the carrier or his agent with customers giving the list of details and description of the goods on board of the vessel and to be landed at the port. It is the cargo declaration.

Form II

A copy of the manifesto is sent to the port by the agents through customers.

Meaning of Import Application

A document in prescribed form is presented to the port by the consignee or agent for the clearance of imported goods on levy of port charges.

Meaning of Bill of Lading

A document is given by the carriers or his agent or master in proof of having taken the goods on board of the vessel.

Meaning of Delivery Order

This is a document given by the carrier or his agent to the traffic manager (port) authorizing the delivery of the goods to the consignee or his agent or representative.

Meaning of Bill of Entry

It is a document in prescribed form which is presented to customs by the importers giving the details of the goods imported, etc. for the purpose of assessment of duty.

Meaning of Consignment

Goods covered by bill of lading.

Meaning of Steamer Agent

Agent or the representative of carrier.

Meaning of FDC (Full Dimension Cargo)

This kind of cargo is not responsible for any damages at the time of export and import. The port is not responsible for any accident or damages. The exporter is completely responsible for the "Full Dimension Cargo".

Meaning of Clearing Agent

Agents or representative of the importer or shippers to look after the port and customs formalities and licensed by customs.

Meaning of Consignee

Person to whom the goods are intended, i.e., the importer.

Meaning of Container

A BOX or unit into which goods are stuffed for transporting from place to place the standard sizes are 20X40X 45.

Meaning of LCL (Less than Container Load)

This container contains cargo
Consigned to more than one importer.

'A' certificate

When goods are landed and not traceable immediately for delivery and later on traced and pointed out to the consignee. A certificate is issued by the trust for the traced goods to enable the importer to avail of the concession on demurrage charges accrued during the period the goods are not available for delivery.

'B' certificate

When goods are not landed and not tallied by trust the trust issues B certificate certifying the short landing of the goods.

'C' certificate

When goods are landed and tallied but not available for delivery and are missing the trust issues certificate for the goods missing.

Port Procedures

Export cargo can be brought into the port after the ship has been allotted a berth and declared for loading. Shippers have to pay the port charges dependent on the procedure followed by each port. Some ports have to pay charges before loading while Bombay port offers the facility of collecting port charges, after loading.

a. Carting Permission

Before bringing cargo to the shipment shed, it is necessary to take "Carting Permission" from the superintendent of the shed and the agent of the shipping company.

b. Vehicle Ticket

At the port gate, while entering with cargo, the shipper has to show carting permission and vehicle ticket, in duplicate, to the gate inspector. The gate inspector examines the goods and the documents to ensure that only the permitted goods are entering into port. The packages, bundles, cases mentioned in the vehicle ticket are tallied with those in the vehicle before the goods are allowed in. Necessary entry is made in the registers in respect of cargo passed through the gate.

c. Mate's Receipt

Soon after the goods are cleared by customs, the exporter/ CHA obtains "Let Ship Order" from the Preventive Officer of customs on the exporter's copy of Shipping Bill. The master of the vessel allows loading of cargo on board, in consultation with Preventive Officers of Customs. The master of the vessel issues mate's receipt to port authorities in respect of shipment taken on board, indicating the condition of goods at the time of receipt. After the payment of port dues, the shipper collects the mate's receipt. This receipt is an important document as it is to be exchanged to Bill of Lading. So, the shipper has to collect it from the superintendent of the shed, soon after it is received to avoid the delay and problems.

d. Bill of lading

The shipper collects blank copies of Bill of Lading from the shipping company and prepares two / three negotiable and required non-negotiable copies of Bill of Lading. The shipping company issues Bill of Lading to the shipper in exchange of mate's receipt. Bill of Lading may be marked "freight paid" if the shipper has paid the freight and "Freight to Pay" when the freight is to be collected from the importer. The shipping company incorporates those clauses that appear in the mate's receipt, before the Bill of Lading is issued.

OBJECTIVES OF THE PAPERS

Primary Objectives

- To know the port process of import and export of goods.
- To know the various documents involved in the exporting and importing procedures followed by the port.
- To identify the areas of improvement in documentation.

Methodology

Type of study

The study will follow an experimental design research method in primary objective and follow a participant observation in second objective.

Experimental research

It is necessary to distinguish clearly between dependent variable and independent variable. A variable is any characteristics that can be taken as different values. Objects are usually not considered, a transparency is not a variable.

Sampling Methods

Convenience sampling (also known as grab or opportunity sampling), a non-probability unrestricted sampling technique, is used as the data have to be collected from readily available sources (multiplex visitors) within a limited span of time. Here the sample population is selected because it is readily available and convenient.

Data Processing

The data required to study the objectives are collected through the primary and secondary data collection method. Primary data refer to the first-hand data collected by the researcher. In this case, it will be the data collected from clearing and forwarding agents. Questionnaire is prepared and sent to different individuals who are considered target population. Secondary data were collected from observation about the port entities by various processings of port procedures, reports and other articles from websites.

Tools for data collection

- Questionnaire
- Interviews

Tools for data analysis

Based on the questionnaire designed and the defined objectives, the following tools are used for data analysis. The SPSS software package tool was used to run statistical tests on the survey data.

- Percentage Analysis
- ANOVA Test

STATISTICAL ANALYSIS

The statistical analysis and data interpretation are done based on the response data using appropriate statistical tools as follows.

Table 1 & Chart 1: Table and chart show percentage of respondents about the berthing facilities in Chennai port

Berthing facilities	Frequency	% of respondent
Highly Satisfied	7	14.0
Satisfied	33	66.0
Neutral	9	18.0
Dissatisfied	1	2.0
Total	50	100.0

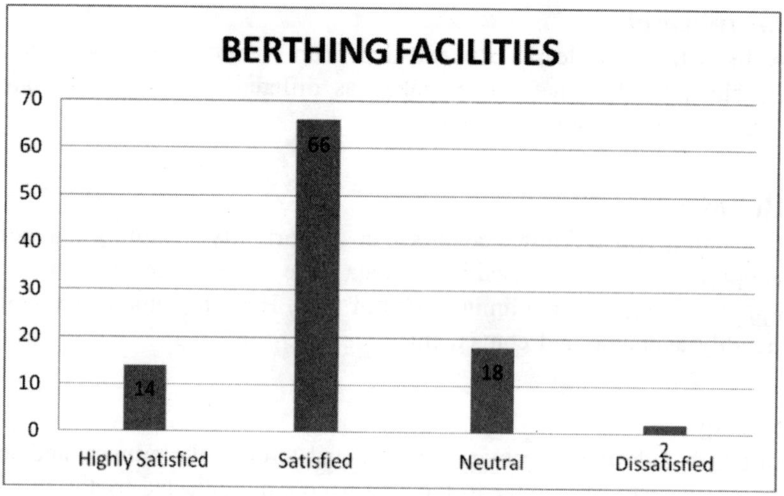

The above table and chart show that 14% of respondents are highly satisfied, 66% of respondents are satisfied,18 % of respondents are neutral and 2 % of respondents are dissatisfied.

Table 2 & Chart 2: Table and chart show percentage of respondents about facility available for smooth handling of cargo and safety of the ship's crew

Smooth Handling of cargo & ship's crew	Frequency	% of respondent
Highly Satisfied	11	22.0
Satisfied	25	50.0
Neutral	13	26.0
Highly Dissatisfied	1	2.0
Total	50	100.0

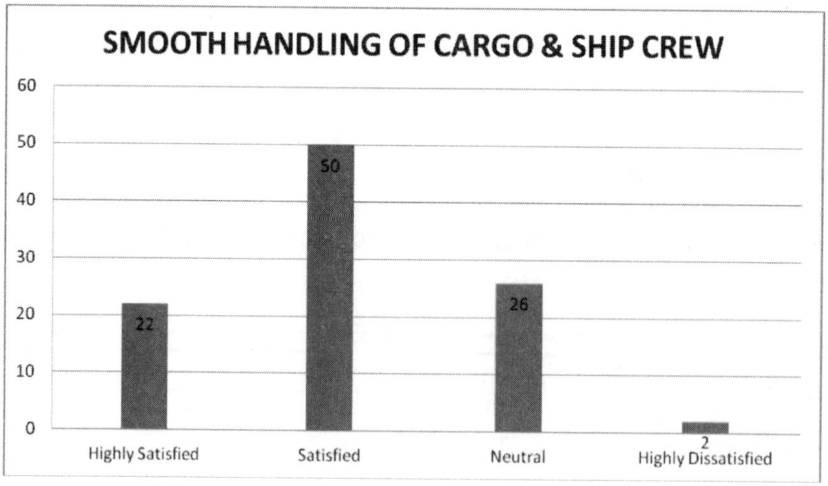

The above table and chart show 22% of respondents are highly satisfied, 50% of respondents are satisfied, 26% of respondents are neutral and 2% of respondents are highly satisfied.

Table 3 & Chart 3: Table and chart show percentage of respondents about performance of cranes & other cargo handling equipment in Chennai port

Performance of cargo handling equipment	Frequency	% of respondent
Highly Satisfied	15	30.0
Satisfied	23	46.0
Neutral	12	24.0
Total	50	100.0

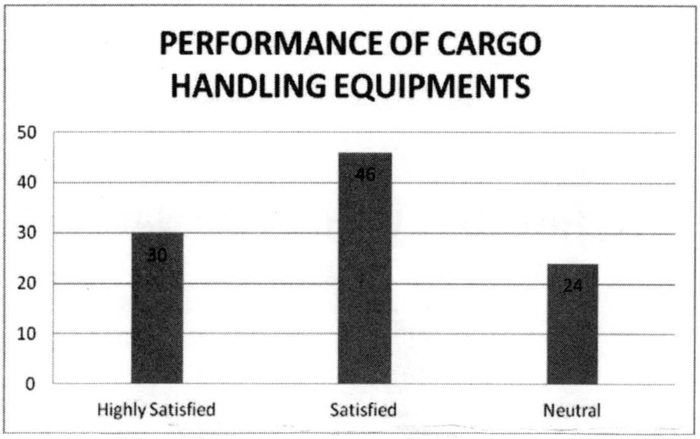

The above table and chart show 30% of respondents are highly satisfied, 46% of respondents are satisfied and 24% of respondents are neutral.

Table 4 & Chart 4: Table and chart show percentage of respondents about opinion of handling cargo

Handling of cargo	Frequency	% of respondent
Highly Satisfied	10	20.0
Satisfied	31	62.0
Neutral	8	16.0
Highly Dissatisfied	1	2.0
Total	50	100.0

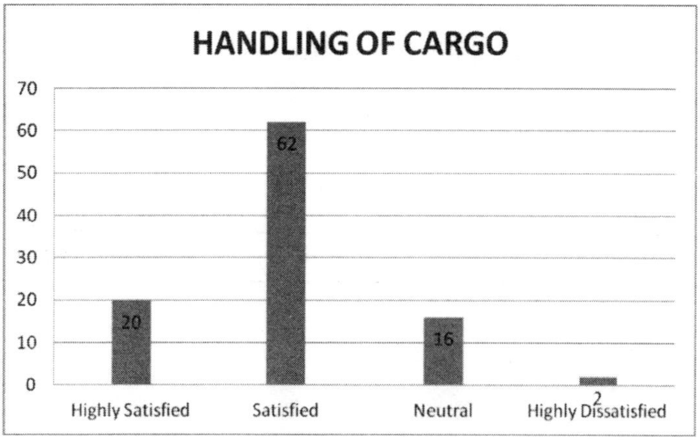

The above table and chart show 20% of respondents are highly satisfied, 62% of respondents are satisfied, 16% of respondents are neutral and 2% respondents are highly dissatisfied.

Table 5 & Chart 5: Table and chart show percentage of respondents about the latest technology used in Chennai port trust

Latest Technology used in Chennai port	Frequency	% of respondent
Highly Satisfied	7	14.0
Satisfied	22	44.0
Neutral	19	38.0
Dissatisfied	2	4.0
Total	50	100.0

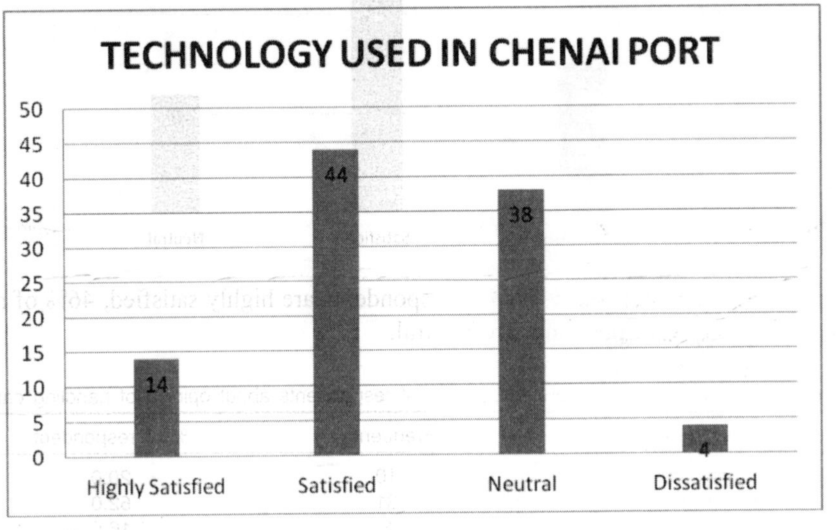

The above table and chart show 14% of respondents are highly satisfied, 44% of respondents are satisfied, 38% of respondents are neutral and 4% of respondents are dissatisfied.

Table 6 & Chart 6: Table and chart show percentage of respondents about cargo clearing procedures (documentation procedure)

Cargo Clearing Procedures	Frequency	% of respondent
Highly Satisfied	16	32.0
Satisfied	29	58.0
Neutral	5	10.0
Total	50	100.0

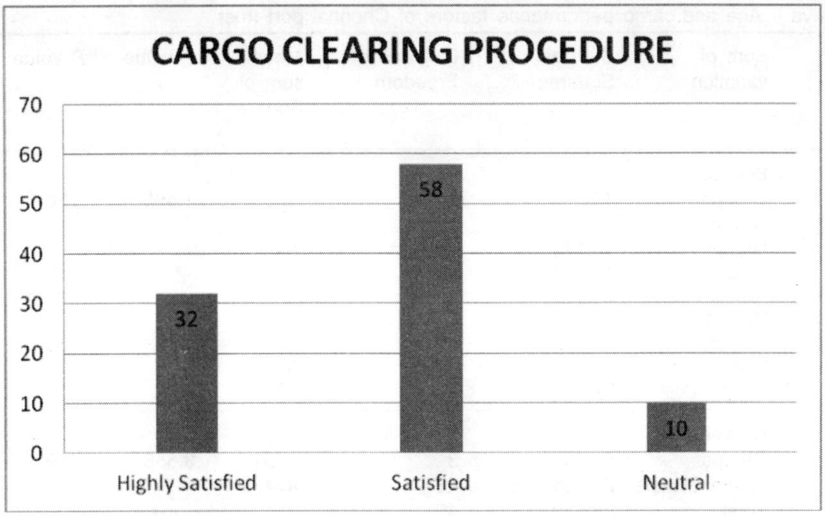

The above table and chart show 32% of respondents are highly satisfied, 58% of respondents are satisfied and 10% of respondents are neutral.

Table 7 & Chart 7: Table and chart show percentage of respondents about the container terminals in Chennai port

Container Terminal	Frequency	%of respondent
Highly Satisfied	11	22.0
Satisfied	27	54.0
Neutral	9	18.0
Dissatisfied	2	4.0
Highly Dissatisfied	1	2.0
Total	50	100.0

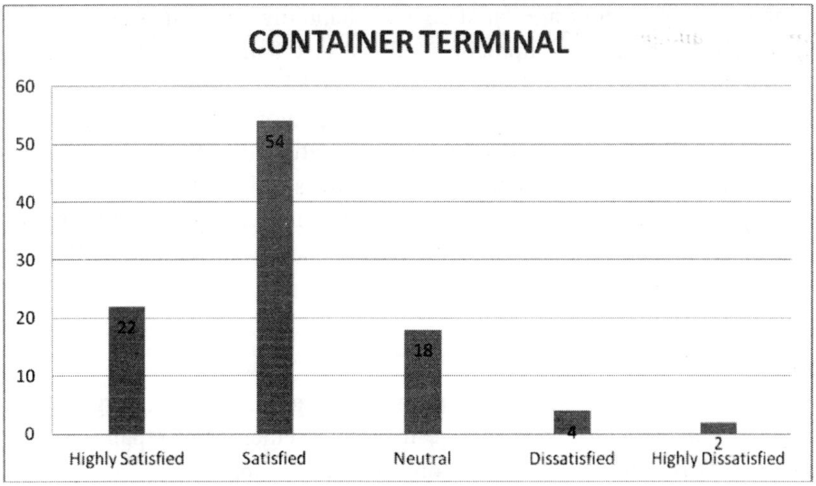

Results of Anova – Age and cargo performance factors of Chennai port trust

Performance factors of Chennai Port Trust	Sum of variation	Sum of Squares	Degrees of Freedom	Mean sum of Square	F value	P value	S/NS
Availability of Berth	Between Groups	1.507	3	.502	1.465	.236	NS
	Within Groups	15.773	46	.343			
	Total	17.280	49				
Performance of cargo handling equipments	Between Groups	1.809	3	.603	1.109	.355	NS
	Within Groups	25.011	46	.544			
	Total	26.820	49				
Handling of cargo	Between Groups	5.194	3	1.731	3.656	.019	S
	Within Groups	21.786	46	.474			
	Total	26.980	49				
Safety	Between Groups	13.808	3	4.603	9.575	.000	S
	Within Groups	22.112	46	.481			
	Total	35.920	49				

It is found from the table that the hypothesis is rejected in two cases (significant) and in other cases (not significant) the hypothesis is accepted. It is concluded that handling of cargo and safety have significant influence on the age of the respondents.

FINDINGS

- Berthing facilities are satisfactory to 66% of agents in Chennai Port Trust.
- Availability of berth is satisfactory to 70% of agents in Chennai Port Trust.
- 50% of the crane operators are satisfied with handling cargo in smooth way.
- The crane and other cargo equipment handling give satisfaction to 46% of agents.
- The service provided in case of emergency is moderate to 44% of employees.
- At Chennai Port Trust, they are using advance technology for all purposes.
- At Chennai Port Trust, 52% of respondents are satisfied with the safety measures.
- Cargo clearing procedure at Chennai Port Trust gives satisfaction to 58% of C&F agencies.
- 54% of respondents are satisfied with the performance of container terminal.
- Handling of cargo and safety have significant influence on the age of the respondents in result of Anova.

Suggestion

- Chennai Port Trust may concentrate on coastal cargo and export cargo.
- Chennai Port may provide more service in case of emergency repairs.
- Chennai Port Trust concentrates more on their traffic dept.

CONCLUSION

This research has been undertaken for the evaluation of the sea cargo, the clearing and forwarding agents to satisfy Chennai Port's services. The overall perception on the evaluation of performance is effective. But Chennai Port wants to increase the cargo handling machineries for handling the goods.

REFERENCES

1. Export & Import procedure, Documentation and logistics, C. RAMGOPAL_New age international publication.
2. International Business- Hill & Jain, Sixth edition, Mcgraw-hill
3. EXIM Policy Manual- 2009 to 2014
4. C.Rama Gopal, Export Import Procedure Documentation & Logistics, New Age International Publisher. 1st Edition.
5. R.K.Jain, Customs Tariff and Process
6. Francis Cherunilum, International Trade & Export management, Himalaya Publishing House, 1984, 1st edition
7. www.chennai port trust.com
8. www.google.com

26

Product Life Cycle to Determine Market in International Business

V.M. Ponniah and A. Chandra Mohan

Professor of Management, School of Management, SRM University, Chennai
E-mail: vmponniah45@gmail.com
Professor of Management, School of Management, SRM University, Chennai,
E-mail: dracmohan_mannava@yahoo.com

ABSTRACT

One of the most important decisions made in international business is the market coverage. This is based on internal and external factors. If the product fails to satisfy the consumer, any amount of effort through other elements in marketing mix- price, promotion and place will not yield success of achieving sales in the long run. Hence, it is imperative to focus on the product. In a business enterprise, financial managers normally make use of the arbitrage, making use of difference in time, towards the success and hence more profitability. Similarly there is scope for marketing manager also, to continue success for a longer period, by making use of the difference in time of the use of the product, by consumers of different countries. This study focuses on why and how a life cycle of a product can be leveraged in the international business.

NEED TO DO INTERNATIONAL BUSINESS IN INDIA

Trade balance in India as obtained from Economic Survey of Government of India reveals the status as furnished below:

(Rs in crore)

Year	Exports	Imports	Trade balance	Rate of change in exports (%) over previous year	Rate of change in imports (%) over previous year
1949-50	485	617	-132	–	–
1959-60	640	961	-321	10.2	6.1
1969-70	1413	1582	-169	4.1	-17.1
1979-80	6418	9143	-2725	12.1	34.2
1989-90	27658	35328	-7670	36.7	25.1
1999-00	159561	215236	-55675	14.2	20.7
2008-09	840755	1374436	-533680	28.2	35.8

Source: Government of India, Economic Survey, 2003-04,2005-06, 2006-07 and 2009-2010.

It is discerned that both exports from and imports to India have increased manifold. Rate of change over the previous year is fluctuating. Important factor to be noted is that the trade gap is widening, leaving a lot of scope for business promoters to enter in export activity.

Commodity Composition of India's International Business

During 2008-2009, the composition of exports from and imports to India are furnished below:

Sl.No.	Major Commodity exported	% age	Sl.No.	Major Commodity imported	% age
1.	Engineering goods	21.6	1.	Petroleum oil and lubricants	30.1
2.	Gems and jewellery	15.1	2.	Capital goods	15.5
3.	Chemical and related	12.3	3.	Electronic goods	7.7
4.	Textiles and readymade garments	10.2	4.	Gold and silver	7.2
5.	Agriculture and allied	9.1	5.	Pearl and precious and semi-precious stones	5.1
6.	Ores and minerals	4.2	6.	Chemicals	5.0

Source: Government of India, Economic Survey 2005-06 and 2009-2010

It is observed that engineering goods are contributing to a maximum of 21.6% of exported commodity from out of India. Further on the import side, capital goods contributed to 15.5 % (next only to petroleum oil and lubricants). Hence, it is stated that any enterprise, engaged in manufacturing sector, can identify a good business opportunity in international business. This paper identifies that a Product Life Cycle can be used to determine a market in international business.

Definition of Product

Product has been defined as anything that can be offered to a market for attention, acquisition, use or consumption that might satisfy a want or need, according to Philip Kotler. In a very narrow sense, a product is a set of tangible physical attributes assembled in an identifiable form. Each product carries a commonly understood descriptive (or generic) name such as apples, steel or baseball bats. In broader interpretation recognises each brand as a separate product.

In International business important product decisions are Market segmentation decision, Product Mix decision, Decision regarding product specifications and Positioning and communications decision. In this paper Product Mix decision is discussed in detail. In simpler terms, it pertains to the type of product and the variants to be offered to the target market.

Product Mix

The product mix normally covers width, depth and consistency. The width of product refers to the number of different product lines. The depth of product refers to the average number of items offered by the enterprise within each product line. The consistency of the product refers to the extent to which various product lines are closely related in end use, production requirements, and distribution channels.

It is widely accepted that in international business, product mix decision mainly depends on market characteristics. In general, enterprises do not introduce their full range in the target country, particularly in the developing countries. It is also observed that in developing countries, enterprises may introduce only after the product has become obsolete or has reached the maturity or declining stage in product life cycle. The situation is discussed in the following paragraphs.

Product Life Cycles to Determine Market in International Business

At a particular point of time, a product could be at different phases of the life cycle in different markets. Even after the sale in one market has reached the maturity stage, the sales could be kept growing by exporting it to foreign markets. Normally the products will be exported to developing countries, where the product is not yet introduced or where the sales are very less.

Suppose a product has Product Life Cycle in four different countries as follows:

Country A: Product is in the declining stage
Country B: Product is in the maturity stage
Country C: Product is in the growth stage
Country D: Product is in the introductory stage
Country E: Product is not yet introduced

Domestic sales curve may decline in country A. By exploring the possibility of market in country D or E, export of the same product can be tried. Now total sales is domestic sales in country A and export sales to country D or E. In the absence of international business, there would be drop in total sales achieved by the enterprise.

Justification for using Product Life Cycle to Determine Market in International Business

There are more chances for a time lag between developed country and developing country in the adoption of technology and its application. Even with the developing countries, technology updating may not be simultaneous. Black & white television penetrated in households in USA ten years before they reached same number of viewers in Europe and Japan. Further black & white televisions were introduced in India only after it had reached the declining stage in advanced countries.

Importer to become an Exporter due to International Business

The location of production bases may shift between countries along with different stages of product life cycle. According to the Model developed by Vernon, an innovative product is first introduced in an advanced country like USA. This is because of availability of market, ease of organising facilities for manufacture, availability of appropriate technology, etc. The product is then exported to other countries, may be West European countries and Japan.

After the market is expanded in these countries, the manufacturers start their subsidiaries to manufacture the product in these countries. These subsidiaries not only cater to the countries where located, but also export to less developed countries or developing countries and also to USA.

Later manufacturing facilities are established in such less developed countries or developing countries. When the technology and product get standardised, such location is advantageous due to low cost of production. They would start exporting to the developed countries.

CONCLUSION

The draft paper for the Twelfth Five Year Plan (2012-2017) released in August 2011 targets an annual GDP growth rate of 9%. This is challenging, but not unattainable. Past record showed that India had already achieved average growth rate of 9% during 2004-2008, which was interrupted by the global financial crisis. This growth should also result in substantial presence of India in the Global Trade.

REFERENCES

1. Francis Cheurnilam, (2010). *International Business*, PHI Learning Private Limited, 5th ed., New Delhi.
2. Philip Kotler and Gray Armstrong, (2005). Principles of *Marketing*, Prentice-Hall of India, 11th ed., New Delhi.
3. Government of India, (1984). *Report of the Committee on Trade Policies.*
4. Deepak Mohanty, Executive Director, Reserve Bank of India, (2011). *Indian Economy: Progress and Prospects*, and Speech delivered at the Harvard Business School, Boston.
5. William, M.K. (2007). Trochim, Cornell University, *Research Methods,* Himal Impressions, New Delhi.

Index